Spoiling the peace?

MANCHESTER
1824

Manchester University Press

Spoiling the peace?

The threat of dissident Republicans to peace in Northern Ireland

S.A. WHITING

Manchester University Press

Published by Manchester University Press
Altrincham Street, Manchester M1 7JA
www.manchesteruniversitypress.co.uk

British Library Cataloguing-in-Publication Data
A catalogue record for this book is available from the British Library

Library of Congress Cataloging-in-Publication Data applied for

ISBN 978 0 7190 9572 6 hardback

First published 2015

The publisher has no responsibility for the persistence or accuracy of URLs for any external or third-party internet websites referred to in this book, and does not guarantee that any content on such websites is, or will remain, accurate or appropriate.

Typeset in 10.5/12.5 Adobe Garamond by
Servis Filmsetting Ltd, Stockport, Cheshire
Printed in Great Britain by
CPI Group (UK) Ltd, Croydon, CR0 4YY

Contents

Figures and tables

Acknowledgements

I would like to express my appreciation to all the interviewees in this book who took the time to offer their insight and warmly welcomed my enquiries. Without such openness I would have never been able to carry out this project.

I would also like to thank all at Manchester University Press for supporting this publication.

Glossary and abbreviations

32CSM	32 County Sovereignty Movement. Political organisation, created in 1997. Linked to the RIRA.
ANC	African National Congress
Ard Chomhairle	National executive of a political party
Ard Fheis	Annual conference
CABHAIR	A republican prisoner association. Linked to RNU. Translated to 'assistance'.
CIRA	Continuity IRA. Republican paramilitary organisation linked to RSF.
Cogús	A republican prisoner association. Translates to 'conscience'.
Dáil Éireann	Lower house of the Irish parliament
DDR	Disarmament, Demobilisation and Reintegration
DEA	District Electoral Area
DUP	Democratic Unionist Party
éirígí	Socialist Irish republican political party, created in 2006
GFA	Good Friday Agreement. Also referred to in this book as 'the Agreement'.
IMC	Independent Monitoring Commission
INLA	Irish National Liberation Army. Republican Socialist paramilitary organisation, created in 1974 over split in the Official republican movement.
IRA	Irish Republican Army
IRPWA	Irish Republican Prisoners Welfare Association
IRSP	Irish Republican Socialist Party. Irish republican socialist party formed in 1974 after splitting from the 'Official' movement. Formerly linked to the paramilitary group INLA.
LVF	Loyalist Volunteer Force
MI5	Military Intelligence Section 5. British internal security services.
MLA	Member of Legislative Assembly
NILT	Northern Ireland Life and Times

Official IRA	Republican paramilitary organisation, linked to the Official republican movement.
ONH	Óglaigh na hÉireann/'Soldiers of Ireland'. Title claimed by various republican factions.
PIRA	Provisional IRA. Republican paramilitary organisation, created in 1969/70. Linked to Provisional Sinn Féin, fully decommissioned in 2005. Also referred to in this book as 'the IRA'.
PSNI	Police Service of Northern Ireland. Successor police force to RUC, created in 2001.
RAAD	Republican Action Against Drugs. Republican paramilitary organisation operating mainly in the Derry area. Engage in violence against suspected drug dealers and other 'anti social behaviour'.
RIRA	Real IRA. Republican paramilitary organisation formed in 1997 by those unhappy with the direction of the peace process, particularly the Mitchell Principles.
RNU	Republican Network for Unity. Irish republican organisation opposed to the direction of the peace process.
RUC	Royal Ulster Constabulary. The former police service, replaced by the PSNI in 2001.
RSF	Republican Sinn Féin. Republican organisation. Split from the Provisional movement in 1986 over the dropping of abstention from Dáil Éireann.
SDLP	Social Democratic and Labour Party
Sinn Féin	Irish republican political party. Also referred to as the 'Provisional movement' to differentiate between RSF and to collectivise the PIRA and Sinn Féin.
Taoiseach	Irish Prime Minister
Teach na Fáilte	A republican prisoner association linked to the IRSP
UUP	Ulster Unionist Party

Introduction

Those who defend status quo relationships of power, or see them as natural and normal, tend to treat any opposition or critique as tantamount to treason or terrorism. That 'another world is possible', to invoke a popular refrain, is nothing less than an ontological challenge to the world that is today.[1]

As various organisations strive to display their loyalty to the principles of national independence and allegiance to their republican forefathers who provided impetus to the struggle for Irish sovereignty, the centenary commemorations in 2016 of the Easter Rising are set to reflect the multifaceted nature of modern day Irish republicanism. Yet the claim to the mantle of true republicanism, as supposedly embodied in those involved in the Rising, remains contested. Competing military and political organisations emerged in what became the Irish Republic, whilst militarism as a tool of Irish republicanism remained in the form of a continuing Irish Republican Army, which was concentrated predominantly in Northern Ireland. For decades, Irish state ideology viewed 'the North' as illegally occupied by the British government, yet rejected the claims of legitimacy of successor IRAs to the 1916–23 version. Dissidence over what constitutes the IRA, the legitimacy of 'armed struggle' and the extent to which British sovereignty over Northern Ireland ought to be acknowledged has long been evident.

The movement of Sinn Féin from the position of abstention to recognising and participating in Dáil Éireann and the Northern Ireland Assembly, accompanied by the removal of the 'party's army', the Provisional IRA, revived the tensions over compromise evident within the republican movement early in the twentieth century. Dissenting voices against the compromises of Provisional Irish republicanism were evident from the mid-1980s and became more significant from the 1990s onwards.[2]

Most peace processes generate organisational divisions. The Taoiseach at the time of the 1998 Good Friday Agreement (GFA), Bertie Ahern, commented: 'It is an observable phenomenon in Northern Ireland, and elsewhere, that tension and violence tend to rise when compromise is in the air.'[3] Within peace processes more generally the groups involved in negotiations are rarely the monoliths presented by their opponents, but instead, are described as complex organisms that perform different functions and provide umbrellas for different interests.[4] It is during ceasefire periods that these interests diffuse and fragment. This observation, combined with the republican movement's volatile nature, indicates the likelihood that the Northern Irish peace process at the end of the twentieth century and the compromises involved would produce dissenting voices.

Armed conflict remains a popular method of attempting to resolve disputes over territory, sovereignty or other resources.[5] The commonalities between the ethno national conflicts in Northern Ireland, South Africa and Israel-Palestine, such as high civilian casualties and violations of human rights, have highlighted the possibility of comparison between each situation.[6] The intractability of the conflicts in deeply divided societies, along with the high likelihood for inter communal tension, means that these separate cases are often brought together in an attempt to form international perspectives.

It is vital nonetheless to remember that each conflict is essentially parochial, with its own distinct culture, history and social development. The task of implementing a peace agreement is highly reliant on the situation in hand where details vary greatly from one conflict to another. The fact that 'peacemaking processes cannot be lifted wholesale like templates and applied to other locations',[7] makes the study and comparison of peace processes seem rather futile. However, it is possible to look beyond certain variables to see how techniques used in one location may be investigated and adapted for use in another.

One of the commonalities is the continuation of violence and the emergence of 'spoiler groups'. As Darby and Mac Ginty note, 'violence precedes peace processes and continues as an unavoidable background during them'.[8] When violence lowers in scale, the policy agenda shifts rapidly from military containment towards a new set of problems, such as reforms to policing and the embedding of a new justice system. Approaching such sensitive issues within a negotiated settlement often produces leaders or factions who are unsatisfied with the outcome.[9] Those who use violence, the 'spoilers', to undermine negotiated peace, can be identified in almost all peace processes.

Armed dissident republicanism remains a feature, if mainly at a low level, of the post GFA context in Northern Ireland. From April 2002 to March 2012 the Police Service of Northern Ireland (PSNI) recorded 528 shootings and 375 bombings.[10] Today militant republican groups that continue to advocate the legitimacy of armed struggle operate far below the capabilities of the PIRA during the peak of the troubles in the early 1970s, yet have inflicted serious casualties – as incidences such as the Omagh bomb in 1998, killing 29, the killing of two soldiers at Massereene army barracks and Constable Stephen Carroll in Craigavon in March 2009; the car bomb that killed Constable Ronan Kerr in April 2011 and the killing of a prison officer in November 2012 all demonstrated. The GFA therefore failed to signify a definitive moment in finally ending armed republicanism. Indeed, dissidence pre-dated the 1998 deal. In addition, given the inevitable presence of 'spoilers' within peace processes more generally, it is striking that the continued use of armed tactics by republican groups was underestimated by policy makers and the security services.[11]

The term 'dissident' is commonly used in the Northern Irish context to denote those republican groups and individuals who oppose the GFA.[12] The label itself should be utilised with caution, as it is ambiguous on several counts. Firstly, the term does not provide insight into what dissent actually constitutes. Does it mean dissent from Sinn Féin, or from peace, or from a political process, or a constitutional process, or does it constitute all of these things? Secondly, it denies any acknowledgement of republicanism as a heterogeneous entity, a varied and diverse phenomenon, reducing it as an ideology to what one particular party (Sinn Féin) offers, even though those offerings have varied hugely in recent times. The term 'dissent' indicates that there is a settled and definitive checklist of what constitutes republicanism, a creed from which dissident groups have strayed. Dissent is therefore somewhat hollow in a description, a term lacking in substance and explanation.[13] As demonstrated in figure 1 the term dissident is also used to incorporate those groups who have, at different times, splintered from the Provisional movement and those who have been formed since the end

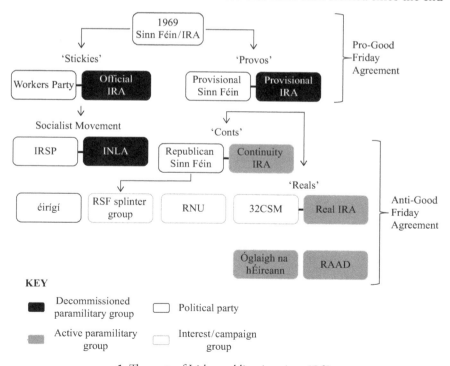

1 The roots of Irish republicanism since 1969

of the Provisional IRA (PIRA). It is also used to include organisations that are linked to paramilitary groups and those which are not.

The republican movement's propensity to split and the subsequent array of groups claiming lineage to the same tradition demands that any research into dissident republicanism requires clear parameters. Specifying a time frame and geographical area, and being selective in regard to the groups under examination, have refined the focus for this book. The dissident groups explored here have emerged since the 1986 division within the Provisional movement on the issue of abstention from Dáil Éireann, a split which led to the formation of Republican Sinn Féin ('conts'). This date provides a logical and clear moment in Irish republican history to begin to evaluate contemporary dissent within the movement. The exception is a short analysis of the Irish Republican Socialist Party (IRSP), formed in 1974 after a split in the 'Official' arm of republicanism ('stickies'). Including the IRSP provides an alternative view by offering insight in to the socialist wing of the movement and their opposition to the GFA. The geographical focus of this research is mainly Northern Ireland with some focus on activity in the Republic. The majority of the interviews conducted are with organisations/individuals in Northern Ireland, with a handful in the Republic of Ireland.

This book covers the following political groups: Republican Sinn Féin (RSF), the 32 County Sovereignty Movement (32CSM), Republican Network for Unity (RNU), éirígí and the Irish Republican Socialist Party (IRSP). These groups present a significant presence within the current context, yet have all emerged at different times and from different roots of the republican tradition (see figure 1). They all therefore, provide points for comparison and contrast. The fractured, evolving nature of violent dissident republicanism has forced groups to split as well as merge. As a result, the task of outlining the subject of interest is made difficult for researchers. This project therefore focuses on several key groupings of armed republicanism: the Real IRA (RIRA), Continuity IRA (CIRA), the Irish National Liberation Army (INLA), Óglaigh na hÉireann (ONH) and Republican Action Against Drugs (RAAD).

In assessing the emergence of anti-state violence and how it is sustained, English indicates that there are two main issues concerning political violence. One is practical, the other is analytical, and our difficulties in responding to the former have been significantly exacerbated by our failings in regard to the latter.[14] This is certainly true in the case of Northern Ireland and armed dissident republicanism; whilst continuous observations of these groups have been made through the media, government reports and intelligence services, few attempts have been made to form a comprehensive understanding of 'dissident' actions. There is a need therefore to provide further insight into the ideology and functioning of 'dissident' groups in order to expand beyond the descriptive analysis. For example, do these groups have ideological and political purpose or is it simply enough to explain their actions as possessing an affinity to violence? 'Emergent principles' dealing with the problem can be enhanced in their effectiveness by contextualisation via knowledge of local circumstances and causes of violence.[15]

Aims of the book

The core purpose of this book is to analyse whether contemporary dissidence forms part of an inevitable cycle of resistance to compromise by republican leaders. Furthermore, what does this reveal about the modern day nature of dissent and does the term 'dissident' have an agreed definition within Irish republicanism? To what extent has fidelity to principle made inevitable republican divisions? Can Sinn Féin, or only the dissidents, or all competing groups, be labelled republican? How do dissidents defend the continued use of armed struggle as a core republican feature?

These questions represent specific research areas that need to be explored in order to understand dissent (violent and non-violent) in the Northern Irish context. At a broader level such questioning may reveal further insight into the issue of violence during and after negotiations of intra-state conflict.

Previous research exploring actors within the republican movement has focused heavily on the use of qualitative data, especially through the use of interviews. The review of literature in chapter 1 highlights the reliance that has been placed upon qualitative research methods when analysing and exploring previous forms of Irish republicanism, with academics employing in-depth interviews, archival research and scrutiny of policy documents. Yet, whilst the existing literature does contain interview data with some dissident organisations, there is a need to build upon this in order to consider the position of organisations, leaders and grass-roots members. Therefore, the use of interviews has the potential to contribute further original data to the literature on dissent. Research output on dissident republicanism is steadily increasing (although very little was written until the mid-2000s) and with it, quantitative methods. Databases of dissident activity (Horgan) and survey data expressing attitudes to dissident groups (Evans and Tonge) are beginning to provide researchers with more demographic and geographic information about violent and non-violent dissident republican activity.[16]

This book continues the trend of attempting to add to the qualitative understanding of Irish republicanism by utilising in-depth, semi-structured interviews and scrutinising primary sources such as policy documents, newspapers, pamphlets and speeches. This is in order to draw inferences in relation to how individuals interpret the principles and tactics of republicanism and how this translates into activity.

It is not the aim of this research to provide a judgement on the morality of certain actions, but rather to gain insight into how others justify their own position and seek to maintain a particular republican political position and methodology. In terms of legal compliance, boundaries have to exist, such as not asking interviewees to divulge information on personal involvement in violent incidents. Rather, questions on contentious issues such as armed struggle are asked in such a way to investigate why interviewees believe it to be a necessary aspect of republican activity. The general outlook supplants the personal positioning in terms of the thrust of questioning. Interviews were conducted with members of dissident organisations, as well as 'mainstream' republicans in Sinn Féin between the period September 2009 and April 2013.

Structure of the book

The opening chapter provides historical and contextual backdrop to this book by examining the existing research. The discussion opens by considering how the splits and tensions within the republican movement can be explained. This is then followed by an evaluation of the (still very limited) existing literature on dissident republicanism as a modern phenomenon. This is in order to address the gaps that exist in the literature and so go beyond the description of dissidents as 'irritants, embarrassing Sinn Féin through the use of traditional republican rhetoric'.[17]

The following chapter explores the basis of republicanism and consider how republican ideology has been adapted and accommodated within the Irish variant of the tradition. The chapter continues by considering the evolution of republican political thought and its application within the Northern Irish context. Such an exploration of the roots of the tradition is necessary to determine how the many shapes and forms of Irish republicanism today deviate from the supposed principles, yet claim attachment to the same tradition. The chapter questions whether it is possible to define Irish republicanism through set principles.

The intent of chapter 3 is to build upon the existing academic analysis examining the extent of ideological and political evolution within Sinn Féin, which contributed to the emergence of the dissidents. It considers the internal and external forces impacting upon the development and electoral rise of Sinn Féin. The chapter then goes on to consider the extent and limits of ideological and policy changes within Sinn Féin and assesses the rationale behind dissolution of the PIRA, exploring how the ascendancy of constitutional politics within what has now become labelled as 'mainstream' republicanism created space for the emergence of dissident groups in opposition to such change.

Chapters 4 and 5 draw on original data from research interviews with members of a wide range of dissident groups to assess motives and rationale for their membership and to assess their political beliefs. These chapters also examine dissident policy documents to explore the origins, strategies and campaigns of various republican groups. This section attempts to consider the commonalities and differences amongst groups under the 'dissident' banner in terms of their position on electoral politics, the appeal of creating a 'broad front', future challenges, their critique of Sinn Féin and whether they possess an alternative strategy for a united Ireland. This enquiry ascertains whether 'dissident' republicanism exists as an identifiable entity, assessing whether the term has sufficient meaning in any analytical application of these groups.

Chapter 6 considers the armed aspect of dissident republicanism. More specifically it explores the current nature of the armed campaign, and how (if at all possible) these tactics are justified by dissidents in the current context. Militant republican groups that continue to advocate the legitimacy of armed struggle operate below the capabilities of the PIRA but have proven their ability to maintain a sporadic yet sustained campaign. This chapter places its focus on several groups that differ in terms of origin, strategy and affiliations to explore what is the aim, if one exists, of armed struggle.

Drawing upon the broader concept of 'spoiler' violence, the final chapter contextualises dissident republican violence within a post-peace agreement setting. It also explores the state's response to dissident violence and considers the interaction between the two actors in an action-response cycle of violence, as well as assessing the relevance of contextual factors such as socio-economic inequality and political grievances.

The illustration of 'dissident' republicanism today is used to encompass a range of groups, individuals and political parties. It has also come to represent those who advocate a range of tactics. The nature of dissidence ranges from those who adopt electoral politics and political campaigning to others who advocate 'revolutionary' tactics and armed struggle. Therefore, 'dissident' has become a term to collectivise all forms of opposition to arrangements under the Good Friday Agreement and the Sinn Féin agenda. Throughout history Irish republicanism has by no means been immune to dissent. Yet, the lack of academic enquiry into the current phase of factionalism has left ideological and empirical aspects untouched. Despite valuable research beginning to emerge, further exploration of dissent as a phenomenon within Irish republicanism can provide an outline to 'some of its contours … and put an end to the taboos that too often exist in relation to what "mysteries" it holds'.[18]

Notes

1   R. D. Lipschutz, 'Foreword', in L. Coleman and K. Tucker (eds), *Situating Global Resistance: Between Discipline and Dissent* (London, Routledge, 2012), p. 1.
2   M. Taylor, 'Introduction', in P. M. Currie and M. Taylor (eds), *Dissident Irish Republicanism* (London, Continuum, 2011), p. 2.
3   Bertie Ahern, cited in the *Observer*, 22 September 1997.
4   J. Darby and R. Mac Ginty, 'Coming out of Violence: A Comparative Study of Peace Processes', in O. Hargie and D. Dickson (eds) *Researching the Troubles: Social Science*

Perspectives on the Northern Ireland Conflict (London, Mainstream Publishing, 2004), p. 275.

5 M. Smyth, 'Introduction', in M. Smyth and G. Robinson (eds), *Researching Violently Divided Societies* (Tokyo, United Nations University Press, 2001), p. 2.

6 See B. Gidron, S. N. Katz and Y. Hasenfeld (eds), *Mobilizing for Peace: Conflict Resolution in Northern Ireland, Israel/Palestine and South Africa* (Oxford, Oxford University Press, 2002); C. Knox and P. Quirk, *Peace Building in Northern Ireland, Israel and South Africa* (Basingstoke, Palgrave Macmillan, 2000).

7 J. Darby and R. Mac Ginty, *The Management of Peace Processes* (Basingstoke, Palgrave, 2000), p. 1.

8 *Ibid.*, p. 8.

9 See S. J. Stedman, 'Spoiler Problems in Peace Processes', *International Security* 22, no. 2 (1997), pp. 5–53.

10 Police Service of Northern Ireland, *Police Recorded Security Situation Statistics: Annual Report Covering the Period 1st April 2011 – 31st March 2012* (Belfast, Northern Ireland Statistics and Research Agency, 2012).

11 Security services admitted to being unprepared for the continued republican security threat and having a slow response to dissident violence. See chapter 6.

12 For further insight in to the meaning of the term 'dissident' see J. Evans and J. Tonge, 'Menace without Mandate? Is There Any Sympathy for Dissident Irish Republicanism in Northern Ireland?', *Terrorism and Political Violence* 24, no. 1 (2012), pp. 64–65; A. McIntyre, 'Of Myths and Men: Dissent within Republicanism and Loyalism', in A. Edwards and S. Bloomer (eds), *Transforming the Peace Process in Northern Ireland: From Terrorism to Democratic Politics* (Dublin, Irish Academic Press, 2008); M. Frampton, *Legion of the Rearguard: Dissident Irish Republicanism* (Dublin, Irish Academic Press, 2011), pp. 1–9.

13 It is necessary to note that there is concern within the mainstream media that the term 'dissident' may also add some kudos or respectability. For example, the term dissident in the past has been attached to citizens in the Soviet Union who dared to criticise the authoritarian regime under the Communist Party. The term therefore carried positive attributes that meant the actions of these individuals were brave and positive. Whilst media outlets are also aware of the positive connotations attached to the label used in Northern Ireland today there is a sense that there were no alternatives.

14 R. English, *Terrorism How to Respond* (Oxford, Oxford University Press, 2009), p. ix.

15 Smyth, 'Introduction', p. 4.

16 See J. Horgan and P. Gill, 'Who Are the Dissidents? An Introduction to the ICST Violent Dissident Republican Project', in Currie and Taylor (eds), *Dissident Irish Republicanism*, pp. 43–64; Evans and Tonge, 'Menace without Mandate?', pp. 61–78.

17 R. Mac Ginty, 'Irish Republicanism and the Peace Process: From Revolution to Reform', in M. Cox, A. Guelke and F. Stephens (eds), *A Farewell to Arms? Beyond the Good Friday Agreement* (Manchester, Manchester University Press, 2006), p. 133.

18 McIntyre, 'Of Myths and Men', p. 117.

1

Evaluating historic splits in Irish republicanism: is there space for the emergence of 'dissidents'?

From abstentionists to institutional participants, from the margins to the mainstream, Sinn Féin has undergone numerous reincarnations since its founding in 1905.[1] The republican movement has always been a mixture of intellectuals, constitutional politicians, political activists, militants and revolutionaries, although these categories have never been mutually exclusive. It is the versatile and complex nature of the republican movement, allied to the difficulty of realising its core ambition of a united, independent Ireland that has made it so prone to ideological divisions and political or military splits. Major splits have occurred on several occasions: 1921, 1926, 1969–70, 1986, 1997 and post 1998. Despite the many ups and downs, splits and schisms that Sinn Féin has gone through, the party has maintained its adherence to the principle of self-determination. Yet, the means of achieving this goal, whether by armed struggle or electoral politics, has often differed and caused the movement to splinter. Moreover, the *modus operandi* of self-determination – and what it constitutes – has been altered by Sinn Féin in recent times. The republican movement has been repeatedly pulled in conflicting directions since its creation, a feature which continues to characterise the movement to the present day.

The literature on both Sinn Féin and the IRA is vast and wide ranging, with the various accounts often highlighting the republican movement's propensity to split. Since the Good Friday Agreement (GFA), a significant amount of literature has been produced in order to form an understanding of where Irish republicanism now stands.[2] This chapter will trace the evolution of Irish republicanism through the academic literature and provide details of where the movement currently stands. The trajectory of Sinn Féin from abstentionism into Dáil Éireann in 1986 and then a Northern Ireland Assembly at the end of the twentieth century, followed by the Provisional IRA's decommissioning of weapons in 2005, revived tensions within republicanism. Significant variation within the literature emerges between those who view the phenomenon as a reoccurring cyclical trend inherent within the Irish republican movement and those who emphasise the importance of contextual realities and stress the unique characteristics of each split.

Divisions within Irish republicanism: is it still about 'the split'?

The multifaceted and diverse nature of the Irish republican movement was evident from the time of partition as the movement fragmented between constitutional moderates and those unwilling to accept anything short of an independent all-Ireland republic. The cyclical pattern within republicanism has been to replace those willing to moderate their agenda with new militants. The divisive issue in 1921, the oath of allegiance to the British Crown, split the movement into moderates and hardliners, pro- and anti-treaty factions.[3] It is the nature of this split that is often viewed as prototypical and therefore essential in the understanding of subsequent divisions, which have been played out over the roles of abstentionism, armed struggle and the tacit acceptance of the need for unionist consent for change.

The works of Brian Feeney, Agnes Maillot and Joost Augusteijn examine the history of the IRA and Sinn Féin, highlighting the consistent republican tendency to split, in order to identify the common themes and as a result produce a transferable model that makes sense of each division.[4] Feeney develops comparisons between the various incarnations of Sinn Féin from the early twentieth century through to the 1990s peace process, arguing that 'all the major splits have taken the same form'.[5] He stresses that comprehending the 1921–22 split is vitally important in understanding the 'theology' of the movement for the rest of its existence.[6] The emergence of the IRA in 1921 as the 'pre-eminent component in the republican movement and its resistance to any political or pro-democratic authority'[7] had a profound effect on the future of the republican movement. Feeney sees the impact of the 1921 republican split and the emergence of the IRA as the prominent partner in the relationship with Sinn Féin as key to understanding the republican movement's tendency to fracture throughout the twentieth century.

Maillot also explores the evolution of Sinn Féin and the IRA. She suggests the emergence of a new Sinn Féin with a distinctly changed outlook as the organisation moved into the twenty-first century. Despite acknowledging that tactics in the last decade of the twentieth century represented a watershed for republicanism, Maillot also makes the valid point that to truly understand the tensions and divisions within republicanism it is important to go back to the origin of the party and its principles.[8] Whilst both Feeney and Maillot emphasise the importance of understanding the history and origins of the movement as establishing a propensity to split, they both comment on the past through the prism of the peace process. Neither offers a discussion of the military breakaway groups caused by Sinn Féin's involvement in the peace process. There is no consideration for the tension caused by the compromises made in the peace process; instead there is a tendency to view the peace process as an end point. This leads to a premature and optimistic interpretation of the unity in which the agreement was made.

Although those who broke away from Sinn Féin in 1986, 1997 and beyond were small minorities, their justifications are still essential in understanding republican heterogeneity. The form of dissent is also largely neglected because the term tends to be associated with those committed to violent methods. However, dissent can assume various forms and rarely constitutes a single entity. Despite their acknowledgement of the republican tendency to splinter Maillot and Feeney surprisingly do not appear to countenance the possible 'replacement' of the PIRA by an alternative IRA as a likely result of the compromises in which mainstream republicans engaged during the peace process.

The republican tendency to split has long been recognised by political historians, yet each split has been treated separately and little recognition has been given to the similarities between them. In analysing the tension within Irish republicanism, Joost Augusteijn attempts to address this by highlighting the similarities and consistencies within republican responses to political change over ninety years.[9] Augusteijn presents splits as a cyclical phenomenon where the tension between political struggle and military conflict provide the recurring catalyst in dividing the movement. Whilst this 'vicious cycle' provides a helpful visual demonstration of the splits, the comparison element, which Augusteijn himself claims to be so necessary, is somewhat limited. Due to the circular and repetitive description of divisions, they are portrayed as almost identical, providing very little scope for comparison between the contextual realities behind each break.

Feeney, Maillot and Augusteijn all look for generalised models and theories to explain the republican tendency to split. Yet the cyclical description appears one-dimensional because it pays little consideration to the contemporary circumstances which, when looked at individually, highlight distinctive republican approaches adopted at each juncture.[10] Patterson warns that too much emphasis on a supposedly unchanging movement 'can blind us to the need to examine the very specific historical circumstances in which republicans operated'.[11] He instead calls for 'a more discontinuous "conjunctural" analysis that breaks with the fatalism of traditional approaches'.[12] Therefore, in order to consider the various transformations the republican tradition has undergone, it is vital to look beyond an all-serving explanation and consider the evolution of republicanism within each specific context.

The 1969 Sinn Féin/IRA split epitomises the importance of taking context into account. In the early 1960s, IRA Chief of Staff, Cathal Goulding, espoused a neo-Marxist analysis of the troubles and pushed for change in the movement. He argued that the British state deliberately divided the Irish working class on sectarian grounds in order to exploit them and keep them from uniting and overthrowing their bourgeois oppressors. Within five years of Goulding's leadership, the movement had turned from one with an often right-wing nationalist and reactionary conservative outlook (albeit with some left-wing tendencies) to 'one which professed to be socialist'.[13] However, whilst the 1969 split and the emergence of the Provisionals was to some extent the result of antagonism towards socialism, it cannot be oversimplified as a left–right division but was instead one based on local circumstances.

The Provisional movement was not primarily motivated by reform in the North; instead the objective was one of defence and Catholic self-protection. After the Catholic demonstrations against discrimination in pursuit of equal citizenry failed, armed activity grew and it was the Provisionals who were at the epicentre of such 'resistance'.[14] It was claimed the PIRA was 'born out of the desire for self-preservation rather than from any overtly patriotic inspiration, still less any abstract ideological commitment to socialism'.[15] It is therefore possible to view the emergence of the Provisionals as situational rather than ideational. As Conor Cruise O'Brien aptly noted, 'The formidable thing about the new IRA – the Provisionals – was its simple relevance to the situation.'[16] Yet, whilst the Provisionals pursued objectives far more relevant to the working-class Catholic population than those of the Official movement they also managed to retain a commitment to the politics and militarism of the 1916 rebellion. Whilst violence rather than politics defined the Provisional self-image – 'legitimised' by its protective role – it is important not to interpret this attachment to resistance and military thinking as a severance from republican tradition and history.

Walsh's analysis of the relationship between socialism and republicanism goes further in highlighting the latter's socialist tendencies and the resulting tensions. The Marxist leanings of the movement under Goulding distracted from the need for self-protection during the Civil Rights era.[17] With the aim of political change, resources had been redirected towards the Civil Rights movement at the expense of military training.[18] Yet, a significant number of republicans remained unconvinced that the Civil Rights strategy bore any validity to their overarching aims, which concerned sovereignty and territory, not equality within the northern unionist state. For many, democratic reform was not a republican objective and the movement's drift leftwards proved too much for a significant number of republicans. The Provisionals developed as a result of an apparent need for self-protection and the resulting philosophy was one which fused localised reactive defence and defiance to broader aspirations of national sovereignty and anti-imperialism. Nonetheless, the Provisionals emerged as a response to the reality of life in the North for nationalists: subordination, discrimination and secondary economic and political status. Without these structural conditions there would have been little growth in the movement. Provisionalism was therefore a fusion of the situational and structural with the ideological. The result was another republican split based loosely upon what Bowyer Bell acknowledged as a somewhat one-dimensional analysis: one between Communist Radicals (Officials) and Catholic Gunmen (Provisionals).[19] Due to the leadership's misdirection and the resulting failure to 'defend' its northern population, the Provisionals emerged, shaped by the circumstances of that time, even if their antecedents within a long narrative of 'struggle' were also evident.

Similarly, English goes about highlighting the importance of contextual realities. In examining the reasons behind each split, he goes deeper than other investigations into republican schisms. English explains how socio-economic realities and the direction taken by the republican movement at various junctures have been influenced by the socialist tendencies of various figures. Irish republicanism has often attracted a Marxist analysis, from the 1916 rebel James Connolly to Peadar O'Donnell in the 1920s and Cathal Goulding in the 1960s. It is therefore possible to argue that 'Marx's ideas helped to create a strain of revolutionary republicanism which in turn jolted Irish politics in a powerful – if not quite a desired – fashion.'[20] These figures realised that in order to understand the workings of nationalism in Ireland it was first essential to understand material and social relationships. English goes on to contend that, 'even for those of us who do share Marx's and Connolly's leftist faith, it remains true that nationalism in Ireland can only be explained properly if one takes account of social and economic forces'.[21] This is not to say that English disregards the importance of the role that history and tradition play in moulding republican strategy. Rather, it is the contemporary circumstances which seemed to highlight and validate certain aspects of the republican tradition to carry forward. As a result, English suggests that each split was situational, but also consequential upon aspects of the long-standing republican tradition; fractures were defined by continuities and discontinuities.[22]

In a similar way to English, the literature produced by White and O'Brien stresses the importance of context, claiming that it is only possible to fully understand the splits within republicanism in terms of the time- and place-specific evolution of the Irish conflict itself. It is therefore essential to look beyond generalised templates or theories.

White and O'Brien account for contemporary circumstances within each split by highlighting the evolutionary nature of the movement. They successfully present each division as logical and necessary for the progression of the movement. The strong focus on oral history by White offers something new in the analysis of republican splits. He points out that 'To understand why people engage in violence we need to understand the actor's interpretation and not the experts.'[23] The evolution of republicanism is therefore very much viewed from a 'bottom-up' perspective and he considers 'how the timing of recruitment affects an individual's perception of the republican movement'.[24] White argues that the two social conditions of geography and timing of recruits have a direct influence on the direction of the movement. He goes about explaining this by highlighting the differences between recruits before and after 1969. In the first half of the twentieth century, 'because the recruitment base was narrow and because new recruits shared common social backgrounds, the movement became an insular, tradition bound, conspiratorial clan shaped by the experience of those still involved from the 1920s'.[25] However, post-1969 republican recruits entered a qualitatively different republican movement. Events such as internment, Bloody Sunday and the hunger strikes generated relatively large numbers of recruits who were 'less likely to be from republican families and are less likely to be committed to the traditions and principles that sustained the movement during the bleak years'.[26] Such an analysis exemplifies how response to the reality of political events gives the republican movement an ever-evolving characteristic. White therefore adds another dimension to the republican movement's tendency to split. The timing of recruitment is vital to that particular generation's perception of the republican movement. As a new generation with differing perceptions question the direction, tension is caused and ultimately leads to a split.

O'Brien provides a detailed account of the Sinn Féin/IRA relationship and stresses the gradual engagement with the political process as an evolutionary, logical step. It is a common conception in many histories of republicanism to describe the divisions as tension between the military and political components. However, O'Brien suggests that rather than the IRA being marginalised it was instead evolving. As he puts it: 'Sinn Féin was not separating itself from the IRA. Rather the IRA was being politicised ... the military and political efforts were being fused together'.[27] The military struggle was justified as a response to the political circumstances of that time. Rather than explaining the splits within Irish republicanism as politics versus military strategy, O'Brien suggests that contextual realities have determined the prominence of either tactic.

Sinn Féin justified the actions of the IRA by arguing that violence arose from political conditions that it alone had no power to change.[28] However, O'Doherty makes the valid point that if the 'violence can in fact be switched on and off to suit electoral purposes, it clearly isn't generated by the political conditions, it clearly isn't the passion of the aggrieved in action; rather it is a tool of a thinking movement'.[29] Therefore, whilst the arguments from English, White and O'Brien highlight the relevance of context in understanding the direction of the republican mmovement, O'Doherty reminds us such pragmatism was not at the expense of stretegic planning and tactical decision making. Some decisions may be made to satisfy internal constituencies or because the leadership *wants* change.

Tension from 1986 onwards

In 1986 the key strategic decision was made to drop abstention in respect of Leinster House from party policy, resulting in another organisational split. Abstention was judged by some to be a fundamental and basic principle that had been prevalent within republican ideology since the end of the Irish Civil War. In no circumstances short of an independent thirty-two county republic could it be compromised. There was apprehension that the recognition of a 'partitionist parliament' governing the twenty-six counties might be extended to recognising a six county northern variant, once the principle of the thirty-two county sovereign Republic, declared in 1916 and seen as inviolable, was breached. Given this outlook, 'anyone who therefore sought to revive the question of abstention was going to have to face the situation where not only a policy was going to have to be amended, but a state of mind'.[30] From the early 1980s, the epicentre of the movement had started to gravitate away from Dublin towards the North and the Adams-McGuinness leadership who were more willing to relegate republican dogma and replace it with pragmatic judgement and tactical assessment. Under the dual strategy of 'armalite and ballot box' deployed after 1981, Sinn Féin was given a far more equal role to the IRA than had previously been the case.[31] The IRA's militarism and Sinn Féin's traditionalism of the first phase of the troubles had masked the political problems likely to surface as the 'war' dragged on without obvious gains.

The emergence of Republican Sinn Féin (RSF) in 1986 constituted a rearguard restatement of fundamental republican principles. The 1986 split, led by former Provisional Sinn Féin leader Ruairí Ó Brádaigh, was not because there was unease towards politics *per se*; RSF emerged because of the refusal of fundamentalists to participate in a twenty-six county parliament, an act that would formally recognise partition and a step towards 'complete absorption in to the British system'.[32] In 1983 Ruairí Ó Brádaigh claimed:

> I am very proud of two things: firstly, I regard the period 1969–1983 as having marked a high point on the graph of the Irish people's struggle for freedom, ranking alongside the 1798 Rising, the Land War of 1879–82 and the 1916–1923 period; secondly during my 14 years as head of Sinn Féin there were no splits or splinters – long may it remain so, as it will, provided we stick to basic principles.[33]

It is this delicate balance between ideological fundamentalism and principle that has so often produced tension within republicanism. A fault line between politics and armed struggle is often highlighted as the fundamental rationale behind each split, but armed struggle persisted beyond 1986 and that fault line, whilst of great importance, has not always run along the same contours. RSF remains abstentionist, with the principle still firmly part of the group's position that the only true Dáil Éireann was formed by the 1918 all-Ireland elections. The group insists: 'we are not for sale ... by any group with one foot in the constitutional grave ... we shall maintain our own identity as the republican movement'.[34]

The emergence of the Real IRA in 1997 and the 32 County Sovereignty Movement (32CSM) was predicated more on the centrality of armed struggle and rejection of the six county state. The 32CSM's members had accepted the 1986 downgrading of republican fundamentals amid the leadership's pledge of continuing armed actions. Therefore, whilst the 32CSM attack 'those who have lost their nerve and compromised the republican position'[35] such criticism is based less on the principle of abstention and more on the perceived role of militarism and opposition to the movement's absorption into the northern state.

Richards places the politics versus armed struggle tension into a wider context. Firstly, he generically discusses the role of political fronts, 'subordinate to the terrorist organisation'.[36] This premise is then applied to Sinn Féin and the IRA. However, from the 1990s onwards Sinn Féin ceased to be a 'political front' and moved to senior partner, providing the driving force of the movement. Whilst Richards is thought-provoking in terms of highlighting the concessions and political weight the threat of violence has brought to the movement, he fails to consider why this relationship between violence and politics has unbalanced and even split the republican movement.

Smith does however explore the friction between politics and armed struggle as ever-present in the republican tradition.[37] He provides a valuable study evaluating the various strategic goals of the IRA and ways it sought to realise them through the use or threat of violence. The emphasis placed on the strategy of the republican movement considers that the use of violence is 'not simply about the crude application of military might, but is a more calculating and competitive environment'.[38] Smith also considers the tension caused within the movement by using tactical violence, suggesting it is 'possible to reinterpret its history as a struggle for and against political control over military'.[39] Agitation among some factions of the movement who can see the potential of political participation causes the movement to split. Whilst within each split the tension between politics and violence is apparent, this argument tends to be more descriptive than analytical. The strategic goals that underscore the politics of Sinn Féin and the gradual supplanting of force are to an extent pushed aside in favour of a straightforward dichotomy between armed struggle and political activity.

Munck criticises this tendency of academic analysts and the media to draw upon the simplistic distinction between armed struggle and politics or, as he phrases it, 'hawks' and 'doves'. He argues that these 'categories are simply inadequate to convey the complexity, and often, contradictory component elements, of republican ideology'.[40] Careful not to replace one simple dichotomy for another, Munck proposes the alternative distinctions of 'theological' and 'realists'. The theological is essentially utopian, where '"principles" prevail over tactics, the past appears more real than the present', whereas realists, 'seek pragmatic changes and are less pessimistic about achieving them through institutional means'.[41] Yet, the important observation is that 'within each of these categories we find both "hawks" and "doves" according to the prevailing categorisation'.[42] There is a tendency within the media and mainstream political arena to view the conduct of 'dissidents' as actions with little logic, an analysis that therefore places them in the 'hawks' or 'theological' camp. Whilst the media are happy to reduce the actions of 'dissidents' to simple pathology or criminal activity, an emphasis which obscures any political dynamic, Munck's argument highlights the complex nature of Irish republicanism where various strands within each grouping do not allow for simplistic categorisation. Thus, there is a need to look beyond the perspective of 'dissident' groups simply having an affinity with violence and explore the ideological underpinning of armed struggle.

Kevin Rafter has attempted to chart the defining periods within the Sinn Féin/IRA relationship and, similarly to Richards and Munck, highlights the fault lines between pragmatists and hardliners which he claims became apparent immediately after the 1985 Anglo-Irish Agreement. Rafter explores the history of the party in relation to the politics of pragmatism, where the flexibility of the republican movement under the Adams-McGuinness leadership has been paramount to the success of the ballot box over armed struggle. He states that the 'IRA, for so long Sinn Féin's masters – came to play the role of servant'.[43] Within the Provisional IRA/Sinn Féin relationship, politics may have triumphed, yet, with such comments as 'acceptance has been signalled that violence did not succeed'[44] one can assume that Rafter has been too quick to accept the entire erosion of militarism. It was evident from an early stage of the Northern Ireland peace process that there remained classic peace process 'spoiler groups' and splinters from the Provisional IRA who believed in the utility of violence. The 32CSM newspaper, *Sovereign Nation*, demonstrates that there is still a strand of republicanism with a preference towards hard-line tactics, in highlighting how 'Pearse and the people who fought with him during Easter week did not view sovereignty as an obscure concept on piece of paper (or an intellectual discussion theologising what should be done) but a crucial issue worth fighting for.'[45] Pragmatism is sometimes portrayed as far too appealing to resist and there is little consideration for those who fail to adhere to the culture of compromise. This is surprising considering that within peace processes it is very unlikely all leaders and factions will see negotiated peace as beneficial, making spoilers a prevalent feature of negotiated settlements.[46]

As Darby and Mac Ginty observe, violence precedes peace processes and continues to remain an unavoidable background during them.[47] The sensitive issues within a negotiated settlement often produce leaders or factions who are unsatisfied with the outcome. As Stedman notes, 'Even the best designed settlements must be prepared for violence from leaders and organisations who decide that the kind of peace in question is not in their interest.'[48] Those who use violence to undermine negotiated peace, or spoilers, can be identified in almost all peace processes. Moreover, the emergence of rejectionists (the modern 'spoiler groups' in the language of contemporary peace processes) is hardly unprecedented in Irish politics. Whilst discussing general trends between peace processes and spoiler group violence, Darby states that during negotiations, 'it is difficult to find any instances when such a move was not accompanied by a split between two main groups – *zealots* and *dealers*'.[49] The *zealots* represent the less compromising and more theological groups who 'picked up the torch – sometimes literally – they believed had been surrendered by the *dealers*'.[50] It is the aim of such groups not to influence the content of any agreement, but to disrupt negotiations to prevent any agreement being reached. Northern Ireland is no exception to Darby's universal observation and, considering the history of republican splits, the emergence of spoilers was not only more likely during the peace process but inevitable.

Evaluating external inputs to the compromise

Since the end of the Cold War, political and academic focus has shifted from inter-state to intra-state conflict. Such global realignment therefore caused a rush to 'examine critically attitudes and perceptions towards conflict ... and the meaning of resolution'[51] in the search for a new paradigm for conflict resolution. The typical nature of such conflict is protracted, deep rooted and runs along ethnic or identity based lines. It is therefore vital to remember that each 'conflict has its own distinct culture, history and social development'.[52] Despite this, apparent commonalities between the ethno-national conflicts in, for example, Northern Ireland, South Africa and Israel-Palestine have highlighted the possibility of comparison between each situation. The complexity of the conflicts in these deeply divided societies, along with the high likelihood of intercommunal violence, has brought together separate cases in an attempt to form an international perspective. The importance of this comparative function in being able to transfer the lessons learnt from one situation to another has been disputed, but external encouragement to Sinn Féin to compromise its immediate goals was nonetheless apparent.

Guelke and Cox both examine the importance of international influences upon the peace process in Northern Ireland. Cox suggests that a very significant influence on the Northern Irish situation 'was the larger shifts in the international system brought about by the end of the Cold War'.[53] Its closure meant a shift in the focus of global politics towards tension within states. With a conflict ostensibly parochial and deep rooted as Northern Ireland's, it may be hard to see what relationship it may have to events elsewhere. Bearing this in mind Cox is careful not to argue that the peace process was a result of the cessation of the Cold War alone, but contends that whilst 'the IRA may well have been a quintessentially Irish phenomenon it could however, not escape the world or ignore what was happening outside of Ireland. Nor I think did it try to.'[54]

Whilst Cox emphasises the importance of the international perspective to Northern Ireland, Guelke takes this argument a step further by highlighting the connections between various peace processes. Guelke goes about demonstrating a chain of events linking one process to another. South Africa embraced a peace process in the 1990s which culminated in the country's transition to a non-racial democracy, this in turn providing encouragement and a positive basis for comparison with Northern Ireland. By the late 1990s, the Good Friday

Agreement 'came to be seen as a model for the resolution of conflict in other deeply divided societies', especially in the Basque region, and 'despite the difficulties and implications the GFA encountered, the example of the settlement ... was seen as particularly relevant to the continuing quest for peace between Israelis and Palestinians'.[55] Therefore, whilst the comparison of peace processes helps to provide a framework or predictive function, according to Cox and Guelke it also provides 'encouragement to the process of change in the other'[56] seemingly intractable conflicts lacking solutions.

Whilst the peace process in Northern Ireland did not happen in a vacuum and was therefore inevitably touched to some extent by international events, it is necessary to question exactly how much weight should be attached to the importance of international comparisons. The South African peace process left the African National Congress (ANC) as the dominant force in South Africa, where political prisoners were released into a political system of black majority rule. However, in Northern Ireland, Sinn Féin had emerged as one element in a power-sharing coalition in a polity which remains part of the United Kingdom. Sinn Féin had fallen short of their political objectives and had made significant compromises on the road to the Good Friday Agreement. The U-turns made by Sinn Féin have led sceptics such as Dixon[57] to propose that international relations theorists have overemphasised the international dimension. Instead, he argues the international aspect has been utilised 'by political actors to choreograph a settlement in Northern Ireland, creating a theatrical performance to persuade diverse constituencies to accept accommodation'.[58] In other words, the Sinn Féin/IRA leadership were able to present the gains of the ANC to an important constituency of the republican movement to disqualify the claims of abandoning principles and in turn gain support for unarmed struggle.

The GFA provided a stark example of the top-down nature of Sinn Féin's decision making[59] along with the leadership's ability to ensure wide support for political change of such a colossal stature. From Dixon's analysis it is possible to suggest that the republican leadership utilised the success of the ANC solely to ensure that the 'rank and file' would follow the party line and back the GFA despite achieving far lesser gains for republicans in Northern Ireland than the ANC had attained for the black community in South Africa. Put more simply, it suggests that Sinn Féin were utilising the success of the ANC as a smoke screen in order to disguise the scale of the compromise they were making. For the small minority that were unwilling to follow the leadership's directions there was an ultimatum of 'exiting mainstream republicanism and accepting the "high risks, little rewards" world of continuing militarism, or quitting the republican movement (of all shades) entirely'.[60] Dixon's analysis of the international comparative perspective which highlights the extent of the concessions made by Sinn Féin in turn draws attention to the space for dissident groups to emerge as the minority who were unwilling to be led into such substantial political change.

In addition, sharing a platform with the ANC gave the Sinn Féin leadership the opportunity to bask in some of the ANC's international limelight. For example, a visiting ANC delegation to Belfast described Adams as an Irish Mandela and in addition referred to the Sinn Féin leader as Mr President.[61] Significant gestures were also made to the party's wider membership; government ministers and officials of the ANC visited IRA prisoners in the Maze prison. Presented as statesmen of a similar stature to Mandela the Sinn Féin leadership benefited from international adulation whilst the rank and file were in receipt of ANC flattery. Such a portrayal of significance must have been far more appealing than the stark contrast of political isolation that would have undoubtedly resulted from exiting the peace process.

From the early 1990s it was becoming increasingly evident that politics would triumph over armed struggle in the form of a constitutional agreement. At this point Adams admitted 'he could envisage a future without the IRA'.[62] During the 1990s peace process the extent of U-turns made by Sinn Féin and the Provisionals proved remarkable given the adherence to republican orthodoxy during the previous two decades, notwithstanding the move away from twenty-six county abstention.[63]

By the turn of the century the Provisionals had ended their armed campaign and Sinn Féin agreed to share power in a government of Northern Ireland which was to remain in the United Kingdom. These momentous changes yielded the latest splits between those 'prepared to accept the lure of constitutionalism and those for whom fidelity to the supposed principles of republicanism outweighed the benefit of respectability conferred by entry into conventional politics'.[64] The Good Friday Agreement gave an Irish dimension to political arrangements in Northern Ireland but fell markedly short of Irish unity and the IRA's original objective of establishing a thirty-two county democratic socialist republic. Even mainstream republicans themselves readily acknowledged that 'the Agreement did not satisfy their aspirations'.[65]

Spoiling the peace?

For the majority of the Provisional rank and file, the apparent gains of the peace process such as prisoner releases, the reform of policing and the re-allocation of resources to nationalist communities justified the compromises made by Sinn Féin and the party's full absorption into the political institutions of Northern Ireland. Yet, despite a conscious effort to maintain a consensus within Sinn Féin and the Provisional IRA, which to a large degree worked, the GFA was seen as the final betrayal by a small yet significant number of republicans. Whilst there was overwhelming support from the northern nationalist community for the GFA, with 97 per cent voting 'Yes' in the referendum,[66] it is important to touch on the diversity of those who opposed the deal. The form of departure from the Provisionals' future political trajectory was diverse. The spectrum of dissent throughout the 1990s ranged from the resignation of local councillors and Members of the Northern Ireland Assembly (MLAs), and the formation of critical journals and blogs, to the continuation of militant activity by certain groups. This demonstrated the range of antipathy and opposition felt towards the Good Friday Agreement in a small section of the republican community. As a result it appears a more accurate description to refer to the republican divisions of the 1990s as more of a 'shattering' in their nature, as opposed to a split, which implies a far more decisive and clear-cut mass departure.[67]

There is an abundance of literature attempting to explore the evolution of Sinn Féin strategy leading up to the GFA. Considering the compromises made by Sinn Féin in entering a power-sharing executive is fundamental in understanding the dissident justification for their opposition to the political status quo. Yet, whilst there is a broad discussion considering Sinn Féin's adherence to, and adaption of, the republican principles still espoused, this is rarely considered in relation to the emergence of dissident groups.

Sinn Féin has been through a period of profound transition, during which the organisation's overall political outlook has been significantly reshaped. The development of a peace agenda from the 1980s onwards and the formation of a pan-nationalist alliance 'brought with it new possibilities and new problems'.[68] Through involvement in dialogue Sinn Féin was able to present itself as the dominant voice in modern day Irish republicanism, yet the party's future became dictated by a process that it helped shape but by no means controlled.[69] For this reason these fundamental shifts can only be made sense of when placed into the wider context. Whilst considering the compromises made by Sinn Féin it is therefore important to consider the impact of exogenous factors such as the economy, external ideological forces and social, political and military circumstances in dictating the shape of 'mainstream' republicanism. Is mainstream republicanism a product of the changing material conditions and a shifting political context? And if so, to what extent?

There is a need to consider the role of macro-level forces in shaping mainstream republicanism. Whilst considering post nationalism within the broader context of Western Europe, Bean provides a valuable discussion on the 'seismic changes'[70] made by Sinn Féin in both organisational and ideological terms in accepting the GFA. According to Bean, practical politics and the strategic analysis which dominated the Provisionals prior to the 1980s have been replaced with the politics of identity (which dominated the Good Friday Agreement) and the vague language of transition. As he notes, 'the language of transition and the politics of implicit dynamics contained within the structures established by the agreement have replaced the clarity and simplicity of traditional republican discourse'.[71] Bean draws a parallel with the pragmatic changes made by New Labour in the mid-1990s and proposes that it is the nature of republicanism to adapt to contemporary events and experience, relegating portrayals of its party as one of romantic tradition and heritage. Amid this redefinition of republican core ideology New Sinn Féin is portrayed as the epitome of post-modern politics. Identity and culture have replaced territory and sovereignty as key issues, the Sinn Féin 'Ireland of Equals' slogan being the embodiment of this.[72]

Similarly to Bean, Frampton proposes that the period leading up to the Good Friday Agreement was a time in which the nature of the republican movement became utterly transformed; 'by 2007, Sinn Féin was virtually unrecognizable from the entity of a quarter of a century earlier'.[73] Yet, these two accounts differ in that whilst Bean exposes Sinn Féin's removal of traditional republican discourse Frampton claims that despite this transformation Sinn Féin remains on the 'Road to the Republic'. The crux of Frampton's argument is that, rather than abandoning principles, the tactics of the Adams-McGuinness leadership has in fact been based in realism, which 'demonstrated a willingness and ability to modify its strategy'.[74] With this, Frampton has a tendency to take Sinn Féin very much at their word in their argument that the Good Friday Agreement is an 'an agreement, not a settlement'. According to Frampton, despite making such a strategic transformation Sinn Féin has not abandoned its republican principles, but instead has evolved to fit into the situational reality in which it finds itself and continues on the onward march to what the party sees as inevitable success.

Such a position allows Sinn Féin to appear very much in an arrangement where the leadership has the ability to dictate and determine the political form it wishes to take whilst leaving very little room for consideration of the impact context plays in determining the shape of Sinn Féin's republicanism. Whilst considering the seismic changes within Sinn Féin Frampton does not provide any assessment of the wider context within which change occurred, but rather is focused on proving the party's 'long march' through an adherence to traditional republican continuity. To clarify this point, Bean highlights how Frampton fails to consider the impact of the collapse of the Soviet Union and the emergence of post-ideological politics which has dominated international politics since the 1990s.[75] The result 'is that Sinn Féin's strategy is now designed to operate on a much narrower terrain'.[76] In order to assess any political change, context is essential in understanding the result. The transformation of Sinn Féin from a revolutionary party to one of mainstream politics did not occur in a vacuum. To miss the importance of exogenous pressures would be to consider ideological debates within Irish republicanism peculiarly immune (if not hermetically sealed) from external influences.[77] Therefore, an analysis considering Sinn Féin's move from insurgency to electoral politics is somewhat incomplete without considering the wider global political landscape.

In addition there is also a tendency by Frampton to portray Sinn Féin as the sole embodiment of republican principles, despite failing to provide a proper assessment of what republicanism signifies or whether it could be offered by 'outsiders' beyond Sinn Féin. He therefore portrays Sinn Féin as owning the monopoly on republicanism and as a result perceives republicanism as what the Provisionals did and tacitly assumes closure with the Good Friday Agreement. On this reading, there is little political or ideological space for the emergence of 'dissidents'.[78] More specifically there is little cognisance, despite the extent of historical examples, of the likelihood of fracture within Irish republicanism as a consequence of Sinn Féin's absorption into the political mainstream.

Whilst political shifts in the wider context have undoubtedly influenced mainstream republican discourse there is also a need to examine factors at a more localised level. Bean's analysis on the changing politics of Sinn Féin does go on to stress the importance of material circumstances in understanding the shape and tactics of the Provisionals.[79] Through direct interaction with the political economy in Northern Ireland the British state managed to define the context within which republicanism manoeuvred, ultimately characterising the nature of republican strategy. In an attempt to marginalise the Provisionals, the British state developed social and economic policies of amelioration. For example, the Fair Employment Act 1989 and the Northern Ireland Act 1998 were introduced to promote the equality of opportunity. In addition Northern Ireland became the recipient of a significant amount of funding from the Peace and Reconciliation Fund and the European Social Fund to help promote and maintain peace. As a result of direct British and European involvement in the political economy of Northern Ireland, 'the Provisionals were well aware that by the 1990s the British strategy was successfully undermining republican influence in the nationalist community'.[80] The outcome was that republicans reorganised and reoriented their community activism in an attempt to broaden their electoral base in the 1990s. Although it appeared to be successful in terms of building electoral support, this came at a price. Bean suggests that the success of social and economic change brought about by EU programmes and British government policies effectively meant that the Provisionals failed to establish wider hegemony beyond base areas and ultimately became pulled into state structures.[81] The British strategy changed from one of containment by exclusion to that of co-operation and conciliation. In response, the future trajectory for Sinn Féin was re-tailored to fit the changing socio-economic landscape and took on the characteristics of 'discontinuity and contingency rather than adherence to republican tradition'.[82]

Such an assessment of Sinn Féin's movement into constitutionalism on the surface appears to strengthen the argument put forward by 'dissidents' that the Provisionals full absorption into the political structures of Northern Ireland means they cannot be labelled republican in their current form. Yet, republicanism is far from monolithic and has never taken this form. As Bean suggests, 'in some cases it would appear that republicanism was so devoid of political form that it could be argued republicanism was whatever the leadership said it was'.[83]

The Provisionals have never been a static, ideology-bound movement, but rather a fluid entity evolving as time dictates. As emphasised by McGovern, republicanism can be viewed as a discursive ideological paradigm offering 'a range of avenues and possibilities for both action and thought which have, in turn, been profoundly influenced by wider developments, both material and ideological'.[84] Irish republicanism does not constitute a single perspective but instead comprises of competing, even at times contradictory, intellectual and ideological influences. What has been left is 'a range of exemplary models, memories, stories and rational political arguments that can be interpreted and reinterpreted through time'.[85] It is this fluid diversity that enabled the Provisionals to replace revolutionary goals with those of social reformism[86] and maintain the line that they remain adhered to republican principles.

The political context in which Sinn Féin has operated has been heavily influenced by the consociational nature of political arrangements in Northern Ireland. Such an institutional arrangement has resulted in opposing parties on either side of the political spectrum, the Democratic Unionist Party (DUP) and Sinn Féin, becoming the two largest parties in the Assembly.[87] Ruane considers the 'culture of compromise' embraced by both unionists and nationalists in agreeing to the GFA and how each side sold the Agreement to its supporters on the basis that their fundamental concerns would be met. Thus, 'the UUP, PUP, and DUP assured unionists that the union was secure; the Social Democratic and Labour Party (SDLP) and Sinn Féin assured nationalists and republicans that the agreement would secure equality and pave the way to a united Ireland'.[88] Ruane predicts that if both sides cannot simultaneously deliver what they promised and, 'that as trust appears to have been misplaced, the party and its leadership will pay a heavy price'.[89] Against this there is clear recent survey evidence of considerable Catholic contentment with the Union.[90]

But what about those who oppose the political arrangements under the Agreement and are therefore not represented within the political status quo? Those who oppose the Sinn Féin trajectory on the grounds their constitutionalism is a 'sell-out' stress the concession of principles and core values in return for political gains. The difference as they see it between their own republicanism and that of the Provisionals is shown by the claim in the 32CSM's *Sovereign Nation*:

> While republicans emphasise they are for peace they are not for 'peace at any price'; and the view of republicans opposed to the Belfast agreement is the 1998 treaty is precisely peace at the wrong price. The real question is not 'peace' but 'peace' on whose terms?[91]

Inextricably bound to the growing electoral success of Sinn Féin was the consequential downgrading of the IRA 'as the "cutting edge" of community resistance'.[92] As with other nationalist and radical movements internationally, the geo-political framework after the Cold War provided a context that was not conducive to revolutionary tactics. The politics of compromise replaced that of the physical force tradition. The gradual shift from a military strategy in the early 1970s, to the dual strategy of 'armalite and ballot box' in the 1980s, to the gradual decline of the PIRA as an 'armed front' in the 1990s, culminated in the 2005 order to dump arms as the PIRA completed arms decommissioning. The Provisionals found it harder to justify physical force and martyrdom as righteous and necessary. As Shanahan argues, 'the republican world view, with its metaphysics of martyrdom, necessity and destiny, was forced to yield to more pragmatic considerations'.[93]

Martin McGuinness, referring to dissident groups as 'traitors to Ireland' for pursuing armed struggle, demonstrated the extent to which the Sinn Féin leadership want to distance the party from armed actions, but this can also be seen as an attempt to distinguish between the (morally justifiable) actions of the PIRA in the past and unjustifiable contemporary violence. Considering the role of political violence, specifically in the overall evolution of republicanism, Alonso demonstrates how realism and pragmatism defeated the ideological absolutism of the Provisionals, whose previous objectives were considered non-negotiable and could only be achievable through armed struggle.[94] In a wealth of interviews with former republican prisoners the justifications of violence are questioned even by some former IRA personnel, epitomised by comments such as: 'I have been involved in military conflict, right, but I also believe that war is futile.'[95] Alonso highlights the frustration of many republicans who endured long periods in jail for Sinn Féin to accept major compromises. He therefore indicates (if unintentionally) why 'dissident' groups emerged. As one ex-prisoner puts it, 'I have to say that all those years spent in prison by so many people, all those deaths, I don't think it was worth it, when you add all that up, I would say I think it was a net loss.'[96] Stressing the futility of armed struggle as a means for achieving a united Ireland assumes that by pursuing this militarist logic 'dissident' groups are devoid of realism and pragmatism. However, it is necessary to point out that for dissidents armed struggle is about continuing resistance to what they view as 'British imperialism'. Therefore, the basis for continued violence by dissidents is a tactic of defiance emerging from the reality that they would rather resist, making life harder for the British, than compromise on the ambiguous 'long road' to a united Ireland.

Moloney's revealing insight into the inner workings of the IRA provides an invaluable empirical account of modern day republicanism, providing a narrative which details the Provisional's journey towards the peace process. A distinctive theme running throughout Moloney's thesis is the protagonist role played by Adams from the 1980s onwards in constructing an electoral profile for Sinn Féin, whilst building a pan-nationalist alliance with Fianna Fáil and the SDLP largely out of sight from the rank and file. Moloney's argument suggests a very much top-down approach towards the peace process, based upon deception and 'betrayal of the grass roots'. Thus, Moloney claims:

> What was striking about the remarks made to the Executive by Adams and McGuinness was the extent to which both men still encouraged the view that the peace process was a just tactical ploy, designed to bring political advantage ... They similarly bolstered the view that the IRA would go back to war if its goal of achieving a promise of British withdrawal was not realised ... Again actual events have demonstrated how unreliable these assurances were.[97]

When considering the history of Irish republicanism the PIRA/RIRA split of 1997 was hardly unexpected. Indeed, Moloney is correct in his claim that 'the IRA split had been a virtual certainty from the moment that Adams embarked on the peace process, such was the scale of the departure from traditional IRA ideology that the enterprise implied'.[98] What makes Moloney's narrative invaluable to republican critics of Adams and the peace process is that it identifies the Provisionals as the faction who departed from republican principles.

But was armed struggle ever a principle or simply a tactic – an expedient for promoting the desired goal of a united Ireland? Although labelled 'dissidents' for rejecting the mainstream republican policy, the 'ultra' IRAs, Tonge asserts, are continuing advocates of an armed struggle which had nearly always existed within republican tradition. Irish republicanism has an extensive historical tradition of fusing violence with more peaceful methods. At various times the preference towards either has fluctuated, suggesting 'the "dissidents" of the CIRA and RIRA are merely the residual ultra-wing that has always existed within Irish republicanism'.[99] Thus, because the presence of violence is so inextricably bound to the republican tradition these dissident groups 'argue that they have remained true to Republican principles and the label "dissident" is perhaps misleading'.[100] From the viewpoint of these dissident groups it is Sinn Féin and the Provisionals who have deviated from Irish Republican theology. However, the Provisionals defend their movement into constitutionalism stressing how armed struggle was only ever a tactic. Thus, Gerry Kelly claimed, 'As we look back across a century of struggle, we see that each phase on the journey has been different. Each has required different strategies and tactics. Republicans required courage to survive, resourcefulness to find new ways forward.'[101] For the Provisionals, the cessation of armed struggle is presented as a pragmatic move designed to advance republican ambitions. It is this principle/tactic dichotomy that is fundamental in understanding the differing views on armed struggle; as either intrinsically embedded into republican theology or a temporary tool to be utilised according to circumstance.

For some dissidents, the continuing need for violence as a tool to remove the British sovereign claim effectively elevates an armed campaign to a principle of republican struggle, even if violence remains a tool rather than part of republican ideology *per se*:

Republicanism argues that history and experience show that constitutional means alone and on their own are not enough – physical force has evoked a response from the British State, whereas peaceful methods of protest tend to be greeted with indifference. If constitutional methods fail, it is prepared to envisage extra-constitutional means as a last resort to effect political change.[102]

Such a strong alignment to the physical force tradition has led to criticism of dissidents for being 'mired in militarism', or subordinating the planning of Irish Freedom to the visceral urge to fight for it.[103] In reference to the Omagh bomb, *An Phoblacht* commented that there is a danger that 'the continuation of the armed campaign itself becomes the objective'.[104]

The mainstream republican (i.e. Sinn Féin) political condemnation of dissident violence is crucial to the stability of the Northern Irish institutions. Whilst mainstream republicans do not view 'violence as the result of some kind of deep cultural pathology, archaic religious antagonism or straight forward tribal barbarism',[105] they argue that dissidents are bereft of any political strategy.

The Provisional critique of dissident violence has in turn been criticised by commentators who do not support armed struggle. The contributions by Anthony McIntyre, a former member of the Provisional IRA, provide a valuable critique of mainstream republicanism. Whilst opposing the continuation of armed struggle he challenges the Provisionals' claim that the shift towards constitutionalism is simply another step on the 'long road' to Irish unity. Instead, McIntyre has the tendency to present the U-turns made by Sinn Féin, especially in reference to their views on armed republicanism, as hypocritical. He highlights this by stressing the commonalities between dissident violence and the techniques formerly utilised by the Provisionals:

> I totally oppose the use of armed force and criticise it most strongly but never forget that the people using it are in the very same mould as those young men and women who resisted tenaciously the British criminalisation policy in the jails.[106]

The continued use of violence and the supposedly negligible political rationale for their violent activities underlie the common conception of dissident groups as simply having a fixation with violence and typically being described as 'irritants, embarrassing Sinn Féin through the use of traditional republican rhetoric'.[107] Whilst McIntyre stresses the futility of violence he does suggest that the Provisionals are largely responsible for the militarism the replacement IRAs have pursued and 'for Martin McGuinness to denounce them as traitors for following the example he set for decades is to commit an act of treachery against truth'.[108]

In addition to his critique of Sinn Féin's involvement in the peace process McIntyre provides insight into connotations the label 'dissident' provides and highlights the tendency for academics when discussing dissidents only to supply the reader with general descriptive accounts. He notes that, whilst there is an abundance of academic literature on loyalist and republican militia, 'little has emerged about the phenomenon of dissent'[109] which for the most part is simply mentioned in passing.[110] In exploring the meaning of the term 'dissent' he provides the following definition:

> Dissent has taken different forms. On occasion it has been the emergence of individuals at the grassroots level of an organisation who were unhappy with elements of strategy or elements of leadership. On the other hand dissenting voices may emerge from within a dominant bloc at the centre of the movement. Sometimes it can be violent but quite often amounts to nothing more than the expression of an opinion contrary to the dominant line.[111]

Whilst this description is novel and assists in formulating what the term dissent constitutes, it is in need of further investigation as McIntyre himself is well aware; 'There is such a rich history of dissent within the world of Northern Ireland's militia waiting to be written that one chapter addressed to both "sides" is grossly inefficient to explain it.'[112] There is the possibility that the under-researched phenomenon of dissent may indicate the extent to which unity has been maintained, or alternatively, signify that 'the odd voice that broke the silence was all too easily slotted into the crank category'.[113]

Existing research on dissident republicanism?

One of the first comprehensive academic research projects to emerge dedicated to contemporary dissident republicanism is Frampton's *Legion of the Rearguard*.[114] The book provides a very valuable guide to the origins, current activities and claims of historical legitimacy of both violent and non-violent dissident groups. Whilst offering insight into contemporary dissident republicanism there is an over-reliance on certain sources, especially in terms of the evidence of David Rupert. Whilst the FBI informer managed to gain close ties to Michael McKevitt, leader of the RIRA, and therefore may have valuable insight into the inner workings of the group, the points made by Frampton are overly dependent on Rupert's testimony. There is a lack of grass-roots perspectives, with few interviews with dissidents conducted.

More recently, further literature has emerged from Sanders and Evans and Tonge. Research from Evans and Tonge explores the enduring nature of the militant republican tradition.[115] They assess why militant republicanism has never enjoyed popular majority support amongst the Irish people, but has endured, albeit in a limited form.[116] Using original data from the Economic and Social Research Council (ESRC) 2010 General Election Survey this research suggests asymmetric communal dissident threat perceptions and also indicates a modest level of sympathy for dissident violence,[117] nonetheless, concluding that a mandate from the living continues to elude dissident republicanism. For dissidents, their mandate continues to come from the martyrdom of the 'patriot dead'.[118]

Sanders also considers the issue of legitimacy within Irish republicanism.[119] This research considers the historical precedent within Irish republicanism for dissent to emerge. Sanders outlines the complex history of Irish republicanism and assesses the propensity for the movement to split throughout history. He continues to explore how these underlying tensions have persisted beyond the GFA and explains how the fault line between ideology and pragmatism has placed continuing strain on Irish republicanism.

Currie and Taylor's collection on dissident republicanism provides a wide range of analysis from various contributors.[120] This collection gives a detailed overview of the nature of dissident republicanism in terms of origin and the level of threat they pose, as well as offering very detailed analysis. For example, Horgan and Gill's chapter charts the rise of dissident activity since October 2009 offering valuable geographic and demographic data on dissidents. The statistics and analysis offered by Nalton, Ramsey and Taylor on the use of the internet as means of radicalisation also provides valuable quantitative data, adding to the small, yet growing, research analysing the spread of dissent within Irish republicanism.

Conclusion

The diverse spectrum of Irish republicanism has produced a range of academic perspectives attempting to make sense of the movement's volatile nature. Those who are historically determinist in their approach,[121] examine the history of the movement in an attempt to identify common themes and construct an explanation of republican splits through generalised theories. This presents an almost cyclical phenomenon which consistently describes the pressures between political struggle and military conflict as providing the reoccurring catalyst in dividing the movement. There is a tendency here to view republicanism purely through the prism of the past. Such an approach provides very little scope for comparison between the contextual realities behind each break. This intrinsic view of republicanism relies heavily on the movement's internal logic and has the tendency to overlook the impact of exogenous factors such as material conditions and external ideological forces.

Alternatively, there are those who highlight the importance of examining the context within which each division occurred.[122] Such accounts demonstrate which and how certain aspects of republican ideology became prevalent at different times. This has led to various depictions of republican tensions: for example between militarism and politics, 'theology' versus 'realism', left versus right, and hardliners versus pragmatists.[123] So why the various illustrations?

Irish republicanism has never been a static entity. Various strategies and ideas have ebbed and flowed. That republicanism has never been cast in a rigid mould makes it harder to define and therefore easier for Sinn Féin, despite the obvious compromises made, to proclaim they remain the embodiment of republican principles. Similarly, 'dissident' groups fail to represent a monolithic entity, meaning they cannot be slotted into simple categorisations and easily labelled. Yet, whilst there has been a large academic contribution on Sinn Féin's pragmatism and compromises in judging the level of adherence to republican principles,[124] to date, 'dissident' republicanism remains largely an under-researched area.

In common with most ideologies, Irish republicanism is relational. However, republicanism is not simply a product of material conditions, external ideological forces and social, political and military circumstances. It is also indebted to an inherited spectrum of political ideas. Republican core values differ not only over time but between individuals. As a result the various shades of contemporary republicanism are, to varying degrees, products of the interaction between context and tradition.

Minimal effort has been made to understand the dissident ideological standpoint, or the commonalities and dissimilarities amongst the various dissident groups and also what the term 'dissident' actually constitutes. Whilst there has been some analysis of the CIRA and RIRA it is mainly empirical and descriptive.[125] This point however, is intended not as criticism, but simply as a means of demonstrating the need to provide deeper insight. Continuous observations of these groups have been made through Indpendent Monitoring Commission (IMC) reports and security intelligence, yet few other attempts have been made to form a comprehensive understanding. There is a tendency to view 'dissident' group credentials in relation to 'mainstream' republican activities. Instead a more interpretist approach is required. More specifically, what is needed is an understanding of how the differing interpretations of republicanism held by 'dissident' groups frame actions, practices and tradition. Therefore, whilst general republican principles are an important consideration in discussing the various strands of republicanism, more so is the individual's interpretation or understanding.

The literature is therefore in need of enhancement in providing further insight into the ideology and functioning of 'dissident' groups, to expand beyond descriptive analysis. Only then will it be possible to begin to understand their principles within the contemporary context. So in answer to the question, is there space for the emergence of dissident republicanism?: history tells us that there has always been space for the emergence of dissidents within republicanism, whereas context will determine where on the republican spectrum there is space for them to emerge.

Notes

1 A. Maillot, *New Sinn Féin: Republicanism in the Twenty-first Century* (London, Routledge, 2005), p. 1.
2 See, R. Alonso, *The IRA and Armed Struggle* (London, Routledge, 2007); K. Bean, *The New Politics of Sinn Féin* (Liverpool, Liverpool University Press, 2007); R. English,

Armed Struggle: A History of the IRA (London, Macmillan, 2003); M. Frampton, *The Long March: Political Strategy of Sinn Féin, 1981–2007* (Basingstoke, Palgrave Macmillan, 2009); Maillot, *New Sinn Féin*; J. Ruane and J. Todd (eds), *After the Good Friday Agreement: Analysing Political Change in Northern Ireland* (Dublin, University College Dublin Press, 1999).

3 B. Feeney, *Sinn Féin: A Hundred Turbulent Years* (Dublin, O'Brien Press, 2002), p. 127.

4 See Feeney, *Sinn Féin*; Maillot, *New Sinn Féin*; J. Augusteijn, 'Political Violence and Democracy: An Analysis of the Tensions within Irish Republican Strategy, 1914–2002', *Irish Political Studies* 18, no. 1 (2003), pp. 1–26.

5 Feeney, *Sinn Féin*, p. 10.

6 *Ibid.*, p. 127.

7 *Ibid.*, p. 127.

8 Maillot, *New Sinn Féin*, p. 7.

9 Augusteijn, 'Political Violence and Democracy', p. 2.

10 English, *Armed Struggle*, p. 133.

11 H. Patterson, *The Politics of Illusion: A Political History of the IRA* (London, Serif, 1997), p. 12.

12 *Ibid.*, p. 12.

13 P. Walsh, *Irish Republicanism and Socialism: The Politics of the Republican Movement 1905 to 1994* (Belfast, Athol Books, 1994), p. 64.

14 M. Hayes, 'The Evolution of Republican Strategy and the "Peace Process" in Ireland', *Race Class* 39, no. 3 (1998), p. 22.

15 *Ibid.*, p. 23.

16 Cited in M. L. R. Smith, *Fighting for Ireland? The Military Strategy of the Irish Republican Movement* (London, Routledge, 1995), p. 93.

17 J. Bowyer Bell, *The Secret Army: The IRA* (Oxon, Transaction Publishers, 2003), p. 371.

18 Walsh, *Irish Republicanism and Socialism*, p. 86.

19 Bowyer Bell, *The Secret Army*, p. 371.

20 R. English, *Irish Freedom: The History of Nationalism in Ireland* (Oxford, Pan Macmillan, 2006), p. 174.

21 *Ibid.*, p. 174.

22 *Ibid.*, p. 129.

23 R. White, *Provisional Irish Republicans: An Oral and Interpretative History* (Westport, Greenwood Press, 1993), p. 10.

24 *Ibid.*, p. 131.

25 *Ibid.*, p. 131.

26 *Ibid.*, pp. 131–132.

27 B. O'Brien, *The Long War: IRA and Sinn Féin* (Dublin, O'Brien Press, 1999), p. 127.

28 Smith, *Fighting for Ireland?*, p. 2.

29 M. O'Doherty, *The Trouble with Guns* (Belfast, Blackstaff Press, 1998), p. 157.

30 B. Lynn, 'Tactic or Principle? The Evolution of Republican Thinking on Abstentionism in Ireland, 1970–1998', *Irish Political Studies* 17, no. 2 (2002), p. 75.

31 O'Brien, *The Long War*, p. 122.

32 Republican Sinn Féin Poblachtach, *Presidential Address 93rd Ard-Fheis* (Dublin, Republican Sinn Féin, 1997).

33 R. White, *Ruairí Ó Brádaigh: The Life and Politics of an Irish Revolutionary* (Bloomington, Indiana University Press, 2006), p. 293.

34 *Ibid.*, p. 293.

35 *Irish Times*, 16 April 2001.

36 A. Richards, 'Terrorist Groups and Political Fronts: The IRA, Sinn Féin, the Peace Process and Democracy', *Terrorism and Political Violence* 13, no. 4 (2001), p. 73.

37 See Smith, *Fighting for Ireland?*

38 *Ibid.*, p. 2.

39 M. Von Tagen Page and M. L. R. Smith, 'War By Other Means: The Problem of Political Control in Irish Republican Strategy', *Armed Forces and Society* 27, no. 1 (2000), p. 100.

40 R. Munck, 'Irish Republicanism: Containment or New Departure?', in A. O'Day (ed.), *Terrorism Laboratory: The Case of Northern Ireland* (Aldershot, Dartmouth Publishing, 1995), p. 165.

41 *Ibid.*, p. 165.

42 *Ibid.*, p. 165.

43 K. Rafter, *Sinn Féin 1905–2005: In the Shadow of Gunmen* (Dublin, Gill and Macmillan, 2005), p. 3.

44 *Ibid.*, p. 242.

45 *Sovereign Nation*, May–June 2009, p. 4.

46 S. J. Stedman, 'Spoiler Problems in Peace Processes', *International Security* 22, no. 2 (1997), p. 8.

47 J. Darby and R. Mac Ginty, *The Management of Peace Processes* (Basingstoke, Palgrave, 2000), p. 8.

48 Stedman, 'Spoiler Problems in Peace Processes', p. 8.

49 J. Darby, 'A Truce Rather Than a Treaty? The Effect of Violence in the Irish Peace Process', in M. Cox, A. Guelke and F. Stephens (eds), *A Farewell to Arms? Beyond the Good Friday Agreement* (Manchester, Manchester University Press, 2006), p. 219.

50 *Ibid.*, p. 219.

51 J. L. Rasmussen, 'Peace Making in the Twenty First Century: New Rules, New Roles, New Actors', in I. Zartman and J. L. Rasmussen (eds), *Peacemaking in International Conflict: Methods and Techniques* (Washington, United States Institute of Peace Press, 1997), p. 28.

52 Darby and Mac Ginty, *The Management of Peace Processes*, p. 3.

53 M. Cox, 'Rethinking the International and Northern Ireland: A Defence', in Cox, Guelke and Stephens (eds), *A Farewell to Arms?*, p. 428.

54 *Ibid.*, p. 429.

55 A. Guelke, 'Political Comparisons from Johannesburg to Jerusalem', in Cox, Guelke and Stephens (eds), *A Farewell to Arms?*, p. 369.

56 *Ibid.*, p. 375.

57 See P. Dixon, 'Rethinking the International and Northern Ireland: A Critique', in Cox, Guelke and Stephens (eds), *A Farewell to Arms?*, pp. 409–426.

58 *Ibid.*, p. 410.

59 J. Tonge, 'Republican Paramilitaries and the Peace Process', in B. Barton and P. J. Roche (eds), *The Northern Irish Question: The Peace Process and the Belfast Agreement* (New York, Palgrave Macmillan, 2009), p. 179.

60 *Ibid.*, p. 179.

61 See, *Independent*, 'The ANC approves Brothers in arms in change's embrace', 3 March 1998.

62 Rafter, *Sinn Féin 1905–2005*, p. 242.

63 J. Tonge, '"They haven't gone away you know". Irish Republican "Dissidents" and "Armed Struggle"', *Terrorism and Political Violence* 16, no. 3 (2004), p. 676.

64 J. Tonge, *Northern Ireland* (Cambridge, Polity Press, 2006), p. 131.

65 Alonso, *The IRA and Armed Struggle*, p. 2.

66 See Conflict Archive in Northern Ireland (CAIN), 'Results of the Referenda in Northern Ireland and Republic of Ireland', 22 May 1998, www.cain.ulst.ac.uk/issues/politics/election/ref1998.htm.

67 *Saoirse*, 'Interview with Ruairí Ó Brádaigh', April 2010.

68 M. McGovern, 'Irish Republicanism and the Potential Pitfalls of Pluralism', *Capital and Class* 71 (2000), p. 135.

69 *Ibid.*, p. 135.

70 K. Bean, 'Shifting Discourses of New Nationalism and Post-republicanism', in M. Elliott (ed.), *The Long Road to Peace in Northern Ireland* (Liverpool, Liverpool University Press, 2007), p. 143.

71 *Ibid.*, p. 140.

72 For more on the Sinn Féin 'Ireland of Equals' rhetoric, see chapter 3.

73 Frampton, *The Long March*, p. 186.

74 *Ibid.*, p. 183.

75 K. Bean, 'Book Review: M. Frampton, The Long March', *Irish Political Studies* 25, no. 1 (2010), p. 137.

76 *Ibid.*, p. 137.

77 McGovern, 'Irish Republicanism and the Potential Pitfalls of Pluralism', p. 151.

78 Although Frampton later suggests that there is in his next book, *Legion of the Rearguard*.

79 K. Bean, 'The Economic and Social War Against Violence: British Social and Economic Strategy and the Evolution of Provisionalism', in A. Edwards and S. Bloomer (eds), *Transforming the Peace Process in Northern Ireland: From Terrorism to Democratic Politics* (Dublin, Irish Academic Press, 2008), p. 165.

80 *Ibid.*, p. 167.

81 *Ibid.*, p. 167.

82 Bean, *The New Politics of Sinn Féin*, p. 251.

83 Bean, 'Shifting Discourses of New Nationalism and Post-republicanism', p. 137.

84 McGovern, 'Irish Republicanism and the Potential Pitfalls of Pluralism', p. 145.

85 *Ibid.*, p. 146.

86 *Ibid.*, p. 146.

87 J. McGarry and B. O'Leary, 'Power Shared after the Death of Thousands', in R. Taylor (ed.), *Consociational Theory: McGarry and O'Leary. The Northern Ireland Conflict* (London, Routledge, 2009).

88 J. Ruane, 'The (End) of Irish History? Three Readings of the Current Conjuncture', in Ruane and Todd (eds), *After the Good Friday Agreement*, p. 164.

89 *Ibid.*, p. 160.

90 In the Northern Ireland Life and Times (NILT) 2010 survey the most popular constitutional preference amongst Catholics was 'To remain part of the United Kingdom with devolved government' with 46 per cent, the option 'to unify with the rest of Ireland' was the preference of 33 per cent of Catholics.

91 *Sovereign Nation*, April–May 2010.

92 K. Bean and M. Hayes, 'Sinn Féin and the New Republicanism of Ireland: Electoral Progress, Political Stasis, and Ideological Failure', *Radical History Review* 104 (2009), p. 128.

93 T. Shanahan, *The Provisional Irish Republican Army and the Morality of Terrorism* (Edinburgh, Edinburgh University Press, 2009), p. 64.

94 Alonso, *The IRA and Armed Struggle*, p. 193.

95 Interview with Ronnie McCartney, *ibid.*, p. 16.

96 Interview with Martin McKevitt, *ibid.*, p. 194.

97 E. Moloney, *A Secret History of the IRA* (London, Penguin, 2002), p. 470.

98 *Ibid.*

99 Tonge, *Northern Ireland*, p. 131.

100 Tonge, '"They haven't gone away you know"', p. 672.

101 *An Phoblacht*, Speech made by Gerry Kelly, 27 March 2008.

102 *Sovereign Nation*, April–May 2010.

103 Bean and Hayes, 'Sinn Féin and the New Republicanism of Ireland', p. 134.

104 *An Phoblacht*, 'The futile path of militarism', 20 August 1998.

105 Hayes, 'The Evolution of Republican Strategy and the "Peace Process" in Ireland', p. 25.

106 A. McIntyre in *The Pensive Quill*, 'Responding to Seán Mór', 14 September 2010.

107 R. Mac Ginty, 'Irish Republicanism and the Peace Process: From Revolution to Reform', in Cox, Guelke and Stephens (eds), *A Farewell to Arms?*, p. 133.

108 A. McIntyre in *The Pensive Quill*, 'Who is McGuinness to talk of treachery', 16 March 2009.

109 A. McIntyre, 'Of Myths and Men: Dissent within Republicanism and Loyalism', in Edwards and Bloomer (eds), *Transforming the Peace Process in Northern Ireland*, p. 116.

110 See A. McIntyre, 'Provisional Republicanism: Internal Politics, Inequalities and Modes of Suppression in Republicanism in Modern Ireland', in F. McGarry (ed.), *Republicanism in Modern Ireland* (Dublin, University College Dublin Press, 2003).

111 McIntyre, 'Of Myths and Men: Dissent within Republicanism and Loyalism', p. 117.

112 *Ibid.*, p. 117.

113 *Ibid.*, p. 117.

114 M. Frampton, *Legion of the Rearguard: Dissident Irish Republicanism* (Dublin, Irish Academic Press, 2011).
115 J. Evans and J. Tonge, 'Menace without Mandate? Is There Any Sympathy for Dissident Republicanism in Northern Ireland?', *Terrorism and Political Violence* 24, no. 1 (2012), pp. 61–78.
116 *Ibid.*, p. 64.
117 See chapter 4 for a discussion of these findings as well as the response the data received.
118 Evans and Tonge, 'Menace without Mandate?', p. 64.
119 A. Sanders, *Inside the IRA: Dissident Republicans and the War for Legitimacy* (Edinburgh, Edinburgh University Press, 2011).
120 P. M. Currie and M. Taylor (eds), *Dissident Irish Republicanism* (London, Continuum, 2011).
121 See Feeney, *Sinn Féin*; Maillot, *New Sinn Féin*; Augusteijn, 'Political Violence and Democracy', pp. 1–26.
122 See Bean, *The New Politics of Sinn Féin*; English, *Irish Freedom*; O'Brien, *The Long War*; White, *Provisional Irish Republicans*.
123 Bowyer Bell, *The Secret Army*; Munck, 'Irish Repubicanism'; Rafter, *Sinn Féin 1905–2005*; Richards, 'Terrorist Groups and Political Fronts', pp. 72–89; Smith, *Fighting for Ireland?*
124 See Feeney, *Sinn Féin*; Maillot, *New Sinn Féin*; Frampton, *The Long March*.
125 See, Mac Ginty, 'Irish Republicanism and the Peace Process'; McIntyre, 'Of Myths and Men'; Moloney, *A Secret History of the IRA*; Tonge, *Northern Ireland*.

2

Irish republicanism as an ideology: are there agreed components?

Irish republicanism is often associated with physical force, separatism and cultural nationalism. However, republican ideas have a much wider foundation and complex history, with many of these ideas adopted and adapted in their Irish variant. Since the echoes of the French and American revolutions pervaded Irish politics, republicanism has played a protagonist role. Yet, disagreements over the interpretation of Irish history have given way to vast number of varying political understandings of republicanism as an ideal and how it should best be applied. It is the purpose of this chapter to link the variants of Irish republicanism to the ideas of republicanism as a whole. This analysis is needed in order to establish how the many shapes and forms of Irish republicanism today deviate in one way or another from its supposed principles and whether it is even possible to define Irish republicanism through set principles. This chapter then goes on to explore the variations in interpretation and the role of historical legitimacy in validating republican lineage. The discussion finally leads on to the application of republican principles in the modern day context by considering where and how variation occurs on the Irish republican spectrum. Such investigation is necessary to establish whether it is possible to define the notion of true 'Irish republicanism' and what this constitutes, or whether such descriptions are unattainable, rendering the term 'dissident' redundant.

Before discussing the Irish context it is essential to look at the key conceptual apparatus of republicanism *per se*. Classical republicanism can be traced back to the Roman Republic which was then later revived in the Renaissance via Machiavelli, where the ideas of a mixed government became a political model to balance liberty, political stability and equality.[1] Further strands of republicanism emerged from the English, American and French revolutions. Since the global realignment of the 1990s, republicanism has experienced a revival in terms of theoretical discussion and as a result emerged as a strand of political theory carrying equal weight to the normative theories which have been central to philosophical debates such as liberalism and socialism.[2]

The institutional core of republicanism has shifted its focus over time. Classical republicanism is usually associated with a form of government that mixed monarchical, aristocratic and democratic elements.[3] Within classical republican thought is the idea that republican systems should be small and decentralised. It was believed that a large republic posed a threat to civic engagement by weakening the connection between the people and the decision makers. The French and American revolutions reshaped republicanism by removing its monarchical and aristocratic tendencies and applying it to whole nations rather than just small states or communities, as well as attaching modern democratic principles, such as freedom, interdependence and civic virtue to collectively provide the foundations of liberty, equality and fraternity, which are discussed further below.

Principles and aspirations

Republican political thought goes far deeper than a form of government in which sovereignty rests with the people instead of a monarch. Yet from this simple but fundamental idea the principles of modern republicanism have been developed.[4] The core principles of republicanism may be seen as freedom, civic virtue and interdependence, designed to realise the ambitions of liberty, equality and fraternity. It is the conflation of core principles and tactics in which the definition of republicanism becomes blurred.

The first central theme in republicanism is the concern with a particular form of freedom. There are varying notions of how freedom should be interpreted and achieved. The concept of liberty questions what the role of the state should be, what functions or responsibilities the state should fulfil and which ones should be left in the hands of private individuals. It is within the various interpretations of liberty that the balance between state and civil society is found. Therefore, in discussing liberty, the most fundamental question is: in striving for liberty what kind of freedom is being considered and how may it be realised?

In contemplating the aspiration of liberty, Isaiah Berlin proposed two distinct concepts of freedom: positive (freedom to act) and negative (freedom from being acted upon/constraint) liberty. Berlin's discussion of negative liberty approaches the question, 'What is the area within which the subject – a person or group of persons – is or should be left to do or be what he is able to do or be, without interference by other persons?'[5] Negative liberty concerns the idea that no individual or group should interfere with individual activity. This individualistic interpretation of freedom is built upon a liberal analysis of the role of liberty. The liberal tradition advocates freedom from constraint where freedom is possessed by the individual with minimal interference from the state. In other words, negative freedom is unimpeded and un-coerced choice to the degree to which no human being or institution interferes with another's activity on an unwarranted bias. Freedom is viewed as the property of the individual and it is the role of law and government to protect this individual right. Liberals therefore strive to create a minimal state to enjoy the widest reach of freedom. It is the role of the state to operate merely as a protective entity, designed to maintain peace and order for citizens to conduct their lives as they see fit. Liberty is freedom from the state, which should not impinge unnecessarily beyond its basic duty of protection.

Yet, republicanism is also allied to the aspiration of positive liberty, which is concerned with the protection of one person's freedom against domination from others. The positive concept of freedom approaches the question, 'What, or who, is the source of control or interference that can determine someone to do, or be, this rather than that?'[6] Contemporary republicans take into account that threats towards freedom may not always come from individuals but from a range of forces.[7] Economic or political domination also inhibits personal freedom and therefore realising freedom requires political intervention to limit the domination of one group over another. Therefore, positive liberty requires more than the absence of interference; 'while freedom excludes domination by another human being, it does not exclude the extensive rule of law'.[8] It involves the presence and usually the exercise of the facilities that foster self-mastery and self-fulfilment and relies on an effective system of law to safeguard freedom. Overall, republican liberty is based on non-domination, whereas the liberal interpretation of freedom is based upon non-interference. Within republicanism freedom is not understood as a natural given right, but a political achievement.[9] In addition, it is essential that citizens are involved in the political system which safeguards their freedom. It is through civic engagement and a strong legal system that the best interests for all can be recognised and protected.

The second core tenet, developed through classical republicanism is civic participation. The principle of civic engagement centres upon the role of the people as a locus for achieving freedom. Traditionally, republicanism became concerned with the active participation of individuals in political life. The aim of this involvement is to ensure the autonomy of its citizens by encouraging a strong attachment to the political community through active citizenship.[10] Expressed more clearly, 'a large purpose of participation is to monitor the behaviour of representatives in order to limit the risks of factionalism and self-interested representation'.[11] For example, in republican discourse political participants should subordinate their private interests to the public good in a process of collective self-determination.[12] The civic humanist tradition promotes virtue at the level of the 'common people' in an attempt to avoid corruption or self-aggrandisement.

It is the intention that through civic virtue the state is inextricably bound to the people, with politics at the epicentre of everyday life. It is through political institutions designed to facilitate debate and discussion amongst its citizens, decentralisation and citizen control of national institutions that civic virtue can promote the aspiration of equality. One of the main attractions of republican political theory is that it offers a direct alternative to individualistic liberalism. Civic republicanism promotes the idea of active citizens whose instincts are to become involved in political activities. Political arrangements and activities are therefore viewed in utilitarian terms, whereby citizenship is considered in its entirety and the greater good of the whole community is promoted above individual considerations. As a result, citizenship includes the performance of duties and participation in collective action. It is the role, even the duty, of citizens to use the opportunity to participate in the decisions that will determine how they live. The purpose of such action is to promote collective action over self-sufficiency. Such participation offers the reward of honour and respect rather than individual self-advancement or material gain. It is important to note that political solidarity is not viewed as a homogeneous formation of people coming together under the auspices of a shared history or language.[13] Republicanism encourages collective action based on civic organisation, distinct from membership of a political community based on exclusively ethnic terms. Cohesion is therefore seen as the result of the pursuit of shared civic values and equality of political opportunity, rather than being a derivative of ethnic or cultural background.

For civic republicanism equality is seen in terms of political equality, covering the right to speak and seek office, as well as equality before the law. Socio-economic equality is also viewed as a necessity in encouraging interdependence. Economic disparities are therefore viewed as disruptive to the republic's ability to work for a common good. Individual concerns are more likely to be at the forefront of decisions if the parties involved are not economic equals. As a result, achieving political equality rests on limiting economic inequality. Redistributive measures are encouraged to provide a stable foundation for the republic to be built. Yet it is also worth noting that such positive public spiritedness is very optimistic in that it assumes considerable altruism underpinning political participation. Civic virtue relies on the possession of a shared purpose, placing aside calculations of self-interest and prioritising intrinsic values as opposed to the accumulation of personal wealth. For civic virtue to promote equality, individuals must demote self-interest. Such an approach places a great deal of confidence in human nature, via the idea that individuals will collectively function so that community concerns triumph over individualistic considerations.

The third core principle of republicanism is the idea of interdependence as the construct of the political community.[14] The republican tradition of Machiavelli and Madison was understood in terms of those who shared a common political life rather than a cultural homogeneity. Republicanism is based upon the notion of participation as the means of effective representation and articulation of the interests of the citizenry. Being organised to promote interdependence within a political community is to allow deliberation, debate and reflection on how to best run political and social affairs. Interdependence is the realisation of the republican aspiration of fraternity; a brotherhood amongst a disparate body of people. A republic flourishes from the interdependence of all citizens 'whose survival and flourishing depends on the kinds of social framework they inhabit, and who have common, as well as separate and conflicting, interests'.[15]

The aspiration of fraternity is not intended to be homogeneous, but instead allows for contributions from a variety of perspectives, to draw on a wealth of opinion. Therefore, the purpose of republicanism is to provide for the common welfare and interdependence between various factions who collectively have the possibility of reshaping their future.

Such interests mark republicanism as distinct from nationalism, which is built on a common or exclusive identity and culture. In other words republicanism champions citizenship over common background in an all-embracing vision, rather than offering a political vision confined to a selection of people on the basis of their national identity. The aim is that, 'By rooting politics in interdependence rather than commonality, it offers a better way of dealing with the cultural and moral differences that are pervasive in modern society.'[16] In other words, republican citizenship is less exclusive than nationality and by allocating sovereignty to the people as opposed to the nation each person has the right to be self-determining and share in the role of government. Republicanism is based on interdependence rather than pre-political identity and as a result encompasses more diverse forms of cultural ethnicity than a nationalist-based system which encourages separatism.

The appeal of republicanism is to provide a positive form of government in the interests of the common good in order to advance the ideals of liberty, equality and fraternity. Whilst these aspirations are at the epicentre of republican thought there are many interpretations of how best to attain them. Rousseau espoused the doctrine that republics could only flourish in small states as large nation states would lead to corruption.[17] There is also a range of views on the need for economic equality. For example, James Madison stressed the possession of property and the separation of powers over participation.[18] In addition, it is very common, although more an indication of social values at the time, for proponents of republicanism to view citizenship in more exclusive terms (many excluded women in political life). Also evident are the differing opinions of how to best organise a republic, providing various combinations of monarchical, aristocratic and democratic elements. Even when intent is said to be the same, there are different interpretations and how this can best be achieved.

As with most political doctrines it is generally assumed that republicanism can be defined by an adherence to a set of values or defined principles. The complication in defining republicanism is that its ideals (liberty, equality, fraternity) are those which most political ideologies would claim at least two of. For example, socialism appropriates the ideals of fraternity and equality in the creation of brotherhood underpinned by the equality of all citizens. Liberalism emphasises liberty in terms of negative or individualistic freedom and equality through the implementation of equal and indiscriminate laws. Nationalism promotes freedom through self-determination on the basis of a single ethnicity, race, nation or culture and fraternity as a homogeneous bond based upon national identity. The intent of highlighting such an argument is to demonstrate how the aspirations of liberty, equality and fraternity are fluid and highly adaptable notions that can be made relevant to numerous perspectives and situations. Such a point reveals how defining a republican core is problematic as the political ideas and programmes offered may be partially shared by other ideologies. Moreover, the interpretation and implementation of 'republican' ideals can often be contested. It is also worth highlighting the paradox that despite promoting fundamental ideas which stress the importance of interdependence, common good, collective action and the suppression of personal concerns, republicanism has been fraught with division, conflicting interest and separation.

In identifying the central principles underpinning republican ideology it is also essential to consider the context in which it is being discussed. The problem that arises here is that history does not supply conceptions of political life that can be applied mechanically to current problems. Therefore, whilst discussing modern republicanism it is essential to remember that the task is not simply one of excavation. Circumstances change and therefore it is difficult to take theoretical perspectives out of their context without great risk of distortion.[19] Republicanism as an ideology does not operate in a vacuum, and the reality is that 'moral and cultural diversity are increasingly salient in our society'.[20] A politics based on shared values is an idealistic aspiration that ignores the causes of fragmentation within society such as ethnic, racial and cultural differences. Because of such underlying differences republicanism has been forced to adapt to contemporary circumstances, which has led to a fusion of ideological principles with pragmatic reality.

In relation to the contested pliability of republicanism there are two broad lines of argument recognisable in the literature today. Firstly, the work of Pocock highlights the use of republican language found in political thought where both continuities and patterns along with innovations and transgressions can be identified.[21] Pocock attempts to understand political thought not only as an ideology but as a political discourse, specifically in terms of the language used. Not all texts can be attributed to the concern of those people at the time in which they were written; rather they are a function of political or philosophical concern which drives the theorist, hence why they need to be read with a fluid interpretation. Therefore, Pocock argues that historical language can be traced through its various exchanges over time to the point that it has become reworked and furnished with rhetoric and idioms. As a result of this exchange the meaning of the text has been influenced; it is for this reason that Pocock deliberately distances himself from the portrayal of a rigid monolithic concept and avoids the use of the term 'paradigm'.[22]

The second, slightly differing perspective is championed by Philip Pettit's work on republican liberty. He argues that republicanism is accompanied by set values and necessary conditions for securing those values. Yet despite these set values there is still a very strong emphasis on the importance of context:

> To endorse republican freedom is not to accept a ready made ideal that can be applied in a mechanical way ... it is to embrace an open ended ideal that gains new substance as it is interpreted in the progressively changing and clarifying perspective of a living society.[23]

Whether republicanism is made up of set values or pliable concepts, Pocock and Pettit have highlighted the importance of flexibility and context. The aspirations of liberty, equality and fraternity are helpful in identifying the basis of modern day republicanism, yet it is also essential to look at the context in which these principles are exercised. Therefore, in order to investigate the appeal of modern republicanism, further enquiry is needed in terms of its social and political contexts.

In terms of political context, the difficulty of applying republicanism to practical policy and the claims to republicanism launched by so many political actors have made the task of definition and identification of what constitutes republican ideals complex. The use of the term 'republicanism' has been stretched and rearticulated with the use of language and discourse playing a central role. For example, Philps suggests,

> the language of republicanism, rather than providing an integrated and sophisticated explanatory and normative paradigm for politics has become increasingly thinned and accommodated to a wide range of potentially divergent political and philosophical positions.[24]

As a result republicanism can take many forms: abstentionist, pluralist, ethnogeographically determinist, pluralist, civic, accommodationist or militarist. Such diverse embodiments of a single tradition complicate the tasks of definition and explanation. Attention will now turn to the role of remembering and historical legitimacy in interpretation and application of Irish republican principles.

Claiming the mantle: appropriating republicanism in Ireland

> For national communities, as for individuals, there can be no sense of identity without remembering.[25]

Despite the diverse and broad spectrum of republicanism, all the elements claiming to offer the 'true', 'holy and apostolic' version of the ideology are united in one sense: they indulge in a deep nostalgia for a similar past. Across the wide republican spectrum in Ireland a great level of importance is placed on recalling the past, to the point where the events of 1798 or 1916 are presented as moments which transcend time.[26] Such recollections of the past have persistently been used to emphasise a shared heritage, common suffering and a united purpose.

Such interpretations are commonly provided through the mediums of memorials, commemorations, iconography and propaganda. Recollecting the past, that is, recalling key events which culminate to form a republican precedent, performs a significant role within modern day republicanism.

Occasions for commemoration and remembrance are scattered throughout the republican calendar. Key events such as the annual visit to the grave of Wolfe Tone, founder of the United Irishmen and seen as the 'founder' of Irish republicanism, are used as occasions to deliver significant political messages. The reading of the 1916 proclamation outside the GPO in Dublin and the various Easter Commemorations across the island are also noteworthy occasions in the republican tradition as key events for remembrance.

In the context of Irish history, memory provides a powerful and evocative tool. Within Irish republicanism, historical memory is utilised to justify actions through a mandate provided by past generations. As Ford suggests, 'No one can deny the power of political martyrdom in modern Irish history. The blood of those who died for the nationalist faith has repeatedly been invoked to inspire and stiffen the sinews of their successors fighting to free Ireland from foreign rule.'[27] Whilst investigating the historical roots of armed struggle Kearney questions what exactly the native republican tradition is that has enabled generations of republicans to justify the rationale behind armed struggle. Is it based upon armed rebellion or peaceful gradualist transformation? He argues that foundational symbols and ideological origins provided the seeds to enable the Provisional republican movement to justify their actions in relation to their historical roots. The Provisionals conceived themselves as the organic legatees of the past generation, an approach which has been followed by their successors, misleadingly labelled 'dissidents'. Kearney asks:

> Is it possible that the guiding motivation of militant republicanism was, and still is to some extent, less the appropriation of the socio-economic means of production, than an exigency of sacrifice to a mythological Ireland: an ancestral deity who would respond to the martyrdom of her sons by rising from her ancient slumber to avenge them?[28]

Such a theological perspective explains republicanism as an often backward-looking movement with little association with or reflection of external material reality. Actions in the present day are justified and made sense of through the prism of the past. As a result, armed struggle is elevated to a status of inevitability rather than convincingly articulated as a means of providing tactical progression. As Ford argues, 'the criticism was frequently voiced that republicans had made armed struggle an end in itself, that blood-sacrifice was primarily a matter of fidelity to previous generations rather than a means of furthering a practical goal'.[29]

Lineage to past generations was contained in the Provisional IRA's training manual, the 'Green Book'. It insisted that 'For the past 800 years the British ruling classes have attempted to smash down the resistance of the Irish people. Campaign after campaign, decade after decade, century after century, armies of resistance have fought … to cast off the chains of foreign occupation.'[30] Drawing attention to such heritage is also utilised today, with military groups owing allegiance to the past, denouncing settlements short of an independent united sovereign Ireland as 'not what Irish republicans fought, died and went to jail for'.[31] Remembering is not simply about physical representations such as marches or remembrance services; it is also necessary to consider the power of history, and memory, in evoking an attachment to former times.

Similarly to Kearney, Moran describes the use of armed struggle as an alignment to a dogmatic theology ascribed to by past generations. He claims that 'the Irish Republican tradition understands Irish nationalism as a theology with its own morality'.[32] The language identified by Moran is that of martyrdom, self-sacrifice and belief; 'By choosing self-immolation, these people, either consciously or unconsciously, confirm a dogmatic theology of violence held by Irish Republicanism' and 'they intended to kill, and ultimately be killed, in order to resurrect Gaelic Ireland by means of a blood sacrifice which served to expiate sinful complacency and compromise'.[33] The tradition of self-sacrifice and martyrdom is permanently embedded within the republican psyche.

Allegiance to the tradition of republican martyrdom can be seen in discussions concerning hunger strikers. Hunger strikes in Ireland are commonly presented as a feature of political confrontation where the powerless people of Celtic Ireland could force themselves to be heard. Such acts epitomise defiance and self-sacrifice, but most significantly provide martyrs for contemporary and subsequent generations. More importantly, the cult of self-sacrifice can flatter its present day followers because it links them with past historical figures and stresses the longevity and endurance of the republican cause.[34] Therefore, framing actions through a window to the past provides a valuable tool in that it justifies present day actions by highlighting historical continuity, allowing those who utilise such description to claim a mandate from history.

A 'mandate' from republican history has been utilised during times of high internal tension or at the point when divisions have occurred within the republican movement. The 1986 split saw the Provisionals drop the principle of abstention to Leinster House in an attempt to adopt a more flexible and pragmatic form of politics. Such a move signified a seismic change of direction, as constitutionalism had caused major divisions in the past. It was apparent that dropping abstention from Provisional policy was unlikely to be embraced by the entire membership. In 1986, leading Provisional republican Ruairí Ó Brádaigh continued to reject the legitimacy of Leinster House and Stormont and soon criticised the new 'reformism' of the Provisionals as indicative of how the Adams-McGuinness leadership was being 'sucked into' and becoming part of the colonial system.[35] For Ó Brádaigh and others that broke away from the

Provisionals and formed Republican Sinn Féin (RSF) (whose members claimed this was the 'old' Sinn Féin party and that non-abstentionists were part of a new organisation) ideological devotion and loyalty were seen as paramount. For them history played a significant role in legitimising the party's purist position. As Frampton suggests it, 'this was a party, after all, for which the shadow of history loomed large; the present was forever interpreted through the prism of the past (and judged inherently inferior as a result)'.[36] Any movement away from full obedience to republican doctrine was seen as a betrayal to past generations who had fought and died for an Irish republic.

Thus RSF use events such as hunger strike commemorations to highlight the importance of remaining loyal and 'to never, ever give up the struggle for freedom, no matter what the odds are against us. They [the hunger strikers] died rather than submit to British rule!'[37] Such a statement is typical in the way it highlights the dedication and defiance of those who died as being central components to purist republicanism. For those with such dedication and intransigence history takes on quasi-religious undertones where pragmatism and the down-grading of basic principles are seen as blasphemous. Such romantic or spiritual attachment to the republican struggle may have an obvious strength, in that 'vague emotion' can be 'more alluring than more cold measured assessment'.[38] Theological understanding of republican ideals and the eulogising of past events provide an emotive value that surpasses the detached appeal of logic and rationality. Such a statement is epitomised by the Terence MacSwiney quote, 'It is not those who can inflict the most but those who can endure the most who will conquer.'[39]

As Frampton points out, such strong allegiance to past generations and the continued promotion of fundamental republican principles can be juxtaposed with the Provisionals' use of realism. In undertaking the compromises of the peace process Sinn Féin were criticised for being 'indistinguishable from their British master'.[40] For those who broke away from the Provisionals in 1986, integrity and purity were favoured over pragmatism and concessions. The Provisionals were being directed by those who wanted the course of the movement to be set by present day circumstances as opposed to deep-rooted principles which were seen to be outdated. As a result, Sinn Féin attempted to reaffirm their political position as being very much placed in the here and now. Consequently, interpretations of republican history, although still used to legitimise actions, varied from the interpretations of those who split from the movement. At the grave of Wolfe Tone in 1986 McGuinness evoked the memory of James Connolly, stating that he

> once remarked that the real danger to republicanism was that it might become a commemorative organisation that mourned its martyrs, that lamented its heroic defeats. There is an element of romanticism within our ranks that, while not consciously defeatist, continues to look at the past for legitimisation.[41]

Whilst McGuinness used the past as a means of legitimising the future of the Provisionals, he also made it clear that he wanted a pragmatic approach that would deliver results rather than a perpetual attachment to a celebrated yet obsolete past.

There is a danger that dwelling on the indulgence of history and the portrayal of republicanism as extraneous to any contextual influences, such as material conditions or political circumstances, may blind us to the conditions explaining the various forms republicanism has taken. In terms of modern day Irish republicanism it is also worth noting that both the accounts of Kearney and Moran were written before the disappearance of the Provisional IRA. Whilst the peace process was on the horizon, it was unknown the extent to which Sinn Féin would compromise or that the PIRA would accept decommissioning, and ultimately cease to exist. It therefore seems hard to justify how the Provisionals had such a dogmatic alliance to the physical force tradition given their subsequent willingness to 'leave the stage' for a settlement far short of their previously uncompromising goal of a united Ireland. Whilst such interpretations remind us of the historical significance of armed struggle, they fail to identify why this is still relevant within the context of today.

The multifaceted and diverse representations of republicanism in Ireland today all claim lineage to the same tradition. Throughout republican history the disengagement from activism and the subsequent pursuit of a new political direction has been followed by the accusations of betrayal to past generations and a 'sell out' of former principles. Hanley notes that such accusations of betrayal have led to a contradictory immediate response, in that 'republicans have often sought to justify a gradual retreat from militarism by reasserting their military and revolutionary credentials'.[42] Despite the choice of tactics through the use of pragmatism being very much based in the present, the reinforcement of republican credentials and the celebration of a military past are often used in an attempt to legitimise a change of course. In tandem with this 'they have also attempted to undermine the physical force records of their opponents'.[43] Such rhetoric leads to a paradox which can be seen today. Whilst Sinn Féin are quick to denounce dissidents who continue the tradition of armed struggle as 'conflict junkies' or 'Neanderthals', it is interesting to note how they defend their own past actions of a similar nature, which they justify as necessary on grounds of context and greater public support. Therefore, allegiance to the past may be selectively employed today by Sinn Féin to repudiate claims from dissident groups that they have 'sold out'. This highlights the struggle to claim political ownership over the republican tradition. It is therefore possible to argue that splits in the movement have in turn made republican history even more pronounced as factions present an unwavering allegiance to the past and their own lineage.

Emphasising an allegiance to the past can reinforce a mandate from past generations or reinforce republican credentials, but what impact does this have

on republicanism today? Whilst it is important to highlight the significance
of the republican past, there is a danger that such deliberate imagery evokes a
rather pious or even cult-like depiction of republicanism, rather than it being
assessed as an existing political, social or military movement. Whilst analysing
republicanism in a way that highlights historical lineage is important in providing a historical context, there is a danger that it may conceal the contextual and
relational nature of the movement.

However, the tradition of remembering is invaluable in what it tells us about
the present rather than the past. As McBride notes, 'What is so striking about the
Irish case is not simply the tendency for present conflicts to express themselves
through the personalities of the past, but the way in which commemorative ritu-
als have become historical forces in their own right.'[44] Memorials do not just
represent a specific circumstance; rather they represent an 'active process', con-
stantly rearticulated and negotiated as historical circumstances alter.[45] Identity is
inextricably linked to remembering, and memory is usually selective, resulting
in a complex relationship between history and memory, fact and imagination.[46]
Therefore, groups tend to express their values through their interpretation of the
past. As a result, recollection not only identifies historical significance but can
also be utilised to indicate a great deal about the contemporary situation.

Through the use of republican language and iconography it is possible to gain
various interpretations of modern republicanism. This returns us to Pocock's
point on how various readings of republican history have in turn been used to
produce contested meanings and conflicting political prescriptions. McBride
suggests that rather than assuming present day actions are determined and ultimately shaped by the past, we should be aware that what we choose to remember
is dictated by contemporary interests and concerns:

> When we recall the past, then, we do so as members of groups – a family, a local
> community, a work force, a political movement, a church or a trade union. What
> we remember or forget therefore has as much to do with external constraints,
> imposed by our social and cultural surroundings, as with what happens in the
> frontal lobes of our brain.[47]

In other words, interpretations of the past are ultimately viewed and considered
through the prism of contemporary circumstances. The past is interpreted differently not only by various generations, but also through various circumstances at
the same point in time. Due to such factors impacting upon human interpretation, it is possible to suggest that memory has a history of its own depending on
individual differences. As McBride observes: 'Although remembrance is always
selective, the selections depend upon a complex interaction between the materials
available and the dominant modes of political and social organisation.'[48] Strong
association with the past is maintained through a reconstruction of history as
distinct from its recollection. Utilising historical reconstruction to provide a

political function may blur historical fact, but it does not necessarily mean that modern day interpretations of the past are hollow or meaningless. What history individuals and groups are choosing to remember, how they remember it and why it matters, tells us a significant amount. Such recollections may not provide reliable historical insight or accuracy yet they provide an alternative angle through which we can gain insight into certain groups.

Utilising romanticism and sentiment creates an emotional appeal that possesses the ability to transcend social, economic and political lines. Republicanism is heterogeneous and has traditionally gained support across varying socio-political-economic situations. It is possible to suggest that remembering and iconography have a practical role in mobilising support today. This use of historical figures represents the diverse nature of republicanism. Margaret O'Callaghan explains how through the use of historic icons republicanism has broadened its appeal across various socio-economic divisions in society:

> Republicanism was at one level a minority elite movement. At another level, through the forms and iconography, vocabulary and pasted oaths disseminated through defenders adopted at different levels of popular resistance movements, it had a broad political purchase throughout the country.[49]

Pettit takes this argument further by describing how through the use of tactics the definition of what it means to be a republican has been stretched and rearticulated. One prominent tactic is that republicanism 'employs only conceptual distinctions and inferential patterns that no one in the community has reason to reject; it offers a medium of debate which no one has a priori ground for dismissing'.[50] In other words, republicanism utilises ambiguous and indefinite rhetoric that allows for a greater and broader acceptance, resulting in a holistic, universal prescription that has the potential to have a more varied and extensive reach.

To demonstrate this point, against the backdrop of the peace process and possibly influenced by the electoral growth of Sinn Féin, other parties have attempted to restate their republican credentials through the use of open ended and almost ambiguous rhetoric. For example, Fianna Fáil aims to secure a united Ireland through peace and agreement, encouraging cross border co-operation. The party affirms its affiliations by incorporating the term 'The Republican Party' in its title. In 1998, its then leader Bertie Ahern, speaking at the Fianna Fáil Ard Fheis, accepted that the party's notion of republicanism was 'perhaps too narrow in the past'.[51] Ahern stressed the civic rather than ethnic aspects of modern Irish republicanism. Whilst eschewing the use of force as a republican tactic, Fianna Fáil's earlier iteration of Irish republicanism had viewed the unionist tradition on the island as ethnically Irish and effectively an illegitimate political tradition and non-identity. In this narrow outlook, the ethnic republicanism of Fianna Fáil did not differ markedly from that offered by Sinn Féin. The peace process moved Fianna Fáil and, less explicitly, Sinn Féin, to a civic, accommodationist, pluralist republican position.

The SDLP's northern nationalism has embraced civic republican ideals in stressing a 'two traditions' approach. Long prior to the peace process, it formulated the 'agreed Ireland' idea in which both traditions would require accommodation within a political framework. The SDLP argued for the need to engage across cultural divisions and provide assurances to unionists about their position in a united Ireland. The SDLP, which has always remained on the constitutional path, became the lesser political voice for nationalists as they were overtaken electorally by Sinn Féin in 2003. The party leader from 2010 to 2011, Margaret Ritchie, reasserted this point at the 2010 annual conference, insisting that 'the SDLP remain absolutely, unambiguously committed to a united Ireland, where the border disappears and we are no longer governed by Britain. It is without qualification our number one political objective.'[52] Although the party considers itself as being 'worlds apart'[53] from Sinn Féin, the difference does not lie in ultimate constitutional preferment. Rather it resides in a more explicit form of civic nationalism, historically more cognisant of the different identity of unionists than the ethnic republicanism previously espoused by Sinn Féin. Even within the SDLP's language, there have been problems in terms of the accommodation and identification of unionists. The language of John Hume referred to unionists as being of a different 'tradition', not of a different 'nation'.[54] Republicans and nationalists have thus struggled fully to accept the legitimacy and nationhood of unionists, even amid the shift from united Ireland political projects based on absorption to those of accommodation.

Such a point identifies the fault lines between civic- and ethnic-based republicanism.[55] Republicanism centres on an individual's membership of a political community, 'in which those who are mutually vulnerable and share a common fate may jointly be able to exercise some collective direction over their lives'.[56] It is in defining the basis of this membership that differences in interpretation occur. Within ethnic republicanism the membership of a political community is defined ethno-geographically. An identity is formed from a common Irish identity which does not recognise an 'artificial' border. Civic republicanism on the other hand is less deterministic in its composition, providing an interpretation of republicanism that emphasises equality and accommodation far more than ethnicity. This emphasis on accommodation has come to characterise mainstream republicanism post 1998.

These differences reflect alternative approaches to and understandings of the republican ideal. As Kilmurray and McWilliams suggest, 'Republicanism is a word to conjure within Ireland – whether North or South. Emotions and interpretations around the concept, and more important in relation to its implications, are as divided as the island itself.'[57] In the rest of the UK, the label 'Irish Republican' has far more negative connotations, and is at times expressed in a manner that simply implies an association with armed struggle or an aspiration that does not go beyond militant nationalism. In Ireland however, it has a more positive connotation. Normatively speaking, nationalism as a concept does not provide a prescription for inter communal co-operation, often being criticised for not taking into account the diversity of cultural and religious identities of those living in Northern Ireland. Therefore, whilst nationalism reinforces communal divisions republicanism as a concept is universal and all-embracing. The appeal of republicanism is that it is able to provide a holistic vision, alternative to nationalism which is seen as exclusivist.

That distinct groups are all able to claim republican lineage highlights the propensity for republicanism to be so broad as to allow for huge local variation in interpretation. As Cullen argues:

> Republicanism is ultimately an open political doctrine. It proposes great principles but it is not about providing a blueprint that must be followed detail by detail. Rather than claiming to be the final answer, it tries to provide a route towards those answers. While it is important principles are non-negotiable, space is left for democratic debate about what the meaning and content of those principles are or should be.[58]

Republicanism has been influenced by a wide range of intellectual, ideological and contextual sources, creating a variety of perspectives. As English indicatively phrases it, 'features of the modern nationalist vision also begin to fray at the ideology's edges and tough-minded interrogation might lead one to suspect that the intellectual garment as a whole would unravel without too much pulling'.[59] Such a statement makes it hard not to question whether those tactical concerns highlighted by Pettit have outshone the principles of Irish republicanism, suggesting pragmatic concerns may have surpassed republican principles.

Despite this, it is possible to argue that the central criticism of republicanism as a political doctrine is also its main advantage. Its versatile nature makes it malleable to different contexts and perspectives. The republic is a form of government in which sovereignty rests with the people, therefore the principles of modern republicanism were developed over time and are moved along by successive generations. Whilst considering republicanism in the framework of today it is essential to view it as a progressive movement where context and realism play a leading role. Brian Hanley notes that while republicanism is primarily a study of ideas, these are inseparable from the context in which they were formed. This explains why 'innovation or change in republican thinking has almost always come about as a reaction to defeat or stalemate'.[60] This goes some way to explaining the argument that the most striking feature of the republican movement in Northern Ireland is the propensity to split amid the absence of progress.[61]

It is the fluidity of republicanism which needs to be understood when considering the dissident ideological position and examining whether splits have been due to disagreements over 'innovation' and 'change' of republican princi-ples. The term 'dissident' is itself contextual, as Sinn Féin, often now portrayed as the embodiment of republicanism, were the 'dissidents' of their day. Such points need to be taken into account whilst considering 'dissident' ideology and justifications of republicans from prevailing republican orthodoxy.

Irish republicanism is relational and shaped by factors within evolving con-temporary circumstances. Such arguments propose that Irish republicanism can only be understood once put into context and viewed with consideration for wider influences on a global as well as more localised level. For example, at the macro-level wider geo-political forces such as the end of the Cold War and the British government strategy had a huge impact upon the political landscape and defined the parameters in which the Provisionals were to operate.[62] At the micro-level, the lived reality on a localised basis, socio-economic circumstances,[63] along with changes within consciousness and ideology,[64] have created many dynamics for republicanism to interact with and be shaped by such contexts.

Today, Irish republicanism is represented by various groups all symbolising a different interpretation of republicanism. Whilst considering such distinctions it is necessary to take into account the impact of wider influences when question-ing why such differences have occurred. In order to judge the ideological under-pinning of dissident groups today it is therefore important to consider the wider context not only in defining their republicanism but also in understanding why these differences have occurred.

Owing to the malleable nature of republicanism, which has resulted in vari-ous interpretations about what the concept actually represents, it is not ideal to construct a scale of 'true' or 'authentic' republicanism. It is not the place of this analysis to state what does and what does not constitute republicanism. Rather each group has the right to be investigated based on its own republican identity and not in relation to any other representation or what may be perceived as any embodiment of republicanism that pre-dates them.

The evolutionary and fluid nature of Irish republicanism makes the task of identifying agreed components highly problematic. Irish republicanism has over time developed into a multifaceted yet intricate concept, where understanding is guided by varying definitions and interpretations of history and influenced by personal experience. It is possible to ask two republicans the question 'what are the core tenets of republicanism?' and be confronted by two varying responses. In other words Irish republicanism has not just evolved over time, but is dra-matically different even between individuals. Various factions have been formed due to different interpretations of republican history and principles and how they should best be applied. Looking across the various factions which all claim to represent republicanism in Ireland today, republicanism embraces the vio-lent and non-violent, the constitutional and revolutionary, the pragmatic and absolutist.

In the broadest possible sense republicanism can be broken down into the principles of freedom, civic engagement and interdependence to realise the aspirations of liberty, equality and fraternity. The idealistic and vague nature of such objectives embraces a vast political spectrum. Republicanism, in its outworking, has thus taken on a multiplicity of forms. It has been hollowed out by a broad range of modern day representations all claiming lineage to a similar tradition and projecting their visions within a republican framework. Republican principles embrace rights of self-determination, universal sovereignty and representative democracy but prescriptions regarding their enactment often clash. Any analysis of dissident republicanism needs to go much further than the consideration of avowed allegiance to republican principles. It needs to understand specific interpretations of the Irish republican tradition.

Translating principles into political action: liberty, equality and fraternity

Republican principles of liberty, equality and fraternity now need addressing in relation to the Irish context. When such universal political principles are applied to the aspiration of a united Ireland the result is a diverse range of interpretations and tactics in pursuit of its attainment. The methods used to achieve a united Ireland have split the movement between pragmatists and absolutists. Successive splits signified the cleavage between pragmatists who saw the necessity of compromising, rather than being driven by belief or dogma and purists who retain a strict adherence to particular concepts and ideas. For purists, absolutism is reinforced by tradition.

Liberty and republicanism
As stated earlier, republicanism is allied to the aspiration of positive liberty. Such an interpretation revolves around the need for protection against the domination of an individual or group of individuals over another. Therefore a republic is based not simply on political independence but also on the social and economic liberation of its people. The realisation of economic, social and democratic freedom is necessary within a republic. This freedom is put into question when interfering forces adjust people's actions. Republicanism also emphasises that the conditions necessary to achieve freedom can only be realised in a system which limits the domination of an individual or group over another. In such situations protecting freedom requires political intervention in the form of laws or government intervention. Laws are required to protect against domination, where positive liberty is threatened. The sovereign power which implements laws does so on a basis of equality. It is through an equal share of sovereign power that people can be free.

Yet it is important to point out that in realising positive liberty there is an assumption that within the nation state an appropriate framework exists to facilitate economic, social and political freedom. There is a need also to consider the possibility that the state can be an oppressive force. From an uncompromising Irish republican perspective it is impossible to attain economic, social or democratic freedom within a divided Ireland, as a 'foreign state' is claiming part of the island. From a moderate republican perspective, two traditions can comfortably be accommodated on the island of Ireland, within separate jurisdictions, although this does not remove the aspiration for ultimate sovereign independence for the entire island. For 'purist' republicans the root to liberty is separatism.

The border dividing the island of Ireland has been consolidated 'as a feature of the economic, political and social-psychological landscape'.[65] Over successive political agreements the practical and political status of the border has evolved. In the 1973 Sunningdale Agreement, the British agreed to support Irish unity should a majority in Northern Ireland indicate such a wish. In other words there was to be no change in the status of Northern Ireland until the majority of the people indicated this desire. The 1985 Anglo-Irish Agreement reinforced this principle of northern consent. The Agreement saw the institutionalisation of British-Irish political co-operation, whilst leaving British legal sovereignty intact. These arrangements changed the significance of the border by promoting a new level of cross-border co-operation and amounted to recognition of its existence, but not full acceptance, by the government of the Republic of Ireland amid its continuing constitutional claim.[66] The 1998 Good Friday Agreement enshrined the principle of northern consent. It also gave everyone the right in Northern Ireland to choose either Irish or British citizenship or both. Throughout the various agreements and the evolving status of the border it was clear that any constitutional route to a united Ireland would be through an agreed Ireland.

However, in parallel to the consolidation, the border became increasingly permeable, straddled by cross-border bodies and North-South co-operation. The result was a paradox. Whilst cross-border activity increased, the border itself has perhaps become more secure, consolidated by constitutional law and the North no longer the subject of an 'irredentist' claim by another government.[67] Partition has taken on a different meaning, where any eradication of the border would have to follow the path of an agreed Ireland and co-determination. Yet the glimpse at the chance of a united Ireland, however remote a possibility in the near future, allowed pragmatic republicans to state that they remained on the long road to Irish unity.[68]

The principle of liberty and the politics of nation are inextricably linked and symbolically fused; the 'core of republicanism, both philosophically and ideologically, is the people. The people are sovereign. That means government of the people by the people.'[69] Liberty and equal citizenship can only be recognised under national self-determination. Whilst partition remains an objective reality, it is possible to suggest that the reaction to it and the interpretation of partition remain subjective.[70] Such subjectivity allows for the separation in opinions;

purist republicans are unable to accept that they have liberty until complete separation from Britain is achieved. They identify Irish republicanism as the route to liberty. If positive freedom is to be obtained, ending foreign 'occupation' and 'oppression', then all efforts should first be directed to the uncompromising separatist goal, dismissing parliamentary politics as ineffective or any compromise to Irish unity as unacceptable. Others have been more pragmatic in how to move towards the eradication of the border and are comfortable with co-determination formulas which 'agree' Ireland.

Fraternity and republicanism

Positive freedom is a pluralistic ideal, extending across a range of interests, identities and allegiances. Fraternity aims to achieve a form of membership which is polycentric as opposed to ethno-centric and grounds membership on the principle of interdependence. Pettit goes further in explaining the ideal of fraternity within republicanism:

> We can surely identify with the republican polity for the fact that it gives each of us to the extent that it gives all, the measure of non-domination that goes with being a fully incorporated member; a fully authorised and a fully recognised citizen. If we cherish our citizenship and our freedom, we have to cherish at the same time the social body in the membership of which the status consists.[71]

The republican tradition realises that freedom in a political and personal sense may be accomplished through the affiliation to, or membership of, a political community, united in the recognition that they can mutually exercise social and political action to a greater extent than if they were to work separately.

The republican tradition of grounding membership on common political interests can be traced back to the 1790s and Wolfe Tone's plea to unite under the identity of the people of Ireland. In 1791 Tone published the pamphlet, *An Argument on behalf of Catholics*, in which he argued for two main things, the unity of the people of Ireland (to establish interdenominational unity) and severance from England (Irish freedom):

> The people are divided, each party afraid and jealous of the other; they have only the justice of their cause to support them, and that plea grievously weakened by the acknowledged exclusion of three-fourths of the nation from their rights as men.[72]

Tone saw fraternity amongst the people of Ireland and popular sovereignty as a means of achieving Irish freedom, arguing the country would 'recover our rank and become a nation in something besides the name'.[73] Fraternity in the republican ideal is polycentric, as opposed to ethno-centric, where citizenship accommodates the politics of difference under the identity of the people of Ireland.

Irish republicanism promotes a common political life, but not homogeneity, encouraging the principle of interdependence whilst valuing individuality and human diversity. Whether this is done within the framework of a united Ireland or simply an aspiration highlights the difference between the purists and pragmatists. Post-agreement public policy focuses on how to provide favourable conditions to promote a shared future and broaden participation.

In the modern context, fraternity and commonality have been difficult to achieve. Desires for civic republicanism are juxtaposed with an elite-level governing consociation in Northern Ireland which, in the short term at least, legitimises ethnic division.[74] Two main public policy documents endorsed by mainstream republicanism aiming to address the co-existence of commonality and diversity have been *A Shared Future: Improving Relations in Northern Ireland* in 2005 and *Programme for Cohesion, Sharing and Integration* in 2010. *A Shared Future* recognises that Northern Ireland is a deeply divided society whilst aiming to encourage the idea of a collective future to replace ethnocentric markers of identity, promoting pluralism, freedom of expression, social cohesion and cultural diversity.[75] The documents emphasise the government's desire to foster mutual understanding and respect for diversity,[76] placing the responsibility for improving relations at all levels of public sector delivery. *Shared Future* emphasises the need for reconciliation, encouraging positive relations to be built on equality, partnership and respect in order to accommodate difference within a divided Ireland. The *Programme for Cohesion, Sharing and Integration* (CSI), 2010, acknowledges that the promotion of equality is fundamental in improving cross-community relations. The document sets out the goals for a shared future, built on the foundations for a cohesive community. The CSI argues for positive relations to be built on equality of opportunity where the government commits to the recognition that 'the promotion of equality of opportunity is an essential element of building good relations'.[77]

Mainstream republican policy alludes to a broadening of participation and the cohesion of communities. Sinn Féin insists that it would not 'discourage anyone who so wishes from endeavouring to promote their cultural identity socially, culturally or politically by any legitimate and democratic method, including the possession of British or any other citizenship'.[78] Focus on the tension between communities as the problem has the potential to direct attention away from the tensions caused by what was viewed as an 'illegitimate' interference by the British state. Given this situation, republicans have tended to play down the need for cultural pluralism and acceptance of diversity. Fraternity was previously (crudely) seen as an inevitable consequence of liberty.

Equality and republicanism

Although sometimes parochial, the republican movement in Ireland also possesses an international outlook. The socialist leader, James Connolly, viewed the struggle for a united Ireland as a phenomenon to be explained through the prism of class conflict extending beyond the Irish state. The British state divided the

Irish working class on sectarian grounds in order to prevent them from uniting under an all-Ireland citizenship, as a result securing British economic interests. In asking the question 'who are the Irish?', Connolly gave the response, 'the Irish working class, the only secure foundation upon which a free nation can be reared'.[79] Connolly considered the working class to be agents of both national and social freedom. According to this analysis, the social situation, in terms of equality, and the national question are inextricably linked.

Despite Connolly's analysis having resonance throughout the history of Irish republicanism, the idea that national revolution can accomplish radical social and economic change has proved a recurring point of controversy within the movement. In the 1960s, Cathal Goulding, the IRA Chief of Staff, attempted to shift the IRA towards an all-Irish neo-Marxist analysis, an approach which proved a significant factor in the 1969 Provisional–Official split. After the split Goulding continued to argue that the violence utilised by the Provisionals diverted attention away from the ruling-class oppression of the working classes. The Irish Republican Socialist Party (IRSP), a breakaway group from the Officials founded in 1974, uphold the idea that class struggle and national liberation cannot be separated. The IRSP aims to 'end Imperialist rule in Ireland and establish a 32 County Democratic socialist Republic with the working class in control of the means of production, distribution and exchange'.[80] The IRSP provide a version of Irish republicanism that is a working-class vision of an all-Irish citizenship bound by socialism with redistribution at its core.

Nonetheless, a contradiction remains, that the Irish National Liberation Army (INLA), the 'military' wing with which the IRSP was associated, bore responsibility for some of the worst sectarian excesses: 'The organisation sworn to build a secular workers' republic found it hard on occasion to resist the temptation to get involved in catholic revenge attacks.'[81] Particularly in rural areas, INLA members were often drawn into confrontations with loyalists.

Whilst being asked to redefine republicanism from a political perspective Sinn Féin MLA Mitchel McLaughlin stated: 'The Republican vision of the future is one in which the goals of equality, democracy and the maximum welfare of the maximum number will be achieved, with due attention to the needs of the international community.'[82] The post-conflict agenda of Sinn Féin has been projected utilising a language of rights encompassing a broader spectrum of identities beyond the republican/unionist dichotomy. Sinn Féin largely replaced socialism and redistribution as a means of creating an all-Ireland citizenship, but continued to stress equality:

> At the core of our agenda for government is one simple word – Equality. Equality of opportunity and of outcome is central to our priorities … As republicans we are totally committed to ending inequality and to bringing about a society where all are treated equally.[83]

Sinn Féin's stress upon equality often fused socio-economic concerns and conflict-related topics (such as prisoner rights and policing issues).[84] Yet, whilst terminology concerning Irish sovereignty remains, a shift has undoubtedly occurred, giving 'equality' a far more significant role. Moreover, the means of achieving equality have drastically changed. In the 1980s it was stressed by Sinn Féin that liberty could only be achieved via a united Ireland; only once this was achieved could the people embark on political freedom and economic independence. There was a need for 'national independence and a social revolution in all of Ireland'.[85] British withdrawal was a necessary precondition to any equality agenda.

Whilst adaptation to changing political and material circumstances is expected of any political party, Sinn Féin has reconceptualised itself through the party's equality rhetoric. McGovern suggests that 'The concept of equality has become the means of expressing Sinn Féin's worldview in every area of its social, political and economic outlook.'[86] Due to strategic considerations and the altered context leading up to and after the GFA the aspiration of equality has been frontloaded in place of the principle of liberty. The emphasis placed on rights and entitlement has dominated the party's image and election campaigns. Sinn Féin's 2007 Assembly Election Manifesto typifies the style of language used:

> The gap has widened between those with massive wealth and those who must work long hours to house, clothe and feed themselves and their families. People in poverty and on the margins of society don't share in this new prosperity.[87]

Such language is especially prominent in discussions concerning the place of unionists within a united Ireland, where Sinn Féin has employed the language of equality 'in order to marry its appeal as a party of communalist leadership with universal principles'.[88] The equality agenda is a way for Sinn Féin to emphasise their role as ethnic community advocates, but is also used as a means to appeal to unionists for a thirty-two county republic based on equality of traditions within a new state (although unionists show little interest). A significant shift has occurred in the way that Sinn Féin no longer claims that Irish unity needs to be achieved before equality can be realised. Whilst the party still has the national question at the core of its agenda, the route to its successful resolution has been drastically altered. In utilising the 'Ireland of Equals' and, more recently, 'national reconciliation' rhetoric, Sinn Féin has adopted a pluralist approach. Mainstream republicanism has become more about a language of priority over dogmatic principle.

Purists versus pragmatists: a typology

The basic fault line of purist versus pragmatist has always been evident within Irish republicanism; both sides of the divide justify their claims to uphold 'true' republican values. For purists, it is not possible to have full liberty under British

Table 1: Purist versus pragmatist conceptions of Irish republicanism

	Purist (Predominantly ethnic)	Pragmatist (Civic/ethnic)
Liberty	Independence	Agreed Ireland
	Self-determination	Co-determination
Equality	All-Irish citizenship	Pluralist – 'Ireland of Equals'
	Socialism	Parity of esteem
	Redistribution	
Fraternity	All Irish	Pluralism
	'Nation Again'	Accommodation of different traditions
		An aspiration to unity
		Acceptance of 'Britishness' on island

rule and parliamentary routes cannot secure freedom. The root to liberty is therefore separatism, backed by physical force if necessary, with the uncompromising goal of self-determination and a united Ireland. This is the framework within which other aspirations of equality and fraternity can be realised. Therefore purists frontload the principle of liberty and specify the need for liberty and independence before other goals can be achieved.

Pragmatists have relegated the principle of freedom in favour of parliamentary politics and constitutionalism, permissible prior to the establishment of a united Ireland, which is retained as a goal, but with Ireland's constitutional future co-determined by its two traditions, a methodology still dismissed as a 'unionist veto' by militant republicans. Table 1 identifies varying interpretations of the principles of liberty, equality and fraternity.

There are no political prescriptions providing an obvious, comfortable route to reaching the republican ideal. As Arthur suggests, 'all that has been done in Ireland has been to base everything on action, and we struggle to find route maps of what the republican movement is about'.[89] Whilst the purist versus pragmatist typologies provide a helpful tool in analysing the evolution of republican principles and highlight the broad nature of modern day Irish republicanism it is important not to become too reductionist. There is a danger that simply highlighting two contrasting and almost juxtaposed viewpoints may create the impression that there is a clear-cut and neat division between the two. On the contrary, one has to allow for a blurring between the two positions whilst also bearing in mind that there may be transfers made across by either side. Such groupings are not mutually exclusive nor are they always easily defined. Fianna Fáil and, currently, Sinn Féin, have been described as 'extra-constitutional' as they transcended their militarist origins, and their republicanism more broadly is an eclectic phenomenon.

Republicanism is also an evolutionary and contextual movement. The pragmatist versus purist dichotomy does not provide an explanation of the dynamic relationship between activists, movement organisation and the larger social structure. The political environment in which movements operate may change over time. If they do not respond they are then at risk of being archaic and out of touch. If they do however reassess strategy and drop long-term principles they may be criticised 'sell-outs' for betraying fundamental beliefs. Yet the purist–pragmatist distinction can be helpful in two regards. Firstly, it highlights a reoccurring historical trend within the republican movement. Secondly, it identifies the various interpretations of republican principles, which goes some way in explaining how in modern day Irish republicanism such a vast range of interpretations can exist whilst all claiming lineage to the same tradition. The allure of practical politics has often proven too hard to resist for former purists, with recurring tendencies to divide republicans.

Conclusion

In exploring republicanism as an ideology, is it possible to label Irish republican-ism with set characteristics? The foundation of such a question can be laid out by exploring republicanism in general, broken down at base level to the principles of liberty (or positive freedom), equality (the promotion of common good over self-interest) and fraternity (with faith in the utilitarian ideal of the political com-munity). The problem in the interpretation and understanding of such principles is that these values are those to which the majority of ideologies subscribe. This raises two key questions. Firstly, is there an agreed way in which to interpret these principles? Secondly is there an appropriate formula or prescription for how to realise such ideals? It is within these two questions that the problem in defining Irish republicanism arises. Republicanism is broad of principle and multifaceted in terms of application, making it very difficult to define Irish republicanism by a set of established principles. This makes it difficult to ascribe the title of 'true republican' to a single political organisation.

What looking at these principles does do is highlight the fault lines between purist and pragmatist, a fault line which allows the phenomenon of dissent to emerge. It is not for this book to state which interpretations are correct, but rather to understand why and in what form these differences emerge. For both purists and pragmatists the goal is the same yet the methodologies differ. Mainstream republicanism relies upon constitutional tactics to change the con-stitution. Militant, self-ascribed 'purists' believe that in working the existing system, the system changes republicans rather than vice versa, making it harder to attain their desired goal. Thus, according, to Ruarí Ó Brádaigh, such entrants 'end up accepting British rule and collaborating instead of opposing it'.[90]

The evolution of republicanism is often referred to in terms of a collective identity. Such interpretations assume that the understanding and interpreta-tion of republicanism is uniform. It is more appropriate to use an interpretive approach considering the complex relationship between the social structure, individuals and the group organisation when analysing Irish republicanism. Republicanism, whilst it has a history, core principles and an agreed goal, is a construction relative to individual and group experiences. It is therefore not ideal to provide a description of set characteristics in order to construct a definitive 'true republicanism'. Irish republicanism is a more fluid and adaptable construction that moves and reshapes itself, adopting (for most republicans) a profile that contemporary circumstances dictate. So, in response to the question posited of whether there are agreed components to Irish republicanism, the construction of a model of the 'true republican' runs the risk of providing a shallow and restricted model, unable to provide the space in which to explain the reasons behind why different interpretations emerge. However, studying the fault lines between purist and pragmatist goes some way in beginning to understand why these differences occur.

Notes

1 See, N. Machiavelli, *The Prince* (Chicago, University of Chicago Press, 1985); J. E. G. Zetzel, *Cicero: De Republica. Selections* (Cambridge, Cambridge University Press, 1995).
2 D. M. Weinstock, *Republicanism: History, Theory and Practice* (Portland, Frank Cass, 2004), p. 1.
3 P. Zagorin, 'Republicanisms', *British Journal for the History of Philosophy* 11, no. 4 (2003), p. 701.
4 F. Cullen, 'Beyond Nationalism: Time to Reclaim the Republican Ideal', *The Republic* 1 (2000), p. 13.
5 I. Berlin, *Four Essays on Liberty* (Oxford, Oxford University Press, 1969), p. 12.
6 *Ibid.*, p. 122.
7 See P. Pettit, *Republicanism: A Theory of Freedom and Government* (Oxford, Oxford University Press, 1997).
8 I. Honohan, 'Freedom as Citizenship: The Republican Tradition in Political Theory', *The Republic* 2 (2001), p. 9.
9 *Ibid.*, p. 7.
10 D. Kelly, 'Reforming Republicanism in Nineteenth-century Britain', in I. Honohan and J. Jennings (eds), *Republicanism in Theory and Practice* (London, Routledge, 2006), p. 41.
11 C. R. Sunstein, 'The Republican Civic Tradition', *Yale Law Journal* 97 (1988), p. 1,556.
12 *Ibid.*, p. 1,547.
13 A. Oldfield, 'Citizenship and the Community: Civic Republicanism and the Modern World', in G. Shafir (ed.), *The Citizenship Debates* (Minneapolis, University of Minnesota Press, 1998), p. 80.
14 Honohan, 'Freedom as Citizenship', p. 21.
15 *Ibid.*, p. 7.

16 *Ibid.*, p. 22.
17 See J. J. Rousseau, *Discourse on Political Economy and the Social Contract* (Oxford, Oxford University Press, 1994).
18 See J. Madison, 'The Federalist Papers, no. 51', in J. Madison, A. Hamilton and J. Jay (eds), *The Federalist Papers* (New York, New America Library, 1951), p. 322.
19 Sunstein, 'The Republican Civic Tradition', p. 1,539.
20 I. Honohan, *Civic Republicanism* (London, Routledge, 2002), p. 2.
21 See P. G. A. Pocock, *The Machiavellian Moment: Florentine Political Thought and the Atlantic Republican Tradition* (Princeton, Princeton University Press, 1975).
22 M. Philps, 'English Republicanism in the 1970s', *Journal of Political Philosophy* 6, no. 3 (1998), p. 236.
23 Pettit, *Republicanism*, p. 147.
24 Philps, 'English Republicanism in the 1970s', p. 244.
25 I. McBride, 'Memory and National Identity in Modern Ireland', in McBride (ed.), *History and Memory in Modern Ireland* (Cambridge, Cambridge University Press, 2001), p. 1.
26 *Ibid.*, p. 1.
27 A. Ford, 'Martyrdom, History and Memory in Early Modern Ireland', in McBride (ed.), *History and Memory in Modern Ireland*, p. 43.
28 R. Kearney, *Transitions: Narratives in Modern Irish Culture* (Manchester, Manchester University Press, 1988), p. 211.
29 Ford, 'Martyrdom, History and Memory in Early Modern Ireland', p. 14.
30 'The Green Book', cited in B. O'Brien, *The Long War: IRA and Sinn Féin* (Dublin, O'Brien Press, 1999), p. 401.
31 *Belfast Telegraph*, 'Dissidents: interview with terror splinter group', 3 November 2010.
32 S. Moran, 'Patrick Pearse and Patriotic Soteriology: The Irish Republican Tradition and the Sanctification of Political Self-Immolation', in Y. Alexander and A. O'Day (eds), *The Irish Terrorism Experience* (Aldershot, Dartmouth, 1991), p. 9.
33 *Ibid.*, pp. 9, 20.
34 G. Sweeney, 'Self-Immolation in Ireland: Hunger Strikes and Political Confrontation', *Anthropology Today* 9, no. 5 (1993), p. 14.
35 R. White, *Ruairí Ó Brádaigh: The Life and Politics of an Irish Revolutionary* (Bloomington, Indiana University Press, 2006), p. 289.
36 M. Frampton, *Legion of the Rearguard: Dissident Irish Republicanism* (Dublin, Irish Academic Press, 2011), p. 67.
37 Address Given at Bundoran Hunger Strike Commemoration by Sarah Murphy, *Saoirse*, September 2000.
38 R. English, *Irish Freedom: The History of Nationalism in Ireland* (London, Pan Macmillan, 2006), p. 303.
39 T. MacSwiney, Quoted in James Larkin Republican Flute Band Liverpool Address 9 October 2010 and *An Phoblacht/Republican News*, 19 June 1997.
40 Address Given at Bundoran Hunger Strike Commemoration by Sarah Murphy, *Saoirse*, September 2000.
41 M. McGuinness, *Text of Oration to Annual Wolfe Tone Commemoration* (London, Wolfe Tone Society, 1986).

42 B. Hanley, 'The Rhetoric of Republican Legitimacy', in F. McGarry (ed.), *Republicanism in Modern Ireland* (Dublin, University College Dublin Press, 2003), p. 167.

43 *Ibid.*, p. 167.

44 McBride, 'Memory and National Identity in Modern Ireland', p. 2.

45 R. Williams, *Marxism and Literature* (Oxford, Oxford University Press, 1977), p. 115.

46 Ford, 'Martyrdom, History and Memory in Early Modern Ireland', p. 66.

47 McBride, 'Memory and National Identity in Modern Ireland', p. 6.

48 *Ibid.*, p. 13.

49 M. O'Callaghan, 'Reconsidering the Republican Tradition in Nineteenth Century Ireland', in I. Honohan (ed.), *Republicanism in Ireland: Confronting Theories and Traditions* (Manchester, Manchester University Press, 2008), pp. 33–34.

50 Pettit, *Republicanism*, p. 131.

51 Bertie Ahern, Address to the 63rd Fianna Fáil Ard Fheis, Dublin, 22 November 1998. See also G. Ivory, 'The Meanings of Republicanism in Contemporary Ireland', in Honahan (ed.), *Republicanism in Ireland*, pp. 98–99.

52 Margaret Ritchie, Address to SDLP Annual Conference, Ramada Hotel, Belfast, 7 November 2010. Full text available at www.cain.ulst.ac.uk/issues/politics/docs/sdlp/mr061110.htm.

53 *Ibid.*

54 M. Cunningham, 'The Political Language of John Hume', *Irish Political Studies* 12, no. 1 (1997), pp. 13–22.

55 See chapter 3 for a deeper discussion of ethnic and civic interpretations of nationalism and how these have been adopted.

56 Honohan, *Civic Republicanism*, p. 1.

57 A. Kilmurray and M. McWilliams, 'Republicanism Revisited', in N. Porter (ed.), *The Republican Ideal: Current Perspectives* (Belfast, Blackstaff Press, 1998), p. 157.

58 Cullen, 'Beyond Nationalism', p. 14.

59 R. English, 'Defining the Nation: Recent Historiography and Irish Nationalism', *European Review of History* 2, no. 2 (1995), p. 196.

60 B. Hanley, 'Change and Continuity: Republican Thought since 1922', *The Republic* 2 (2001), p. 93.

61 J. Augusteijn, 'Political Violence and Democracy: An Analysis of the Tensions within Irish Republican Strategy, 1914–2002', *Irish Political Studies* 18, no. 1 (2003), p. 1.

62 See K. Bean, 'The Economic and Social War Against Violence: British Social and Economic Strategy and the Evolution of Provisionalism', in A. Edwards and S. Bloomer (eds), *Transforming the Peace Process in Northern Ireland: From Terrorism to Democratic Politics* (Dublin, Irish Academic Press, 2008); K. Bean, 'Shifting Discourses of New Nationalism and Post-republicanism', in M. Elliott (ed.), *The Long Road to Peace in Northern Ireland* (Liverpool, Liverpool University Press, 2007); M. Cox, Rethinking the International and Northern Ireland; A Defence, in M. Cox, A. Guelke, and F. Stephens (eds), *A Farewell to Arms? Beyond the Good Friday Agreement* (Manchester, Manchester University Press, 2006).

63 See P. Shirlow, 'The Economics of the Peace Process', in C. Gilligan and J. Tonge (eds), *Peace or War? Understanding the Peace Process in Northern Ireland* (Aldershot, Ashgate, 1997).

64 See English, *Irish Freedom*; M. McGovern, 'Irish Republicanism and the Potential Pitfalls of Pluralism', *Capital and Class* 71 (2000), pp. 133–161.

65 J. Coakley and L. O'Dowd, 'The Transformation of the Irish Border', *Political Geography* 26, no. 8 (2007), p. 878.

66 *Ibid.*, p. 880.

67 *Ibid.*, pp. 877–885.

68 M. Frampton, *The Long March: Political Strategy of Sinn Féin, 1981–2007* (Basingstoke, Palgrave Macmillan, 2009).

69 M. McLaughlin in Porter (ed.), *The Republican Ideal*, p. 4.

70 B. O'Leary, 'Analysing Partition: Definition, Classification and Explanation', *Political Geography* 26 (2007), p. 887.

71 Pettit, *Republicanism*, p. 147.

72 T .W. Tone, *An Argument on behalf of the Catholics of Ireland (by A Northern Whig)* [1791], in T. W. Moody, R. B. McDowell and C. J. Woods (eds), *The Writings of Theobald Wolfe Tone, 1763–98* (Vol. I) (Oxford, Clarendon Press, 1998), pp. 126–127.

73 *Ibid.*, p. 127.

74 See chapter 3 for a more detailed discussion of the consociation versus integration debate.

75 B. Graham and C. Nash, 'A Shared Future: Territoriality, Pluralism and Public Policy in Northern Ireland', *Political Geography* 25, no. 3 (2006), p. 260.

76 Office of First Minister and Deputy First Minister, *A Shared Future: A Consultation Paper on Improving Relations in Northern Ireland. Policy and Strategic Framework for Good Relations in Northern Ireland* (Belfast, Community Relations Unit, 2005).

77 Office of First Minister and Deputy First Minister, *Programme for Cohesion, Sharing and Integration* (Belfast, Policy Secretariat, 2010), p. 75.

78 McLaughlin in Porter (ed.), *The Republican Ideal*, p. 5.

79 J. Connolly, 'The Irish Flag' (8 April 1916), in *Collected Works* (Vol. II) (Dublin, News Books, 1988), p. 175.

80 IRSP, *Founding Statement of the IRSP* (Dublin, IRSP, 1974), p. 1, available at www.irsp.ie/Background/history/founding.html, accessed 21 June 2012.

81 J. Holland and H. McDonald, *INLA: Deadly Divisions* (Dublin, Torc Press, 1994), p. 227.

82 McLaughlin in Porter (ed.), *The Republican Ideal*, p. i.

83 Sinn Féin, *Agenda for Government: Sinn Féin Assembly Election Manifesto* (Dublin, Sinn Féin, 2003), p. 3.

84 M. McGovern, '"The Old Days are over": Irish Republicanism, the Peace Process and the Discourse of Equality', *Terrorism and Political Violence* 16, no. 3 (2004), pp. 632–633.

85 G. Adams, *The Politics of Irish Freedom* (Dingle, Brandon, 1986), p. 167.

86 McGovern, '"The Old Days are over"', p. 632.

87 Sinn Féin, *Others Promise, We Deliver: 2007 Manifesto* (Dublin, Sinn Féin, 2007), p. 4 .

88 McGovern, '"The Old Days are over"', p. 622.

89 P. Arthur, 'Republicanism and the Implementation of the Agreement: An Academic Perspective', *Working Papers in British-Irish Studies* 5 (2001), p. 10.

90 *Saoirse*, 'Interview with Ruairí O Bradaigh', 1 April 2010.

3

Creating political space for 'dissidents'? The extent of ideological compromise by Sinn Féin and 'Provisional' republicanism

> I can understand why dissident republicans bristle at being called 'dissidents'. After all, it inescapably defines and anchors them as being dissident relative to a much larger, successful republican organisation with which they disagree.[1]

'Dissident' republicanism has assumed various forms and its heterogeneous nature makes it a difficult entity to define and analyse. Although those who broke away from Provisional Sinn Féin in 1986, 1997 and beyond, or created new republican groups with no previous connections, were small in number, their justifications remain significant in understanding the Irish republican ideology. Whilst those republicans who oppose the Sinn Féin agenda are a small and disunited minority, they are important in resisting the idea that the party has a monopoly of what constitutes Irish republicanism.[2] The range of 'dissent' is reflected today in paramilitary organisations, community groups, blogs, forums and journals. Whilst the form of dissent is broad, a key and often overlooked question is, from what, or who, are these groups dissenting? If Provisional republicanism is the yardstick for which to measure the spectrum of republican manifestations in the modern day context then it is vital to consider the relationship between Provisionalism and traditional republican ideology.

To date, the focus of academic analysis has been upon the extent to which the Provisional movement has compromised traditional republican ideals through its involvement in the peace process and acceptance of political institutions in Northern Ireland. The Provisional brand of Irish republicanism has been through a period of profound transition. The movement has evolved and adapted, processes which have brought with them the charge of having 'sold out'. The extent to which Sinn Féin has evolved is indeed startling. This chapter examines the extent of ideological and political contortions within Provisional republicanism, accounting for the changes within Sinn Féin strategy. The chapter considers the impact of exogenous and endogenous pressures, in addition to positive choices, underpinning such drastic change. It then continues to discuss the influences on Sinn Féin as a constitutional party, in order to assess the wider impact of electoral competition on the party's positioning. Within the academic debate surrounding the phenomenon of 'dissent' within modern day Irish republicanism there is a need to create a framework that considers the relationship between the changed political approach of Sinn Féin and the ideological tenets of republicanism.

Tracing the transition

Sinn Féin has been through a period of profound transition. As such it is not surprising that this seismic change is explored in an array of academic literature. A significant amount of academic attention has attempted to understand how Sinn Féin represented continuity and change within the Irish republican tradition.[3] This chapter will dissect these contributions as well as highlight any possible inadequacies within the literature. First, however, it is necessary briefly to illustrate the extent of (Provisional) republican transition.

The development of revisionist republicanism within Sinn Féin can be traced to the 1986 decision to drop the long-standing republican policy of abstention from Leinster House. The Provisionals had emerged in 1969 in opposition to taking seats in Dáil Éireann and Stormont, rejecting the political institutions of the Irish Republic and Northern Ireland as partitionist in residing over only twenty-six counties and six counties respectively. Those determined to maintain abstention pointed out that the Sinn Féin constitution stipulated that candidates standing on an attendance basis for any of the partitionist assemblies were guilty of 'an act of treason'.[4] Considering the existence of the Provisionals derived in part from the safeguarding of abstentionist purism, the recognition, and the ultimate acceptance by Provisional Sinn Féin of the government of the twenty-six counties from 1986 signified a substantial revision to party policy.

The 1994 PIRA ceasefire provided the catalyst for the next major revision to Provisional republicanism, which, despite a brief breakdown in the cessation of violence in 1996–97, culminated in the disbandment of the paramilitary organisation. This was finalised in 2005 with the decommissioning of weapons 'finally accomplished'.[5] Given the previous attachment to the slogan of 'not a bullet, not an ounce' in reference to the surrendering of arms, the completion of decommissioning demonstrated a remarkable revision of the Provisional approach to achieving 'freedom and justice' in Ireland. In 1986 Martin McGuinness had insisted, following Sinn Féin's local election successes: 'We don't believe that winning elections and winning any amount of votes will bring freedom in Ireland. At the end of the day, it will be the cutting edge of the IRA which will bring freedom.'[6] The former PIRA prisoner, Tommy McKearney, describes the culmination of (Provisional) change as indicative that the 'leadership had achieved a certain status by surrendering its old programme and being allocated a place within the British system in Ireland. The era of new Sinn Féin was firmly established.'[7] Whilst there had been previous hiatuses in the military campaigns of the IRA, the ability to resume an armed campaign had always been retained. Full decommissioning therefore represented a new departure.

Accepting the terms of the Good Friday Agreement (GFA) and entering power sharing in Stormont meant the recognition of Northern Ireland as a political entity and the approval of a deal which maintained the existence of a partitioned island for as long as the majority of the citizens of Northern Ireland so wished. This principle of consent, which had previously been vehemently rejected as a 'unionist veto', provided the cornerstone of the GFA. Despite the previous demands upon the British government to pledge withdrawal from Northern Ireland as a prelude to negotiations over the details of departure, Sinn Féin accepted an agreement without any guarantee of reaching their ultimate goal. The declaration of support for the Police Service of Northern Ireland (PSNI) in 2007 by Sinn Féin, which restored power sharing after a temporary collapse, signified the party's acceptance that the road to a united Ireland was to be along a constitutional path which fully accepted the institutions of the northern state it still avowedly wished to dissolve.

For the majority within Sinn Féin and the PIRA, this revision represented the evolution of tactical considerations and a natural development in order to adjust to contextual realities.[8] However, for others this revision went too far and indicated the desertion of principles that are fundamental to republicanism as an ideology.[9] The variation within interpretations of republicanism highlights differences in perception over what is a republican principle and what is merely a republican tactic. It also highlights differences over how, strategically, a united Ireland might be reached. Cognisance of the debate between what are tactics and what are principles is fundamental in understanding the emergence of dissident republicanism.

Whilst the republican movement has generally agreed on final goals, sections have often possessed markedly divergent perceptions of the existing potential of political opportunities. As a result, varying perceptions regarding resources, opportunities and threats have co-existed with uncertainty and disagreement about which strategies would maximise the potential to secure goals.[10] In addition to the disagreements over the effectiveness and suitability of particular strategies and tactics, there have also been very different views of how ultimate goals and the strategies for obtaining them were related. For some, republicanism constitutes a fixed set of unyielding principles and ideas, whilst others are more likely to interpret republicanism as an evolving movement with adaptive strategies, conditioned by military and political opportunities,[11] British state strategies,[12] and public and electoral opinion.[13] Sinn Féin acknowledged in the 1970s that:

> The Republican Movement has always had three tendencies: a militarist and fairly apolitical tendency; a revolutionary tendency; and a constitutional tendency. These terms, as used here, are relative to the conditions, the circumstances and the

historical background against which the Movement functions. Throughout the history of the Movement one or other of the tendencies has periodically been in the ascendancy[14]

Despite the rebranding of Sinn Féin's republicanism, the organisation has remained relatively unified in that it has retained most members and indeed expanded. Today, within the mainstream discourse there is a tendency to place Sinn Féin at a level whereby it has complete possession of the republican franchise. As a result, there is a need to understand Provisional republicanism in its own right in order to consider whether there is space, ideologically and practically, for the emergence of dissident groups. Has Sinn Féin's republicanism maintained fidelity to republican principles, travelling on what it perceives as the 'long road' to the Republic, as argued by Frampton?[15] Alternatively, has the scale of change meant that Sinn Féin have vacated republican space so much as to create opportunities for others? Or, do 'end of history' claims go some way in explaining change, as Irish republicanism has entered an endgame, despite protestations to the contrary, incapable of replacement by fragmented and marginalised dissident groups. This lattermost view has been expressed most stridently by Anthony McIntyre:

> There is no crisis. This is so because there is no longer any social phenomenon that we may term republicanism. The present pockets of the faithful exist here and there, for the most part taking cultural form. But as a social phenomenon of any political import republicanism has ceased to function.[16]

The key consideration here is whether the Provisionals have maintained old values within a new context, as claimed in the very different framework of neoliberalism by 'New Labour'[17] or whether they have adapted to an extent whereby they can no longer be called republican. Or, as articulated by McIntyre, has republicanism expired?

Explaining the transition

Considering this transition is vital in order to understand the dissident rationale. As the opening quote from Danny Morrison encapsulates, the term 'dissident' has been interpreted to view groups in relation to Sinn Féin as opposed to the wider republican framework. As a result, tracing the development of the Provisionals as well as considering how and why this change occurred is fundamental in understanding dissident justifications of their own approach. To understand the dissident ideological standpoint it is necessary to consider Sinn Féin's movement into constitutional politics and to what extent that represented the updating, revising or contorting of Irish republican principles.

There are several lines of reasoning emerging from the academic literature attempting to explain the motives behind the transformation within the

Provisional movement. The first argument suggests that modern Sinn Féin is a product of the failure of tactics (i.e. the IRA's armed struggle) which ultimately forced a reassessment of strategy. The centrality of armed struggle to republican strategy in the first two decades of Provisional republicanism is summed up by the following assertion:

> The IRA strategy is very clear. At some point in the future, due to the pressure of the continuing and sustained armed struggle, the will of the British government to remain in this country will be broken. This is the objective of the armed struggle … we can state confidently today that there will be no ceasefire and no truces until Britain declares its intent to withdraw and leave our people in peace.[18]

The absolutism from the Provisionals on the centrality of armed struggle ebbed away as realism and pragmatism overshadowed the limited potential gains of a military campaign. Emphasis switched to a second front of electoralism. Yet it was untenable to maintain the armed front of the PIRA whilst embarking on a project designed to make Sinn Féin become the dominant force within northern nationalism. Within the Provisional strategy there were insufficient resources and an obvious lack of complementarity, for both the ballot box and the armalite as a permanent duality. Alonso explains this realisation from a grass-roots level where the frustration of the rank and file over the lack of achievements of a military campaign, allied to the stagnation of Sinn Féin's vote, indicated the failure and futility of armed struggle.[19] However, Moloney offers a top-down explanation of change, where the decision to initiate movement away from armed struggle as a tactic was leadership led.[20] Whether this movement away from armed struggle was leadership led or grass-roots driven, the uncomfortable juxtapositioning of militarism with electoralism suggests an inevitability in one element being subsumed. Sinn Féin duly came to surpass the PIRA and became the senior partner in the Provisional movement. Understanding this political versus military friction throughout the history of republicanism is essential in beginning to explain the movement's tendency to split.[21]

An alternative explanation of change is more rooted in the contention that the Provisionals were never fastened by a strong ideological anchor. Rather, the development of the movement relied on pragmatism and therefore the changes made within republicanism were unsurprising.[22] This argument attempts to explain the development of the Provisionals as situational and contextual more than ideational. Under this interpretation, northern Provisionals were not unduly committed to the traditional ideological grounding of Irish republicanism, and the politics and ideology of 1916 (the indivisible republic) were mere bolt-ons to the street politics of 1969. The emergence of the Provisionals was centred more upon a supposed defence of northern communities rather than a level of commitment to republican ideals and tradition.[23] The importance of context in understanding the Provisional movement, and ultimately strategy, is

explained by English in his assertion that, 'the Provisional IRA's violent nationalism was also about a community in struggle; indeed it was one largely defined
by a particular kind of struggle. Constitutional politics were held to have failed,
reformism to have been proved futile.'[24] If the birth of Provisional republicanism was indeed as a result of situational circumstances as opposed to ideological
devotion, it meant that pragmatism and immediate local concerns were placed
before the conventional republican mantras of a thirty-two county republic. As a
result, the evolution of the PIRA and Sinn Féin was based on realism as distinct
from rigid dogma. Eventually this permitted the displacement of the historical
certainties of republican discourse for the vaguer language of transition.

This argument is pursued by McIntyre, who contends that the Provisionals
were an organisation shaped by the situational context, notably British Army
and RUC repression and second-class socio-economic status, rather than a
movement imbued with deep ideological devotion dictating direction. McIntyre
goes on to state that armed struggle was not merely a dynamic towards a united
Ireland, but also a means for achieving reform in the North:

> The modern republican movement has persistently been the product of British state
> strategies rather than a body which has existed for the sole purpose of completing
> the 'unfinished business' of uniting Ireland. It represents the crystallisation of
> nationalist opposition to structural exclusion within the North of Ireland.[25]

The existence of the Provisionals on a mainly situational rather than ideational
basis, meant that if the situation changed on the ground they too could change,
pragmatism displacing purism. Whilst this argument contextualises how the
Provisional movement has functioned, there is a need to question also the
extent to which they have been devoid of ideological foundation. It is difficult
to expand McIntyre's argument across the whole organisation and therefore in
considering the creation of the Provisionals one cannot simply dismiss the role
of ideology. Whilst ideological shallowness was characteristic of many within
the Provisionals, it ignores the commitment of the republican *leadership* at formation in 1969–70 to the politics of 1916–19 and core principles such as the
policy of abstention. That leadership was eventually ousted by northern figures,
with Adams at the forefront. Whilst the founders of the Provisionals may have
been instilled by republican tradition, recruits after 1969 were more likely to
join in response to the situation on the ground such as state violence and socio-
economic disparities.[26] Therefore, it is possible to propose that the formation
of the Provisionals was based upon ideological alignment; however, it was situational reality and the context on the ground that developed and expanded the
movement.

For political movements to gain and maintain support they have to retain
relevance. Therefore, an element of pragmatism is essential in order to respond
to contextual demands and remain significant. However, it is the balance

between ideological adherence and a willingness to adjust to contextual realities that makes Irish republicanism so contested. The dogmatic allegiance to certain principles may force a movement into political isolation whilst the relegation or removal of other tenets may lead to accusations of having sold out. Dissidents allege that the Provisionals relegated principles beyond the point where they could still be considered republican and that republicanism became whatever the Sinn Féin leadership claimed it was on any given day.[27]

Another key argument attempting to explain the shifts within Provisionalism focuses on the impact of structural conditions in determining the shape and nature of modern day mainstream republicanism, emphasising the impact of exogenous factors such as socio-economic and political development. Sinn Féin now operates in a very different socio-economic context compared to when second-class citizenry existed amongst northern working-class Catholics in the 1970s. Economic growth, investment opportunities and a plethora of anti-discrimination legislative measures meant a decrease in economic disparity.[28] The greater economic parity between communities is a consequence of fair employment legislation, political change, and external financial support from the British and American governments as well as peace and reconciliation funding from supranational bodies such as the EU.[29]

There is also a need to consider the impact of a changing political context where 'post-ideological' politics, on an international level, and the changes in British strategy, at state level, dictated the arena in which Provisionalism functioned.[30] According to this analysis it was the result of these external pressures on the Provisionals that meant that it was to become inevitable that Sinn Féin would move into the electoral arena and allow itself to become dominated by electoral concerns, rather than be hidebound by outdated nationalist dogma and ideology, anti-colonial rhetoric and futile militarism. The new electoralism and competition for votes allowed revolutionary goals to be replaced by the rhetoric of social reformism and electoral appeal. Sinn Féin became less the self-ascribed government of Ireland, an untenable position, and much more a competitive political actor in a pluralist electoral marketplace. However, for dissidents this absorption into the political mainstream went far beyond the simple adjustment to exterior pressures.

Diversity and multiplicity have come to define the nature of the republican movement throughout history. For some it is within this history where understanding of the trajectory from the margins to the political mainstream lies.[31] The more 'purist' interpretation of republicanism, by its very nature, has remained so static that any situation that requires adjustment or amendment to policy (a situation that inevitably presents itself to any dynamic political organisation) has been followed by cries of 'sell-out'. This invariably makes the schismatic tendencies within republicanism an inherent trait. Whilst such an interpretation allows for the emergence of dissident groups, it does not explain with precision the growth of dissent and why the fault line between purist and pragmatist is not always clear, evidenced by the way in which different factions left the Provisionals at different times. Whilst each of the arguments above frames the evolution of the Provisionals differently they are all linked by a similar line of thought in that they portray Sinn Féin's movement into constitutionalism as inevitable. Whether the shape of mainstream republicanism can be defined by the failure of armed struggle, the arguments that the Provisionals never had a strong ideological anchor, the impact of exogenous forces and the innate nature of the movement to split, all depict revisionism with a sense of inevitability.

The civic/ethnic dichotomy

There is a tendency within some of the existing literature to explain contemporary Provisionalism as a result of the external influences of socio-economic transformation and localised structures of power within the nationalist community.[32] These arguments highlight accompanying processes of institutionalisation, rather than accounting for what Sinn Féin's modern outlook now represents. Whilst the route of transition taken by Sinn Féin is explained, there is a need to reveal more about the current form of Sinn Féin's republicanism. There is a body of a literature that explains the development of Provisional republicanism in relation to concepts of identity and ideas of the nation.[33]

Debates on Irish identity and the concept of the Irish nation are part of a much wider debate on nationalism. In recent years nationalism has been explained through a 'civic' versus 'ethnic' dichotomy.[34] One of the first to articulate this divide between civic and ethnic forms of nationalism was Hans Kohn, who argued that:

> Nationalism in the West arose in an effort to build a nation in the political reality and the struggles of the present without too much sentimental regard for the past; nationalists in Central and Eastern Europe created, often out of the myth of the past and the dreams of the future, an ideal fatherland.[35]

Civic nationalism, the basis of which is a voluntary constitutional association of people supportive of particular political structures in recognition of ethnic identity, is seen to be a typically western model. Ethnic nationalism, which is distinguished by 'its emphasis on a community of birth and native culture', is identified as an eastern variant.[36] Civic nationalism has its roots in the democratic and secular tradition of the Enlightenment and is typically positively valued for being inclusive, identifying the citizen as the basis of the nation state. The nation state is thus defined as civic to the extent that it recognises the nation as a community of 'equal, right-bearing citizens, united in patriotic attachment to a shared set of political practices and values'.[37] As a result the nation state constitutes all those who align themselves to the nation regardless of race, religion or language. Ethnic nationalism has largely been negatively valued for being exclusive.[38] The eastern ethnic tradition defines the nation in terms of a 'homogeneous' people; what unites people is a common identity. Kearney explains this dichotomy:

> Civic nationalism conceives of the nation as including all of its citizens- regardless of blood, creed or colour. Ethnocentric nationalism believes, by contrast, that what holds a community together is not common rights of citizenship (or humanity) but common ethnicity (or race).[39]

Whilst this civic–ethnic distinction highlights variations within nationalism, it is also criticised for being too rigid a framework, misleadingly offering polar positions.[40] Rather, it is more appropriate to distinguish between various forms of nationalism by considering the inclusive and exclusive nature of classification. As Brubaker notes, 'all understandings of nationhood and all forms of nationalism are simultaneously inclusive and exclusive. What varies is not the fact or even degree of inclusiveness or exclusiveness, but the bases or criteria of inclusion and exclusion.'[41] It is more appropriate to define types of nationalism by considering the basis of inclusion and exclusion as opposed to the more rigid labels that come with the civic and ethnic definitions.

Nationalism can be the collectivist politics of 'blood and belonging', centred on the ethnic affiliation of the *Volk*. Alternatively, nationalism can be the expression of association between citizens in a specific designated area/polity they share where the rights of man trump those of the nation. The latter interpretation frontloads the importance of the nation and the concept of universalism, adopting a more civic position. It is this civic interpretation that is argued to have defined nationalism in modern polities, where movement towards the semi-autonomy of nations, as via devolution in the United Kingdom, is defined by the *demos* as opposed to the *ethnos*.[42] This new nationalism reflects the accommodationist, pragmatic politics that came to typify much sub-state nationalism by the late twentieth century. As nationalism moved away from the specificity of ethnically determined characteristics to one which embraces difference within the nation, national identity ultimately became far more flexible, and as a result it has become harder to distinguish who 'we' are as a nation.

The manner in which national identity is defined and explained varies greatly. The concept of the nation is dependent on several factors, such as geography, sovereignty, ethnicity and culture. Within each factor there are different and contested interpretations. Given this complexity, the criteria of belonging to that state, or deciding what constitutes the 'we' as a nation, has flexible conditions. Today in both the Republic of Ireland and in Northern Ireland the question of 'national identity' is under discussion, posing questions such as what is the Irish nation and who is included within that nation?[43] Key to the evaluation of nationalism is not so much the criteria to which a group is identified but more the degree to which other groups are respected. As Harris contends, 'Far from just articulating identity, nationalism articulates political aims and promotes interests in the name of and on behalf of a group it helped to constitute as a national group.'[44] The Irish conflict is indeed most commonly explained as an ethno-national quarrel involving rival concepts of the nation and national identity.[45]

Two communities within Northern Ireland have distinct identities both with a set of traditional ideals and with a definitive aspiration; they therefore have been described as possessing fundamentally opposing national and cultural identities.[46] At this stage it is necessary to look closely at the republican interpretation of cultural difference and acceptance of other identities, particularly in respect of how this has evolved in parallel to wider debates on nationalism. Interpretation of national identity and treatment of 'other groups' within the understanding of 'Irishness', provide a framework in which to explore the development of what is now the mainstream republican movement within a broader geo-political context.

The civic/ethnic divide in explaining Provisional republicanism

The two Northern Irish communities have long held conflicting national and cultural identities as well as polarised constitutional aspirations. The Provisional interpretation of the conflict in the 1970s identified the British presence in the North as a colonial occupation. A British identity was therefore seen as a product of Britain's imperial presence, one held by the 'forces of occupation', whereas the inhabitants of the island were Irish. As a result, Provisional republican thinking of this time approached the question of national identity with an element of solipsism, where the issues that mattered to one's own republican people could be seen as indistinguishable from those affecting the Irish people as a whole, whether unionist or nationalist, north or south.[47] Gerry Adams offered one example of such discourse:

> Ireland is historically, culturally and geographically one single unit. The partition of Ireland, established by the British 'Government of Ireland Act', divides Ireland into two artificial statelets, the boundaries of which were determined by a sectarian head-count and can be maintained only by continuing sectarianism.[48]

Republican emphasis was placed on a colonial interpretation of the conflict and the need for a decisive break from Britain.[49] The aim was to force the British out of Ireland after which reconciliation between different *Irish* traditions would soon follow. Unionism, according to the 1970s Provisional interpretation, merely served partitionist interests, whilst unionists were barely acknowledged as a distinct community, let alone a different nation. Unionism was portrayed as a product of partition and represented an artificial construct and therefore constituted an empty ideology. As Kearney and Cullen note, 'proposed solutions to the problem of governing Northern Ireland have been couched in terms of the denial of its national identity to one or other of the communities'.[50] This triumphalism of one community over the other reinforced an ethnically determined theory of nationalism.

Having initially offered relatively benign views of loyalists as merely deluded during the 1970s, the republican leadership offered harder-line, anti-loyalist rhetoric into the 1980s, stressing that republicanism 'cannot and should not ever tolerate or compromise with loyalism'.[51] From the 1990s onwards a new discourse began to emerge regarding the republican interpretation of unionism. The Sinn Féin document *Towards a Lasting Peace*, published in 1992 articulated how unionists, could not, and should not, be coerced in to a united Ireland. Unionism was increasingly portrayed as a legitimate identity that could be accommodated within a united Ireland:

> We must be realistic enough to accept that, in the event of a British withdrawal, part of this island will be inhabited by more than 900,000 people whose whole history, aspirations, culture and sense of stability have been formed, nurtured and reinforced within a British political, intellectual and emotional environment.[52]

Such language of acceptance and accommodation marked a clear contrast with earlier assessments. Sinn Féin came to accept that in a 'vision of a united and independent Ireland there must be a place for those who consider themselves British and those who wish to stay British'.[53] Asked whether it was possible to accept the Britishness of unionism, the editor of Sinn Féin's *An Phoblacht*, Peadar Whelan, responded:

> Well that is a hard one for me to answer because I find it difficult to fathom. There is a friend of mine who used to talk about unionism and he used to say to me you would wonder why people would prefer to be the subjects of a British Queen or a British monarch than be a citizen of a united Ireland …Why would you rather be a subject than a citizen?[54]

Whilst the Sinn Féin position on unionism may have evolved, it has struggled to become fully accepting of Britishness as an identity upon the island of Ireland. Sinn Féin's Alex Maskey offered this perspective: 'I accept there are a lot of people who have an affinity with Britain. But there are some people who think they are British. I don't think they are British. They were born here so they're Irish, so I don't see them as British.'[55]

Rather than implying a complete overhaul of previous interpretations of British identity, Sinn Féin's shift in position signified the recognition of the realisation that dialogue and agreement with unionists is essential in achieving an indivisible Ireland. An example of this discourse was demonstrated by TD and Sinn Féin Vice-President, Mary Lou McDonald, who, when asked about working with unionism, rejected the idea of a single sense of identity, asserting: 'The history and tradition of unionism, is the history and tradition of unionism, and as so for nationalism and republicanism.'[56] Consequently the republican strategy became defined by unionist outreach and accommodation of existing identities and traditions, as opposed to the straightforward need for their transformation. The republican position on unionism had not changed dramatically; rather a shift had occurred in how this was presented. Consent and respect therefore became taglines for Sinn Féin to reach out to the unionist community, but as a legitimate political or ideological construct unionism remains contested.

Sinn Féin's brand of republicanism has shifted to the politics of communal equality, rather than the overthrow of the previously conceived 'artificial state' that was Northern Ireland. In terms of defining or expressing national identity, emphasis was given to co-existence between communities. This is typified through the language of Adams, which places less stress upon territorial imperatives and more upon 'Humeite' conceptualisations[57] of an agreed Ireland, with an approved mode of self-determination:

> The vision of an Ireland that is at peace with itself and with our nearest neighbours in Britain is a shared aspiration for most of the people in Ireland … Decisions on these matters, in our view, can ultimately only be arrived at through the most inclusive dialogue, political discourse and negotiation by the people of Ireland. Clearly that includes unionists.[58]

Such language of inclusion and pluralism typifies the reordering of republican principles and the frontloading of equality, agreement and consensus. This process has involved the promotion of a unionist outreach and the centrality of power sharing. Sinn Féin's republicanism evolved from the 1970s interpretation of identity as purely ethnic in terms of definition to that which recognises the island of Ireland as a 'rich tapestry of identities', recognising shared values, shared geography and a shared political culture.[59]

This shift has seen the promotion of the civic republican themes of equality and citizenship, and acknowledgement, at least, of unionist identity and allegiance. As Murray and Tonge explain, 'Sinn Féin had moved towards a civic Republicanism, which acknowledges the plurality of identities in Northern Ireland and recognises an independent existence for Unionists beyond their British "colonial masters".'[60] Sinn Féin has moved from 'ethnically' determined republicanism, which promotes a homogeneous Irish identity, to a more civic and inclusive interpretation. This shift is argued to have 'popularized concepts of Irish identity as malleable and capable of a variety of readings' and, as a result, has created the possibility of remoulding Irish identity.[61]

Whilst the civic/ethnic dichotomy is useful in outlining the changes within Sinn Féin, it does not necessarily add to the understanding of why this shift has taken place. Any attempt to clarify the reasons why changes occurred needs to consider the impact of events on two levels. Firstly, there is a need to take a step back from the Northern Irish context in considering nationalism and reflect on the impact of wider political trends. On an international level it is possible to observe how the relationship between nationalism and self-determination has evolved, specifically the movement away from centralised homogeneous states towards models of multi-level governance. The devolution of powers and the subsequent exercising of authority across different jurisdictions is demonstrated, in various forms, in Catalonia, Wales, Scotland and Quebec, as examples. Therefore, it is no longer assumed that nation states are in the possession of undiluted authority. This shift is argued to have brought about a reduction in nationalist movements that persist in the aim of building entirely separate states and instead the exercising of self-determination without constituting a separate space.[62] Ethno-national communities still exist but they do so by functioning as sub-state nationalist entities within the framework of devolution, a trend outlined below:

> The shift [towards civic nationalism] responds to the need to break with the oppressive governance of cultural minorities to avoid the pain and wanton destruction that results from the disaffection of these minorities and their demands to build new states, as well as the need to find ways to provide national minorities with equal rights, governance and political participation – without dismembering existing states.[63]

Within this context it is possible to consider the environment within which Sinn Féin has evolved and placed the civic interpretation of nationalism before more ethnic understandings.

Secondly, running parallel to the impact of wider geo-political trends is the impact of far more localised factors. In explaining transitions within Sinn Féin, it is necessary to consider more direct impacts within Northern Ireland. Contemporary events and situational reality ultimately shaped the context within which Sinn Féin moved from a revolutionary force to a constitutional player. The increasing consciousness that the PIRA was fighting a stalled war and the realisation that unionism could not be defeated meant that Sinn Féin were in a position where they would have to seriously reconsider their position if they wanted to be a serious nationalist force within the contemporary context.

The impact of trends on a macro-level (such as the shift in nationalisms and the decline of the centralised state) and on a more micro-level (the realisation of a stalemate with the armed campaign, plus the evolving stance of the British government and the onset of limited pan-nationalism), both contributed to shifts in Sinn Féin's position. However, Sinn Féin's movement into mainstream politics did not, as some hastily observed, necessarily represent the end of militant nationalism.[64] Rather, as Sinn Féin vacated that space, others were willing to try to fill that void.

In considering the wider debate on the evolution of nationalisms in global politics, there is a need to question, what does this new politics of Sinn Féin represent? As Kearney asks, 'do we mean, finally, new republicanism – post-nationalist and post-unionist – which would allow the inhabitants of Ireland to reaffirm their local identities while embracing a new nationalism?'[65] There is potential for the modern civic interpretation of nationalism to explain 'new' Sinn Féin and provide a framework in which to start understanding the seismic changes within party policy. The relationship with evolving theories of nationalism is summarised by Bean:

> Provisionalism is probably best described as an ideological configuration rather than a unified body of ideas; it has remained a work-in-progress throughout its history because it is a sight of contestation between elements of the universal and the particular, revealed especially in the tensions between civic and ethnic conceptions of identity and the nation.[66]

The shifting paradigm that has come to define the nature of nationalism in the twenty-first century provides a valuable framework in which to analyse Sinn Féin's republicanism. Assessment of the wider geo-political trend towards post-ideological politics is helpful in highlighting the context within which the organisation has changed, especially in terms of how the party can be considered to fit into the theoretical framework of new nationalism. Within this framework, Sinn Féin's contemporary version of republicanism is dominated by post-ideological and pragmatic politics. The politics of identity rather than territory and sovereignty came to typify the new Sinn Féin framework.

Republicanism is a fragmented and diverse phenomenon and contemporary versions are articulated by a broad spectrum of groups and individuals beyond what Sinn Féin represent. All these elements claiming the republican mantle have functioned in the same broader political context, yet remain diverse in the analysis they offer and the interpretation they provide. Therefore, whilst contextual analysis is helpful at a macro-level in defining Sinn Féin's modern agenda, it fails to explain why dissidents have not followed the same path. If the context is the same, why has the development of new 'nationalism' permeated Sinn Féin far more than 'dissident' organisations? The analysis of Sinn Féin in light of the evolving nature of nationalism does not consider the ideological or functional political space for dissidents to emerge. Whilst it recognises the pragmatic nature of mainstream republicanism and the possibility of dissidence, it does not tell us how such dissent is formulated.

Republicanism and the Good Friday Agreement

The Good Friday Agreement fell markedly short of the ultimate republican goal of a united Ireland. As described by McKearney, the Agreement presented a predicament in that:

The old dilemma for reformed insurgents had resurfaced for Sinn Féin. A group enters parliament intent on making change and finds it difficult to do so without making compromises within the confines of institutions designed to produce glacial progress.[67]

The GFA enticed Sinn Féin into the Northern Ireland Assembly and placed the future of the border within the parameters of the consent principle. In return Sinn Féin retained a commitment to a united Ireland, subject to the consent of a majority of the people of Northern Ireland, whilst gaining an all-Ireland dimension to the Agreement with the creation of a North-South ministerial council and cross-border bodies. Some vehemently proclaim that the Good Friday Agreement represented the consolidation of partition, a significant defeat for Irish republicanism.[68] Such sentiment was pithily expressed by the sister of hunger striker Bobby Sands, Bernadette Sands McKevitt, when she proclaimed that her brother 'did not die for cross-border bodies with executive powers'.[69] For these critics, the deal was seen as a betrayal to past generations.

Sinn Féin was confronted by the position that typically presents itself to previously marginalised organisations once they enter the mainstream political arena. However genuinely intent on delivering change they may be at the time of entering the political mainstream it is eventually revealed how difficult it is to do so without making compromises within the confines of the institutions in which they operate. Peadar Whelan illustrates this delicate balance between ideological devotion and the more pragmatic and tactical considerations that present themselves to political parties:

> But obviously you have to have fundamental tenets, you obviously have to have a foundation and fundamental cornerstones. You have to have your fundamentals and guiding principles … But in the course of government you have to make tactical changes and decisions.[70]

Sinn Féin has attempted to portray the GFA in transitional terms, framing it as a building block towards a united Ireland. The Agreement had massive support North and South within republican and nationalist communities.[71] Sinn Féin therefore did not so much have to sell the Agreement as advocate the settlement on the basis that it was a stepping stone on the path to Irish unity and not to the 'endgame'. As explained by Danny Morrison, 'right okay, we have signed off the Belfast Agreement so we are at the end of it so why are you still going on about the next phase, and then the next phase? That's because republicans don't consider business finished.'[72] In attempting to minimise the shift from traditional republican approaches, the Sinn Féin leadership framed the agreement in 'strategic transitional terms'.[73] Accepted on the grounds that it provided a staging post on the journey to Irish unity, the Good Friday Agreement was portrayed as one fragment within an evolving process, or the 'new phase of the struggle'.[74] Sinn Féin's base stresses that no one signed up to the Agreement thinking it was the final piece of the puzzle, emphasising how the 'language of Good Friday Agreement is explicit in this'.[75] In addition, for anyone who thinks the story is over, they have been starkly warned to 'think again and think hard'.[76]

The Provisionals long rejected the constitutional path, arguing that British policies and unionist resistance meant that republican aims needed to be advanced by militarism in addition to politics. The argument was that there was no gradualist path to a united Ireland, as 'unionist resistance and British backing of unionism precluded it'.[77] For Anthony McIntyre this presented a choice between the militant pursuit of anti-partitionism and the constitutional nationalist route of accepting partition.[78] Consequently, for the Provisionals, the militant path dominated. Over time, the context changed, and with it so did the Provisionals' approach, as electoral strategy came to the forefront. However, the key question here is not necessarily the manner in which this change occurred, but rather how to interpret this change. In other words, is it possible to characterise Sinn Féin's acceptance of the Agreement as 'a new phase of the republican struggle' or did it signify decisive movement away from fundamental republican tenets? For McIntyre, acceptance of the Agreement meant that Sinn Féin moved beyond the parameters of what can be defined as republican, positioning themselves as partitionist nationalists. He argues that, 'while a nationalist can be a partitionist a republican never is. It is the primal ground a republican cannot abandon.'[79] According to this interpretation Provisional revisionism indicated the rejection of core republican beliefs. Sinn Féin's endorsement of the GFA reinforced partition. Such an argument rests on taking a binary position (anti-partitionism versus partitionism) as the fundamental feature in adherence to the core of republican ideology.[80] The key objective of the Provisionals was to secure a British declaration of intent to leave, but instead they endorsed the principles of agreement and consensus, forcing the prospect of a united Ireland to become conditional upon unionist consent, which is unlikely ever to be forthcoming.[81] This interpretation therefore refuses to view the GFA in terms of the pursuit of republican goals on a different platform, or as Adams has termed it, a 'new phase of the struggle ... a transitional stage towards reunification'.[82]

In considering the evolution from armed struggle to constitutional politics, a more flexible interpretation beyond the partitionist/anti-partitionist binary can be adopted.[83] A more benign perspective recognised that the Agreement attempted to acknowledge traditional republican goals whilst accommodating modern democratic principles such as an end to violence; equality; consent and human rights. Sinn Féin followed this lead in frontloading universal principles of democracy, justice, equality and peace.[84] Ultimately, Sinn Féin recognised the need for an agreement which at least provides a possible path to Irish unity and offers advancement for northern nationalists within the existing state. Danny Morrison typifies this far more pragmatic interpretation of the evolution of the Provisional movement, especially in relation to the practical aspect of functioning within constitutional parameters:

> Well principles are a guide. It's objectives and aspirations you know, which are important definitions. I know what you mean by principles. When I was involved in the struggle, I was a fundamentalist and I think the only way you can wage an armed struggle is if you believe in ultimate demands and they have to be black and white. Once you engage in negotiations, or in compromise, then a whole new system kicks in called pragmatism or *realpolitik* and that is what we have to engage with.[85]

Sinn Féin can propose transition arguments which are difficult to challenge entirely in the absence of ultimate predictive capacities over the outworking of the GFA. However, the early evidence suggests little transition to unity and diminished appetite for such a shift amid improved economic and political status for northern nationalists. McKearney describes how this has relegated the national question:

> Irish unity remains an aspiration for many, but only an aspiration, a pleasant thought, but not something in which most people are prepared to invest time or energy. Certainly it is not something many see as worth spilling the amount of blood, sweat and tears that would be involved in doing so without Unionist consent.[86]

Whilst the centrality of the national question remains for Sinn Féin, the purpose of its being has transformed. For some the ideal of a united Ireland is utilised as a vision, a distant and elusive aspiration, as opposed to a directly attainable reality. As a result, for all republicans the ideal of a united Ireland is not forgotten yet the means by which to achieve this, along with the vision of what unity constitutes, differ from the old physical force methodology and Gaelic territorial sovereign entity once envisaged. Such an analysis reveals the fault line between purpose and aspiration, pragmatism and purism, principles and tactics.

The fluid, malleable approach of Sinn Féin has emphasised the importance of context and tactical considerations above what is considered by some to be fundamental principle and tradition. As early as 1988, Guelke noted how 'the grounding of the legitimacy of the Provisional IRA's campaign in a traditional republican interpretation of Irish history is now much less emphasised than it was at the start of the campaign'.[87] The growing level of contemplation given to tactical considerations and the consequent evolving relationship with principles are recognised by Sinn Féin's Sean Oliver:

> Tactically in the last 30–40 years, you know you've judged things and made big departures, you've taken initiatives to get us to where we are today. But, I suppose you could say that you have your underlying principles of what the struggle is about and then tactically you judge things. You know certainly big initiatives … I suppose one of the big ones was in '86 when we decided that if elected we would take [seats] in the parliament in Dublin … taking seats here in the assembly. The

initiative around policing, our engagement with the police, would all be tactics that
you would weigh up and say well does it advance the struggle? But you have your
underlying principles, maybe three or four, which are what we are about and what
we are after.[88]

According to this analysis, change within Sinn Féin centres around the consideration of key principles which are then framed within the parameters determined
by judgement and evaluation. In adapting to context, Sinn Féin uses distinct
political strategies on either side of the border. In the Republic, the party remains
in opposition and staunchly condemns the fiscal cuts being implemented in the
South, yet simultaneously have been criticised for implementing similar policies
in the North.[89] Such an illustration demonstrates the difference in projected
interests, depending on the position of power, and subsequently the relationship
this determines between pragmatism and principles. Danny Morrison acknowledges the questions that would arise for Sinn Féin if they found themselves in a
position whereby they held the balance of power in the Republic:

> So there are dangers of coalition in the future and it could well be that [with]
> Sinn Féin's policies, if they stick to them … it might be very difficult to form a
> coalition … I don't know how to handle that, I don't know whether you sacrifice
> some of your principles and your demands and your well thought out working-class
> policies in the belief, and it is usually a false belief, that you get in to power and
> you are going to be a clear sweep through the regime, and you are going to change
> things so radically, because normally it doesn't turn out like that because people
> become disillusioned and you are going to lose support. On the other hand, what
> are you engaged in politics for? To be in power, all politics is about being in power.
> It is not about being in opposition. It is safe to be in opposition because you can
> say anything in opposition. But when you go in to power, that is when reality kicks
> in and you have to make the budget balance.[90]

The emphasis placed on context and pragmatic considerations implies that
Northern Ireland has evolved from the days of the troubles and Sinn Féin has
moved along with it, acknowledging the alleviation of oppression and inequality
and thus articulating new agendas. The movement away from armed struggle
and towards constitutionalism is seen as a logical development in such changed
circumstances. Such an argument implies that whilst departure from tradition
has occurred, there is no political space for dissidents to hold any relevance.
Small pockets of 'physical force' republicans remain irreconcilable, and their
dejection is understandable. Many participated in the 1970–97 protracted, gru-
elling and costly struggle against the British state to break the union.[91] Sinn Féin
implies that the continuation of armed struggle is the single motivating factor
for such groups, now arguing that armed action is 'anything but political' and
in 'most cases anything but republican'.[92] Alex Maskey asserted: 'It frustrates me
actually you know that there are people out there who will either be a Republican

or are supposed to be a Republican or want to be a Republican and in my opinion they are doing nothing but undermine what Republicanism worked, fought for, for a number of years.'[93] This discourse refutes that those dissenting from the pro-Stormont line are republican or acting for republicanism, thus avoiding the accusations of an ideological departure for Sinn Féin. Republicanism is essentially whatever Sinn Féin does.

Others do, however, go further in considering the evolution of Sinn Féin. As Patterson explains, 'the radicalism of Sinn Féin's departures, not from what simply might be portrayed as republican metaphysics, but from much of what until very recently they defined as their own strategic project, meant that a reaction was inevitable'.[94] Yet, the scale of departure was relatively low considering the extent of change. Testament to the success of the Sinn Féin electoral project is that they remain overwhelmingly in possession of the republican franchise. Dissidents are therefore commonly considered in reference to what the Provisionals, in their modern day form of Sinn Féin, represent. There is a need therefore to analyse these groups in their own right and assess their own republican credentials, in addition to why they disagree with the Sinn Féin interpretation.

Sinn Féin as an electoral force

> The range of areas covered by the [Good Friday] agreement and the span of political perspectives that assented to it were truly remarkable. The agreement extended not only over constitutional issues of extraordinary sensitivity and complex institutional provisions ... it also elaborated fundamental principles in the areas of human rights, policing, criminal justice and equality, and made specific transitional provisions in the areas of decommissioning of weapons, demilitarisation, release of prisoners and reconciliation of victims of violence.[95]

The above perspective encapsulates the complexity of the Good Friday Agreement. Within the literature that explores Sinn Féin's support for the Agreement and their transition into constitutionalism there is a (historically understandable) tendency to concentrate upon the party's relationship with the PIRA, tracing the changing dynamics between republican political and military fronts.[96] Amid the attention applied to the transition of Sinn Féin, there is a need to assess the impact of external agents in prompting ideological adjustment.[97] The literature also underplays how the universal electoral rules and logic that drive political parties were equally applicable to Sinn Féin.

The electoral dynamics of the peace process encouraged republican political moderation, embracing a willingness to reconsider positions that had for a long time been viewed as sacrosanct. Coakley describes the air of unpredictability that surrounded political positions during the peace negotiations: 'It should be pointed out that in this context the metaphor of political theatre needs to be carefully defined: the political parties (or actors) may be grouped within particular "traditions", but the characters they play out are complex – sometimes schizophrenic, and always developing over time.'[98] This flexible and responsive nature of political actors needs to be explored and considered in relation to the general battle for electoral support, as competition for votes is the key factor that ultimately influences the final position of parties in the mainstream political arena.

Due to the potential gains for nationalists, the GFA was a relatively easy sell. The Agreement seemingly ended conflict and established political institutions and structures based on an entirely new approach to overcome the exclusion – and the deep-seated alienation – of nationalists.[99] With the implementation of the D'Hondt system the electoral rewards in terms of political office were for the first time transparent. Under the terms of the Agreement the Executive had to be cross-community representative, guaranteeing Sinn Féin political office. It is hard to imagine that the Agreement would have been so attractive to nationalists if the rewards on offer had not been so clear-cut.

If Sinn Féin had ignored the appetite for peace and the nationalist electorate's support for the power-sharing arrangements set out under the Good Friday Agreement the party would have been confined to the margins of politics. Instead, Sinn Féin has been rewarded electorally for their movement towards a participatory and constitutional form of political involvement. Therefore, in order to fully explore Sinn Féin's full acceptance of the northern political institutions there is a need to consider the extent to which electoral forces influenced Sinn Féin's ideological reassessment, leading to the party's overwhelming endorsement (97 per cent to 3 per cent at the 1998 Ard Fheis) of the GFA. Under the consociational power-sharing terms of the Agreement, the rewards for electoral success, in terms of places in government under the D'Hondt divisor, were unusually explicit.

Realignment of electoral preferences

The results of the first post-Agreement Assembly election saw the moderate nationalists and unionists of the SDLP and the UUP respectively receive electoral rewards for their roles in authoring the historic compromises made. However, Sinn Féin's performance – polling only 4 per cent below the SDLP – was sufficiently strong to indicate a serious threat to the SDLP's position as the largest nationalist party.

Sinn Féin could reasonably assume that, having been rewarded for the PIRA's ceasefires, further movement towards constitutionalism would achieve electoral reward. In October 2001 the PIRA began the process of putting their weapons beyond use. As Arthur explains: 'The significance of the decommissioning gesture lay in the fact that it implied that at long last republicans were prepared to play by the democratic rules of the game. And it was truly historic ... never,

ever in the history of republicanism had such a gesture been made'.[100] The process of decommissioning was confirmed by General John de Chastelain to have been completed in 2005. Furthermore, by accepting the legitimacy of the PSNI through the 2006 St Andrews Agreement (a decision confirmed at a special conference in January 2007) Sinn Féin had completed the final phase in their transformative journey. They had moved from a party vehemently opposed to power sharing in a northern state to one committed to working in a cross-community executive and assembly within Northern Ireland. Electoral reward duly ensued. The 2007 Assembly elections saw the DUP and Sinn Féin become the electoral beneficiaries at the expense of more moderate parties in their own bloc as they were made joint leaders of a new power-sharing government, positions consolidated in the 2011 Assembly contests.

The Sinn Féin electoral project had been successful in mobilising new supporters[101] (including first-time and previous non-voters) and gained backing from voters previously supportive of the SDLP.[102] Pre-PIRA ceasefire Sinn Féin was perceived as a party of the Catholic working class, with little support amongst middle-class nationalists, an area where the SDLP were seen as dominant.[103] In a post-conflict Northern Ireland there has been an increase in cross-class support for Sinn Féin. Whilst the manual classes remain the most likely to vote for Sinn Féin, structural voting determinants have diminished as the party becomes 'partly de-ghettoised' and increasingly draws more middle-class support.[104]

Explaining the electoral rise of Sinn Féin: ethnic outbidding or moderation?

Northern Ireland remains a polity where ethnicity and identity are still very strongly linked to voter preference. Twelve years after the GFA, there was still no evidence of a thawing of ethnic bloc voting, only 5 per cent of unionists and 9 per cent of nationalists claiming to be either 'very' or 'fairly' likely to consider a vote for a candidate from the opposite ethnic bloc.[105] Parties are therefore competing for votes within the same ethnic bloc. Electoral competition is exercised within an ethnic dual-party system.[106] Because of the largely closed nature of both electoral blocs, nationalist parties are considered to be bound by the rules of a two-party system. The DUP and Sinn Féin quickly established themselves as the largest parties with the opposing blocs at the expense of the UUP and the SDLP.

There are two possible explanations for party change. The first is that voters move towards parties that are deemed more able to represent their concerns and protect their interests.[107] Secondly, and more cogently as an explanation for Sinn Féin's change, parties move towards the median voter (in this case the median nationalist voter). Sinn Féin moved towards a position that could be reconciled with the immediate aspirations of the bulk of the nationalist electorate whilst retaining an image of robustness and promoting continued communal defence.[108]

Whilst most voters want peace and power sharing, they simultaneously want the strongest tribune to protect their ethno-national interests. Policy outcomes therefore depend heavily on inter-ethnic bargaining. Individuals turn to parties that possess a reputation for successfully protecting the interests of their representative bloc, based on policy positions and belligerence.[109] As a result, voters are more inclined to switch their preference from the 'moderate' to the supposedly more 'extreme' parties, as a result of 'ethnic tribune appeal'.[110] The 2010 General Election Survey found that 61 per cent of Catholics were of the opinion that Sinn Féin had been the more effective party for nationalists, with only 13 per cent believing that the SDLP had been the 'more effective'.[111] The perception is that Sinn Féin are more successful in representing the nationalist community given their stridency, but this stridency is welcomed within the constitutional sphere, not as support for political violence. Competition creates a centrifugal dynamic of party positioning as parties mobilise 'their' community, engaging in emotive ethnic appeals that suggest that, without the defence offered by a particular party, their group's vital interests are in danger of being 'sold out'.[112] This goes some way to explain why support has moved away from the SDLP to Sinn Féin. However, this argument perhaps overemphasises the 'extreme' nature of parties such as the DUP and Sinn Féin and does not fully account for the scale of concessions made by either.

Another argument emphasises the need to consider the position of Sinn Féin in the context of a political party subject to electoral logic. Sinn Féin's support base tended to precede the party in terms of expressing support for power-sharing political institutions of Northern Ireland. Popular attitudes amongst Sinn Féin's voters were very much in favour of mandatory power sharing and decommissioning at the time of the 1998 GFA referendum, whilst, even on the morning of the GFA, Sinn Féin's Chair, Mitchel McLaughlin, insisted that notwithstanding his party's support for the GFA, it did not support an Assembly.[113] Between the signing of the Agreement in 1998 and the second Assembly election in 2003 support for the Northern Ireland Assembly increased from 76 to 94 per cent amongst Sinn Féin voters.[114] This was more than the support demonstrated by any other party's electoral base. By 2011, Sinn Féin 's supporters were more likely to 'very satisfied' with the devolved power-sharing government than those of any other party.[115] In order to explore Sinn Féin's endeavour to encapsulate the desires of the median nationalist voter and overtake the SDLP as the nationalist's electoral preference it is necessary to consider their strategy in terms of the electoral logic that determines the final shape of constitutional organisations.

Within any political context it is the fundamental concern of a party to gain and maintain electoral support. As Downs asserts, 'No party, new or old, can survive without gaining the support of a sizeable fraction of the electorate – a support active enough to be expressed by votes in elections.'[116] The key concern in assessing the ideological shift of Sinn Féin is what influences ideological change or political re-evaluation. Political parties are faced with the dilemma that they wish to capture as many voters as possible whilst also wanting to retain a strong appeal to each voter. They therefore have to present a wide spectrum of policies whilst simultaneously tailoring these policies to the ideological viewpoint of whichever voter is being pursued. During the consolidation of Sinn Féin as a constitutional entity the party has progressed from absolutistism that demanded full independence, 'Brits out' and socialism, to an agreed Ireland based on co-determination and a rhetoric that promotes an 'Ireland of Equals'.[117] With the military aspect of republicanism stalled, Sinn Féin became far more pragmatic as the party was increasingly bound by the rules of electoral competition pertaining to other constitutional parties. Whilst Sinn Féin maintains that the national question remains dominant and the goal of a united Ireland retains prominence within the electoral literature, the strategies of attainment have had to be considerably adjusted (in two different jurisdictions) to bolster the party's electoral project.

In terms of electoral competition it is seen as a form of electoral logic for parties to try and be as ambiguous as possible about their precise political positions.[118] If parties are ambiguous about the specific details of individual policies, every policy can cover a wider spread of voters. The result is that this 'vastly widens the band on the political scale into which various interpretations of a party's net position may fall. Ambiguity thus increases the number of voters to whom a party may appeal.'[119] This allows voters to place a different weighting on policies and each individual can also interpret the meaning of each policy differently, considering it in terms of what brings it closer to their own position. Sinn Féin are bound by the rules of electoral competition and have therefore moved their positioning in order to attract the median voter. The party has had to redefine what republicanism constitutes in practical policy terms, leading to the overthrow of positions that were once viewed as non-negotiable. For 'dissident' groups, rather than viewing Sinn Féin's transformation as a reinterpretation of republicanism in an attempt to function within an electoral marketplace, the party's pursuit of voters has been at the expense of republican principles.

These electoral concerns are of no importance to dissident groups whose appeal remains very narrow and localised.[120] Indeed there is almost a sense of pride in being relatively small and conspiratorial. Mainstream criticism that dissident groups have little support does not necessarily have as hard-hitting impact as intended. That these groups do not endeavour to appear electorally attractive in turn means there is less pressure on dissidents to accommodate a wider spectrum of individuals. It is far easier for dissident groups to present a more continuous and uninterrupted interpretation of republicanism.

Conclusion

An analysis that considers the impact of electoral logic and competition on political parties is beneficial in that it highlights the space Sinn Féin vacated in their move towards the constitutionalism where lay the median nationalist voter. As the party gained support, there has been a minority of republicans left behind that refuses to go along with the Sinn Féin electoral project. Consideration of the electoral rationale underpinning the transformation of Sinn Féin is vital in order to understand fragmentation within Irish republicanism. It is common within modern political discourse to utilise the term 'dissident' in reference to groups being considered in relation to Sinn Féin, rather than deploy a broader and less restrictive republican framework. In order to begin understanding the dissident ideological standpoint it is necessary to consider Sinn Féin's movement into constitutional politics and to what extent that represented the updating, revising or contorting of Irish republican principles.

Changes within Sinn Féin have involved the broadening of ideas (such as a more pluralist conception of identity), the rearranging of principles (equality has been frontloaded ahead of freedom, with self-determination and territorial sovereignty demoted in favour of a vaguer 'Ireland of Equals'), a change of tactics (full movement into constitutional politics) and the relegation of imperatives (British withdrawal and a united Ireland) to aspirational ultimate objectives, albeit still prominent in Sinn Féin discourse. The sum of these parts is considerable transition. Yet, no representation of republicanism across the broad spectrum would deny that the tradition is evolutionary and contextual. Ultimately, it is unrealistic to expect political parties to remain static over time and unchanged in policies. When bound by laws of electoral competition (as Sinn Féin became) with office-seeking priorities, parties have to respond, to external (e.g. electoral, governmental) and internal (e.g. incentives to achieve tangible results) pressures that develop. The academic literature that considers the evolution of Sinn Féin is wide-ranging in assessing the impact of military fortune and British state strategy, but has appeared reluctant to comprehend Sinn Féin as essentially an ordinary political party in modern times, conditioned by the rules of the electoral game and successfully adapting to those rules.

Sinn Féin appears in a position of dominance in their representation of the republican tradition. Such a position is testament to the overall success of the rebranding of the party. As a result, the party is often portrayed as standing as the mouthpiece or the single representation of the Irish republican tradition, possessing the republican franchise. Other groups and individuals who claim to represent republicanism are considered in relation to what Sinn Féin represent. As McGovern observes, 'it is necessary to understand the extent to which Sinn Féin has successfully recast itself as the primary political mouthpiece for this complex northern Nationalist outlook. In doing so they have rearticulated the meaning of Republicanism.'[121] Yet a restricted understanding of Irish republicanism is risked via exclusive concentration upon Sinn Féin. The party has a dominant position within the republican community, but for some this has come at the cost of ideological commitment and full absorption into a state the party once vowed to defeat.

Whilst considering the splits within the republican movement it is not so much a question of creating a distinct division between firstly, Sinn Féin having adapted their strategy according to contextual demands, and secondly, others who have remained loyal to a rigid republican mantra. Rather, whilst considering dissidence within modern day Irish republicanism, it is more important to question whether the scale of change within Sinn Féin has created space for others to move in and occupy. Whilst it is important to consider the ground that Sinn Féin now occupies, it is even more important to consider the space that they have left behind. Rather than considering republicanism in binary terms, that is to suppose that groups fit into one of two categories, 'Sinn Féin republican' or 'other', it is more beneficial to adopt a multi-dimensional model when considering the republican tradition. In order to contemplate further the range of groups that proclaim a republican heritage it is necessary to consider republicanism as a spectrum that demonstrates the possibility of groups representing a multiplicity of ideals, concepts and beliefs.

To explore the possibility of constructing such a paradigm, the following chapters will consider several groups and their position on a broad spectrum of ideas, concepts and beliefs. For example, there is a need to explore the context in which 'dissident' groups emerged along with their claims of legitimacy and possession of a mandate. In addition it is also necessary to consider these groups' goals and objectives, strategy, membership and future trajectory, along with their position on key topics such as their attitudes towards unionism and the use of armed struggle as a tactic. The intention is to construct an understanding of groups across the contemporary republican spectrum, in order to consider their position in their own right, as distinct from measurement merely in relation to modern Sinn Féin.

Notes

1 D. Morrison in *Daily Ireland*, 'When one doesn't mind being called a Provo', 6 September 2006.
2 This chapter focuses primarily on republicanism in Northern Ireland and Sinn Féin's position in the North as opposed to the Irish Republic.
3 See, as examples R. Alonso, *The IRA and Armed Struggle* (London, Routledge, 2007); K. Bean, *The New Politics of Sinn Féin* (Liverpool, Liverpool University Press, 2007); R. English, *Armed Struggle: A History of the IRA* (Basingstoke, Macmillan, 2003); M. Frampton, *The Long March: Political Strategy of Sinn Féin, 1981–2007*

(Basingstoke, Macmillan, 2009); A. Maillot, *New Sinn Féin: Republicanism in the Twenty-first Century* (London, Routledge, 2005); E. Moloney, *A Secret History of the IRA* (London, Penguin, 2002); J. Ruane and J. Todd (eds), *After the Good Friday Agreement: Analysing Political Change in Northern Ireland* (Dublin, University College Dublin Press, 1999); J. Tonge, *Northern Ireland* (Cambridge, Polity Press, 2006).

4 Sinn Féin Education Department, 'The Split', *Republican Lecture Series* No. 1 (1979).

5 *BBC News*, 'IRA "has destroyed all its arms"', 26 September 2005.

6 *New York Times*, 'Irish Issue: a look at both sides', 18 February 1986.

7 T. McKearney, *The Provisional IRA: From Insurrection to Parliament* (London, Pluto Press, 2011), p. 182.

8 See Sinn Féin, 'Defending the Good Friday Agreement', Sinn Féin submission to the Mitchell Review, 23 September 1999, www.cain.ulst.ac.uk/events/peace/docs/sf23999.htm.

9 See for example Republican Network for Unity (RNU), 'Critique of the Good Friday Agreement', 14 September 2011, www.republicannetwork.ie/; A. McIntyre in *The Pensive Quill*, 'Republicanism: alive or dying?', 1 January 2008.

10 C. Irvin, *Militant Nationalism: Between Movement and Party in Ireland and the Basque Country* (Minneapolis, University of Minnesota Press, 1999), p. 21.

11 See English, *Armed Struggle*; Frampton, *The Long March*; Maillot, *New Sinn Féin*.

12 See Bean, *The New Politics of Sinn Féin*; K. Bean and M. Hayes, 'Sinn Féin and the New Republicanism of Ireland: Electoral Progress, Political Stasis, and Ideological Failure', *Radical History Review* 104 (2009), pp. 126–142.

13 See G. Murray and J. Tonge, *Sinn Féin and the SDLP: From Alienation to Participation* (London, Hurst, 2005).

14 Sinn Féin Education Department, 'The Split'.

15 See Frampton, *The Long March*.

16 A. McIntyre in *The Pensive Quill*, 'Republicanism: alive or dying?', 1 January 2008.

17 See Bean, *The New Politics of Sinn Féin*.

18 IRA spokesperson quoted in *An Phoblacht/Republican News*, 17 August 1989.

19 Alonso, *The IRA and Armed Struggle*.

20 Moloney, *A Secret History of the IRA*.

21 A. Richards, 'Terrorist Groups and Political Fronts: The IRA, Sinn Féin, the Peace Process and Democracy', *Terrorism and Political Violence* 13, no. 4 (2001), pp. 72–89; M. Von Tagen Page and M. L. R. Smith, 'War By Other Means: The Problem of Political Control in Irish Republican Strategy', *Armed Forces and Society* 27, no. 1 (2000), pp. 79–104.

22 Maillot, *New Sinn Féin*; A. McIntyre, *The Good Friday Agreement: The Death of Irish Republicanism* (New York, Ausubo Press, 2008).

23 M. Hayes, 'The Evolution of Republican Strategy and the "Peace Process" in Ireland', *Race Class* 39, no. 3 (1998), pp. 21–29.

24 R. English, *Irish Freedom: The History of Nationalism in Ireland* (Oxford, Pan Macmillan, 2006), p. 372.

25 A. McIntyre, 'Modern Irish Republicanism: The Product of British State Strategies', *Irish Political Studies* 10, no. 1 (1995), p. 98.

26 Also see R. White, *Provisional Irish Republicans: An Oral and Interpretive History* (Westport, Greenwood Press, 1993).

27 K. Bean, 'Shifting Discourses of New Nationalism and Post-republicanism', in M. Elliott (ed.), *The Long Road to Peace in Northern Ireland* (Liverpool, Liverpool University Press, 2007), p. 137; also see H. Patterson, 'Towards 2016', *Fourthwrite* (Spring, 2000), p. 5.

28 K. Bean, 'The Economic and Social War Against Violence: British Social and Economic Strategy and the Evolution of Provisionalism', in A. Edwards and S. Bloomer (eds), *Transforming the Peace Process in Northern Ireland: From Terrorism to Democratic Politics* (Dublin, Irish Academic Press, 2008); Bean, *The New Politics of Sinn Féin*; P. Shirlow, 'The Economics of the Peace Process', in C. Gilligan and J. Tonge (eds), *Peace or War? Understanding the Peace Process in Northern Ireland* (Aldershot, Ashgate, 1997), p. 136; P. Shirlow and B. Murtagh, *Belfast: Segregation, Violence and the City* (London, Pluto, 2006).

29 See Bean, 'The Economic and Social War Against Violence', p. 165. See also for impact of armed struggle on economic stability M. McGovern, 'Irish Republicanism and the Potential Pitfalls of Pluralism', *Capital and Class* 71 (2000), pp. 133–161.

30 Bean and Hayes, 'Sinn Féin and the New Republicanism of Ireland', pp. 126–142.

31 J. Augusteijn, 'Political Violence and Democracy: An Analysis of the Tensions Within Irish Republican Strategy, 1914–2002', *Irish Political Studies* 18, no. 1 (2003), pp. 1–26; White, *Provisional Irish Republicans*; B. O'Brien, *The Long War: IRA and Sinn Féin* (Dublin, O'Brien Press, 1999).

32 Bean, *The New Politics of Sinn Féin*, p. 135.

33 See R. Kearney, *Post Nationalist Ireland: Politics, Culture and Philosophy* (London, Routledge, 1997); Bean, *The New Politics of Sinn Féin*. See also Murray and Tonge, *Sinn Féin and the SDLP*, pp. 263–267 for a discussion on post-republicanism.

34 For broader discussion on nationalism, see E. Harris, *Nationalism: Theories and Cases* (Edinburgh, Edinburgh University Press, 2009); J. Hearn, *Rethinking Nationalism: A Critical Introduction* (New York, Palgrave Macmillan, 2006).

35 H. Kohn, *The Idea of Nationalism* (New York, Collier, 1967), pp. 330–331.

36 A. D. Smith, *National Identity* (Harmondsworth, Penguin, 1991), p. 11.

37 Kearney, *Post Nationalist Ireland*, pp. 2–3.

38 O. Zenker, 'Autochthony and Activism among Contemporary Irish Nationalists in Northern Ireland, or: If 'Civic' Nationalists are 'Ethno'-cultural Revivalists, What Remains of the Civic/ethnic Divide?' *Nations and Nationalism* 15, no. 4 (2009), p. 697.

39 Kearney, *Post Nationalist Ireland*, p. 57.

40 See D. Brown, *Contemporary Nationalism: Civic, Ethnocultural and Multicultural Politics* (London, Routledge, 2000); W. Kymlicka, 'Misunderstanding Nationalism', in R. Beiner (ed.), *Theorising Nationalism* (New York, SUNY Press, 1999); T. Nairn, *Faces of Nationalism* (London, Verso, 1997).

41 R. Brubaker, '"Civic" and "ethnic" nationalism', in R. Brubaker (ed.), *Ethnicity without Groups* (Cambridge MA, Harvard University Press, 2004), p. 141.

42 *Ibid.*, p. 166.

43 See H. F. Kearny, *Ireland, Contested Ideas of Nationalism and History* (Cork, Cork University Press, 2007), p. 36.
44 Harris, *Nationalism: Theories and Cases*, p. 33.
45 B. O'Leary and J. McGarry, *The Politics of Antagonism: Understanding Northern Ireland* (London, Athlone Press, 1996).
46 Kearney, *Post Nationalist Ireland*.
47 See English, *Irish Freedom*, p. 401.
48 G. Adams, *The Politics of Irish Freedom* (Dingle, Brandon, 1986), p. 22.
49 J. Todd, 'Nationalism, Republicanism and the Good Friday Agreement', in Ruane and Todd (eds), *After the Good Friday Agreement*, p. 56.
50 R. Kearney and B. Cullen, 'Rethinking Ireland: A Proposal for a Joint Sovereignty Solution', in R. Kearney, *Post Nationalist Ireland: Politics, Culture and Philosophy* (London, Routledge, 1997), p. 2.
51 *An Phoblacht*, 5 November 1981.
52 Sinn Féin, *Towards a Lasting Peace in Ireland* (Dublin, Sinn Féin, 1992), p. 4.
53 J. Gibney in *An Phoblacht*, 2 March 1995.
54 Peadar Whelan, interview with author, Belfast, 25 September 2009.
55 Alex Maskey, interview with author, Belfast, 25 September 2009.
56 Mary Lou McDonald, speaking at Sinn Féin fringe meeting, Labour Party conference, 'Ireland and Britain: Towards a New Relationship', Liverpool, 25 September 2011.
57 See M. Cunningham, 'The Political Language of John Hume', *Irish Political Studies* 12, no. 1 (1997), pp. 13–22.
58 G. Adams Press Release, 'Rights for all charter', January 2004, www.sinnfein.ie/contents/6804.
59 Mary Lou McDonald, Labour Party conference, 'Ireland and Britain: Towards a New Relationship', Liverpool, 25 September 2011.
60 Murray and Tonge, *Sinn Féin and the SDLP*, p. 263.
61 Bean, *The New Politics of Sinn Féin*, p. 164.
62 E. Nimni, 'Nationalism, Ethnicity and, Self-Determination: A Paradigm Shift', in K. Breen and S. O'Neill (eds), *After the Nation? Critical Reflections on Nationalism and Postnationalism* (Basingstoke, Palgrave, 2010), pp. 21–37.
63 *Ibid.*, p. 24.
64 Arthur Aughey in the *Observer*, 'Completely and verifiably beyond use', 7 May 2000.
65 Kearney, *Post Nationalist Ireland*, p. 26.
66 Bean, *The New Politics of Sinn Féin*, p. 135.
67 McKearney, *The Provisional IRA*, p. 190.
68 See Slugger O'Toole, 'The Good Friday Agreement represents a significant defeat for republicanism', 14 April 2009, available at http://sluggerotoole.com/2009/04/14/the-good-Friday-agreement-represents-a-significant-defeat-for-republicanism/.
69 Bernadette Sands quoted in *Magill* – S. Breen, 'The ideals Bobby died for are ideals I hold dear and which have always motivated me', 1 January 1998.
70 Peadar Whelan, interview with author, Belfast, 25 September 2009.
71 See Conflict Archive in Northern Ireland (CAIN), Results of the Referenda in Northern Ireland and Republic of Ireland, 22 May 1998, www.cain.ulst.ac.uk/

issues/politics/election/ref1998.htm. The Good Friday Agreement was approved in referenda across communities with 71.12 per cent in the North voting 'Yes' and 94.4 per cent in the Republic.

72 Danny Morrison, interview with author, Liverpool, 8 October 2011.
73 A. McIntyre, 'Modern Irish Republicanism and the Belfast Agreement: Chickens Coming Home to Roost, or Turkeys Celebrating Christmas', in R. Wilford (ed.), *Aspects of the Belfast Agreement* (Oxford, Oxford University Press, 2001), p. 203.
74 See for example, *An Phoblacht*, 'Plotting course for future – Adams', 18 November 1999, cited in McIntyre, 'Modern Irish Republicanism and the Belfast Agreement', p. 210.
75 Mary Lou McDonald, Labour Party conference, 'Ireland and Britain: Towards a New Relationship', Liverpool, 25 September 2011.
76 *Ibid.*
77 Todd, 'Nationalism, Republicanism and the Good Friday Agreement', p. 56.
78 A. McIntyre, 'Modern Irish Republicanism: The Product of British State Strategies', *Irish Political Studies* 10, no. 1 (1995), pp. 97–122.
79 Anthony McIntyre in *The Pensive Quill*, 'Responding to Seán Mór', 14 February 2010.
80 See Todd, 'Nationalism, Republicanism and the Good Friday Agreement', p. 57.
81 See L. O Ruairc in *Weekly Worker*, 'A Republican Versailles, not an honourable compromise', 26 May 2005.
82 *An Phoblacht/Republican News*, 'Gerry Adams: presidential address', 23 April 1998.
83 See G. Adams, Speech, *Irish News*, 8 January 1999; P. Doherty, Speech at Noraid Dinner, *Irish News* , 28 January 1999; M. McLaughlin, 'The Republican Ideal', in N. Porter (ed.), *The Republican Ideal: Current Perspectives* (Belfast, Blackstaff, 1999), pp. 62–84.
84 For a more in-depth discussion on the use of language from the Provisionals, see Todd, 'Nationalism, Republicanism and the Good Friday Agreement', pp. 56–62.
85 Danny Morrison, interview with author, Liverpool, 8 October 2011.
86 McKearney, *The Provisional IRA*, p. 188.
87 A. Guelke, *Northern Ireland: The International Perspective* (Dublin, Gill and MacMillan, 1988), p. 41.
88 Sean Oliver, interview with author, Belfast, 25 September 2009.
89 See *Belfast Telegraph*, 'Sinn Féin's McGuinness defends budget spending cuts', 16 December 2010; World Socialist Website, 'Sinn Féin's McGuiness stands for Irish presidency', 27 October 2011, www.wsws.org/.
90 Danny Morrison, interview with author, Liverpool, 8 October 2011.
91 Mary Lou McDonald, Labour Party conference, 'Ireland and Britain: Towards a New Relationship', Liverpool, 25 September 2011.
92 *Ibid.*
93 Alex Maskey, interview with author, Belfast, 25 September 2009.
94 H. Patterson, 'Beyond the "Micro Group": The Dissident Republican Challenge, in P. M. Currie and M. Taylor (eds), *Dissident Irish Republicanism* (London, Continuum, 2011), p. 66.

95 J. Coakley, 'Constitutional Innovation and Political Change in Twentieth Century Ireland', in J. Coakley (ed.), *Changing Shades of Orange and Green: Redefining the Union and the Nation in Contemporary Ireland* (Dublin, University College Dublin Press, 2002), pp. 1–2.

96 See Alonso, *The IRA and Armed Struggle*; B. Feeney, *Sinn Féin: A Hundred Turbulent Years* (Dublin, O'Brien Press, 2002); Augusteijn, 'Political Violence and Democracy', pp. 1–26; O'Brien, *The Long War*, p. 127; M. L. R. Smith, *Fighting for Ireland?: The Military Strategy of the Irish Republican Movement* (London, Routledge, 1995); Richards, 'Terrorist Groups and Political Fronts', pp. 72–89; Von Tagen Page and Smith, 'War By Other Means', pp. 79–104; K. Rafter, *Sinn Féin 1905–2005: In the Shadow of Gunmen* (Dublin, Gill and Macmillan, 2005).

97 For some exceptions see, Bean, 'The Economic and Social War Against Violence'; Bean, *The New Politics of Sinn Féin*; McGovern, 'Irish Republicanism and the Potential Pitfalls of Pluralism', pp. 133–161; Murray and Tonge, *Sinn Féin and the SDLP*.

98 Coakley, 'Constitutional Innovation and Political Change in Twentieth Century Ireland', p. 10.

99 See Sinn Féin, 'Defending the Good Friday Agreement', Sinn Féin submission to the Mitchell Review, 23 September 1999, p. 2, www.cain.ulst.ac.uk/events/peace/docs/sf23999.htm.

100 P. Arthur, 'The Transformation of Republicanism', in Coakley (ed.), *Changing Shades of Orange and Green*, p. 85.

101 I. McAllister, '"The armalite and the ballot box": Sinn Féin's Electoral Strategy in Northern Ireland', *Electoral Studies* 23, no. 1 (2004), pp. 123–142.

102 See P. Mitchell, G. Evans and B. O'Leary, 'Extremist Outbidding in Ethnic Party Systems is Not Inevitable: Tribune Parties in Northern Ireland', *Political Studies* 57, no. 2 (2009), pp. 397–421.

103 See Murray and Tonge, *Sinn Féin and the SDLP*; G. Evans and M. Duffy, 'Beyond the Sectarian Divide: The Social Bases and Political Consequences of Nationalist and Unionist Party Competition in Northern Ireland', *British Journal of Political Science* 27, no. 1 (1997), pp. 47–81.

104 J. Evans and J. Tonge, 'Social Class and Party Choice in Northern Ireland's Ethnic Blocs', *West European Politics* 32, no. 5 (2009), pp. 1,012–1,030.

105 See J. Tonge, J. Evans, P. Mitchell and B. Hayes, 'The 2010 Election in Northern Ireland: Evidence from Aggregate and ESRC Survey Data', Data presented at the 2010 Electoral Change in Northern Ireland Conference, Queen's University, Belfast, October 2010.

106 See Evans and Duffy, 'Beyond the Sectarian Divide', pp. 47–81.

107 See P. Mitchell and G. Evans, 'Ethnic Party Competition and the Dynamics of Power Sharing in Northern Ireland', in R. Taylor (ed.), *Consociational Theory: McGarry and O'Leary. The Northern Ireland Conflict* (London, Routledge, 2009), pp. 146–64; Mitchell, Evans and O'Leary, 'Extremist Outbidding in Ethnic Party Systems is Not Inevitable', p. 402.

108 See A. Downs, *An Economic Theory of Democracy* (New York, HarperCollins, 1957); J. Evans and J. Tonge, 'From Abstentionism to Enthusiasm: Sinn Féin,

Nationalist Electors and Support for Devolved Power Sharing in Northern Ireland, *Irish Political Studies* 1 (2012), pp. 9–11; K. Strom, 'A Behavioural Theory of Competitive Party Politics', *American Journal of Political Science* 34, no. 2 (1990), pp. 565–598; J. McGarry, 'Consociationalism and Its Critics: Evidence from the Historic Northern Ireland Assembly Election 2007', *Electoral Studies* 28, no. 3 (2009), pp. 458–466.

109 Mitchell, Evans and O'Leary, 'Extremist Outbidding in Ethnic Party Systems is Not Inevitable', p. 402.

110 *Ibid.*

111 See Tonge, Evans, Mitchell and Hayes, 'The 2010 Election in Northern Ireland: Evidence from Aggregate and ESRC Survey Data', Belfast, 2010.

112 Mitchell, Evans and O'Leary, 'Extremist Outbidding in Ethnic Party Systems is Not Inevitable', p. 400.

113 See B. Hayes and I. McAllister, 'Who Voted for Peace? Public Support for the 1998 Northern Ireland Agreement', *Irish Political Studies* 16, no. 1 (2001), pp. 73–93.

114 Mitchell, Evans and O'Leary, 'Extremist Outbidding in Ethnic Party Systems is Not Inevitable', p. 409.

115 Evans and Tonge, 'From Abstentionism to Enthusiasm', pp. 1–19.

116 Downs, *An Economic Theory of Democracy*, p. 128.

117 For a more detailed description of the policy shifts within Sinn Féin see chapter 2.

118 Downs, *An Economic Theory of Democracy*, pp. 135–137.

119 *Ibid.*, p. 136.

120 32CSM affiliated Gary Donnelly stood as an Independent in the 2011 elections polling 612 votes, placing him fifth. Donnelly ran again in 2014 and topped the polls in Moor DEA, see chapter 4.

121 M. McGovern, '"The Old Days are over": Irish Republicanism, the Peace Process and the Discourse of Equality', *Terrorism and Political Violence* 16, no. 3 (2004), p. 628.

4

Continuity or dissidence? The origins of dissident republicans and their mandate

> Republicanism is discursive in that it offers an internally differentiated series of ideological possibilities. It contains within it a range of exemplary models, memories, stories and rational political arguments that can be interpreted and reinterpreted through time. The 'Republican tradition' may therefore be conceived as a discursively constituted, culturally and politically specific collective resource by which power is contested at the level of the idea.[1]

Dissident republican groups are often described as having no support and no political or electoral mandate amongst the republican community. They are seen as out of touch and antediluvian, and labelled as anti-republican. In a typical denunciation, the Tánaiste referred to 'these deluded criminals [who] fail to comprehend the true meaning of republicanism and quite clearly have nothing but contempt for this country and its people'.[2] Currently, dissident groups either refuse to stand candidates in elections, or fail to register a significant impact on the rare occasions when they do enter the electoral arena. The idea that these groups may have support in Northern Ireland is dismissed amid the apparent absence of even a modest mandate. As one example, the actions of dissidents sparked the following collective reaction from a range of political representatives after a bombing in Derry:

> The latest bomb attacks on Londonderry/Derry demonstrate the contempt in which you hold each and every citizen of this city. You have chosen to exclude yourselves from the political process and because of this you have no voice, and certainly no mandate.[3]

The decisions of dissidents to avoid the mainstream political arena mean they are portrayed as 'cowards who are afraid to face the electorate'.[4] However, for dissident groups, their self-ascribed 'mandate' goes beyond the remit of constitutional political representation and is instead based upon historical claims of legitimacy, drawn from the 'right' to oppose British rule in Ireland amid loyalty to previous generations of republican dead. The concerns for fidelity and continuity are often placed before the need for modern popular consent within the current political dispensation, tendencies one might ascribe to previous Irish rebellions from 1798 onwards and certainly since 1916. The irony here is that in highlighting the absence of an electoral mandate for dissidents, former PIRA members, most notably the Deputy First Minister, Martin McGuinness, have been accused of deploying the same arguments against dissidents which were dismissed by him when used against the Provisionals in the 1970s and, to a much lesser extent, the 1980s and 1990s.[5] During the PIRA's violent campaigns of the 1970s, Sinn Féin, which declined to contest elections, was accused of lacking a popular mandate on similar grounds to the charges made on dissident groups today. Even when republicans contested elections from 1981 onwards, their 'mandate' was confined (with the exception of the hunger strike crisis) to support from a minority of the minority Catholic community in the North. Those groups who in today's political context reject the constitutional transition of Sinn Féin can find some refuge in the context of history. Support for dissident groups today is considerably smaller than it was for the PIRA/Sinn Féin. Yet, support for the PIRA or Sinn Féin was never a majority taste amongst nationalists in Northern Ireland when the PIRA's armed campaign was operational, but the 'armed struggle' of that era has not been retrospectively delegitimised by Sinn Féin despite that lack of mandate.

Sinn Féin has, however, increasingly acknowledged the hurt caused during the PIRA armed campaign. In *An Phoblacht*, Sinn Féin's National Chairperson, Declan Kearney expressed the following:

> Regardless of the stance of others, we should recognise the healing influence of being able to say sorry for the human effects of all actions caused during the armed struggle. All sensible people would wish it had been otherwise … The political reality is those actions cannot be undone or disowned. It would be better they had never happened.[6]

Whilst Sinn Féin are open in expressing regret in terms of the hurt the actions of the PIRA caused it remains a step too far to retrospectively render their campaign as illegitimate. Such a claim would render their war as having been futile and wrong. Kearney is also keen to stress that the socio-economic and political conditions that contributed to armed struggle are no longer present in the current context, also insisting: 'Armed struggle is not a point of principle or an end in itself. It arose from political conditions, as a last resort and those conditions no longer exist.'[7] According to this analysis the conditions that justified the existence of the PIRA no longer exist, even though British sovereignty over Northern Ireland – which the IRA was supposed to have been about ending, not making more pleasant its application – remains in place. Kearney's analysis leans towards a perspective that recasts the IRA as a reformist, civil rights vanguard movement, one more concerned with equality than national sovereignty. However, more important at this stage is that neither Sinn Féin nor dissidents today have ever enjoyed majority popular endorsement – but at what point and to what extent is minority support large enough to claim a mandate and legitimacy? Or is, as the dissidents assert, the 'right' to bear arms against a 'foreign occupier' an item not reducible to such electoral considerations?

The emergence of republican violence at the end of the 1960s is justified by Sinn Féin as a response to social inequality, discrimination by the state and lack of political representation. This feeling of defencelessness supposedly justified violence to 'counter-balance the feeling of weakness'.[8] Today, those who defended the use of violence from 1969 until almost the turn of the century, claim that the context has changed and armed struggle can no longer be justified. In July 2005, the PIRA called off its campaign stating, 'All volunteers have been instructed to assist the development of purely political and democratic programmes through exclusively peaceful means. Volunteers must not engage in any other activities whatsoever.'[9] According to the Sinn Féin narrative violence was justifiable between 1969 until 1997, but in today's context it is no longer a credible position.[10] In response, dissidents offer historical determinism – that the 'lessons of history' suggest that armed struggle is inevitable and that such armed struggle will not enjoy popular support at the time, but may be viewed more favourably retrospectively. It is certainly not the first time in the history of the republican movement that 'renegades' have been relegated to the past, with the supposed vanquishing of the IRA in 1921, 1923 and 1962 offering obvious examples.

There is a need to consider the interaction between ideological, structural and personal factors such as historical interpretation, background and individual motivation, which may explain why individuals join dissident organisations. This chapter acknowledges the influence of wider networks and the dynamics between localised and historical contexts. Accordingly, emphasis is placed on human experience, interpretation and meaning. In considering groups such as Republican Sinn Féin (RSF), the 32 County Sovereignty Movement (32CSM), the Irish Republican Socialist Party (IRSP) and éirígí, the analysis of this chapter focuses on why dissent occurs, the political and ideological context that sustains it and the capacity for participants to envisage a possible solution to key issues. It is therefore important not only to consider the wider context in defining the republicanism of supporters of dissident groups, but more specifically to examine how beliefs frame certain actions, practices and organisation, as well as understanding the differences under the umbrella label of 'dissident'. This chapter will explore the different origins of these dissident organisations, their claims of a mandate, their interpretation of Sinn Féin's position and their stance on electoral politics.

Republican purism? The origins of Republican Sinn Féin

In 1986 a split within the Provisional movement saw the formation of Republican Sinn Féin (RSF). Many of those who broke away to form RSF were those who led the walk-out in 1969–70 to form Provisional Sinn Féin and the Provisional IRA. The 1986 split was led mainly by pre 1969 southern-based individuals, such as Ruairí Ó Brádaigh, his brother Sean, Des Long and Denis McInerny. Of the twenty-one members of the first RSF Ard Chomhairle (national executive) only two came from north of the border.[11]

Similar to the earlier split in 1969, abstention was again the key to their walk-out at the 1986 Ard Fheis. The tension within the movement was evident from the early 1980s. At the 1981 Ard Fheis, the 'armalite and ballot box' speech by Danny Morrison confirmed that the future of the Provisional movement was one where armed struggle and electoral politics would be merged. According to White's analysis, this was a key moment in that it undermined a decade's worth of work by people like Ó Brádaigh, who, although not opposed to elections, argued that the IRA and Sinn Féin were separate and distinct organisations whose roles could not be married.[12] However, it is important to question the extent to which the PIRA and Sinn Féin were ever truly separate organisations. Whilst in structural terms it was true in that two distinct entities existed, the membership was often overlapping, with individuals spanning both organisations. In addition there was no distinct separation within the decision-making process, given that the IRA approved Sinn Féin's actions and the political party was hardly autonomous. It is therefore possible that the 'ballot box and armalite' strategy actually separated the organisations further by outlining their distinct roles, designed to complement each other.

By 1986 the younger, more dominant northern-based leadership had created a forceful argument for dropping abstention to Leinster House. For those who went on to form RSF the dropping of abstention indicated the abandonment of fundamental principles, a betrayal of republican martyrs, amounting to a catalyst to an inevitable chain of events. Abstentionists charged that recognising Leinster House would shift the movement away from revolutionary struggle and would lead to the ultimate acceptance of Stormont and Westminster. As a result the walk-out during the 1986 Ard Fheis was depicted by RSF as a movement in defence of traditional republicanism. As former Vice-President Geraldine Taylor explains:

> The very basis of the republican movement, the rock on which republicanism was founded on was not to recognise Stormont, Westminster or the Dáil and they in 1986 decided to recognise Dáil Éireann by saying they would take their seats there. That was the first step down that road, that was the time we moved away from them. We walked out but we walked out with the republican movement intact.[13]

According to the Taylor interpretation, because the Provisionals moved away from the Sinn Féin constitution by accepting an ending of abstention, RSF alone is representative of the continued republican tradition. This timeless and uncompromising claim was epitomised in 2005 when RSF celebrated their centenary;

therefore, placing their origins in the 1905 creation of Sinn Féin as opposed to
the more recent 1986 division.

'There is no room for another Sinn Féin':[14]
the beginnings of the 32 County Sovereignty Movement

The 32CSM initially took the form of the 32 County Sovereignty Committee
(32CSC), a pressure group within Sinn Féin organised to lobby against the direction Sinn Féin was moving in and persuade them to refocus on the key issues
of national sovereignty. The 32CSC came into existence in Fingal in December
1997. Most of those individuals involved were members of Sinn Féin who were
finding themselves 'increasingly marginalised due to their open concerns at the
direction which the party was being led'.[15] These members were soon expelled
from Sinn Féin and were barred from entering the 1998 Ard Fheis.[16] Prominent
members included former Sinn Féin district councillor Francie Mackey, who
became chairperson, Bernadette Sands-McKevitt who took the role of vice-
chairperson, Rory Dougan, Joe Dillon, Ciaran Dwyer, Michael Burke and
Marian Price.[17]

The creation of the 32CSM centred on what they termed 'the ideological
retreat within Republicanism preceding the signing of the Belfast Agreement in
April 1998'.[18] Departure from Sinn Féin focused on the direction of the peace
process, most specifically acceptance of the Mitchell Principles of non-violence
(adherence to which removed the prospect of a re-ignition of the IRA's armed
struggle even if the outcome of talks was unsatisfactory) and the principle of
unionist consent.[19] Minutes from the first gathering point out that 'it was felt
that the peace talks, based on the Mitchell and joint framework documents
which guarantee a Unionist veto, will ensure an internal Six-county settlement
and prohibit the probability of the end to partition'.[20] The 32CSM offers a
republican critique of the peace process and Good Friday Agreement, arguing
that they produced a 'partitionist solution that would only pump the life force
back into the rotten 6 county corrupt state'.[21] A 32CSM member explained their
perspective:

> Republicanism is about ending British rule in Ireland, ending parliamentary and
> modern day accommodation in Ireland, that's quite clear. Stormont, the British
> can put up as many puppet parliaments as they want in East Belfast, it's not going
> to change the nature of a republic.[22]

The 32CSM describes itself as a movement rather than a political party and
pre 2011 its members insisted that they had no intention of running in elections.[23] They therefore do not promote themselves as the original republican
party, or explain their roots as being in the 1905 creation of Sinn Féin: 'We do
not claim to be the "Real Sinn Féin" and we are not trying to steal the thunder

from any group that does. The 32CSM is democratic; there is no room or no need for another Sinn Féin.'[24] Thus the 32CSM set themselves apart from the new moderation of Sinn Féin (although their policies are very similar to the 1980s offerings of that movement) and the militant dogmatism of Republican Sinn Féin. Leading members of the 32CSM have refuted the accusation of being members of the RIRA. However, it has been suggested by Frampton that the 32CSM was set up purely as support for the RIRA, and was always the subordinate of the partner. Frampton states that:

> From the outset, then, the 32CSC/32CSM was close ideologically – and personnel-wise – to the RIRA. Indeed, the founder of the Real IRA, Michael McKevitt, would at one point confide to the FBI agent David Rupert that the '32 were all military people and they were put there for that purpose to keep army politics in the hands of the military'.[25]

Due to legislative restrictions on the advocacy of terrorism and terrorist groups, the 32CSM does not seem to be as active in presenting itself alongside the RIRA in its literature or statements as it may have been when the group first emerged. In recent years there has been a toning down, but not complete removal, of reporting RIRA activity within 32CSM publications and on its website.[26]

Eschewing electoral politics

The most frequent criticism facing dissidents is that they are unable to demonstrate their legitimacy in representing any section of society, not being in possession of any form of electoral mandate. The following statement from Martin McGuinness epitomises the questioning of the lack of a mandate for groups such as RSF and the 32CSM:

> I suppose it begs the question, given that they would say they're committed to Irish reunification, how do you bring about Irish unity without the support of the people of Ireland? That is the big question they need to answer.[27]

In terms of creating an effective electoral alternative to Sinn Féin, dissident groups fail to register even a minor threat. RSF occasionally stand candidates as independents in local elections and on an abstentionist ticket in Westminster and Assembly elections, but the 32CSM as a whole eschews such contests. Beyond the obvious lack of votes, it is difficult to measure if there is any support, or sympathy (the 'sneaking regarders') for 'dissident' groups. In the BBC Northern Ireland 'Hearts and Minds' poll in 2002, 3.3 and 3.8 per cent within the nationalist community claimed that the 32CSM and RSF respectively, would best represent their views.[28] This was at a point when support for the GFA was at its lowest since it was signed in 1998, with the Assembly suspended amid considerable intra-unionist division and allegations of a PIRA 'spy ring' at

Stormont. In 2006, however, these figures for support fell slightly showing 2.4 per cent RSF support amongst the overall electorate (circa 4 per cent of nationalists) and 0.6 per cent for the 32CSM (1 per cent of nationalists).[29]

It is thus easy, as demonstrated below, for critics to dismiss the legitimacy of such groups in reference to them failing to secure support from the electorate:

> They have no mandate. The arrangements in this country have been settled by the Good Friday Agreement. It has been voted on by the people of this country and nobody has any right to challenge that in the way that these people are doing.[30]

Although they rarely engage in such terms, dissidents argue that democratic methods of full Irish 'self-determination' have never been permitted and that those stressing democracy need to examine the dubious democratic credentials of partition, implemented despite an absence of electoral mandate for such following Sinn Féin's 1918 final all-Ireland election victory. Eighty years after that election, the GFA referendum did not allow Irish electors, north or south, to express their support for a united Ireland, as this was never an option on the ballot paper. Ireland was partitioned at a time when Sinn Féin held three quarters of the parliamentary seats on the island.[31] Dissidents highlight that republicans today could also hold the majority of seats but a united Ireland would be prevented by the 'unionist veto'. In the most unlikely event that the Irish Republic's electors had voted to retain Articles 2 and 3 in 1998, it would not have mattered in terms of creating a thirty-two county republic: the North retained a 'veto'. Even Gerry Adams noted this at the Sinn Féin Ard Fheis in May 1998, insisting:

> It is clear that the referendums do not constitute the exercise of national self-determination. Self-determination is universally accepted to mean a nation's right to exercise the political freedom to determine its own social, economic, and cultural development without external influence and without partial or total disruption of the national unity or territorial integrity. These criteria are not observed in Ireland.[32]

Voters in the Irish Republic were, however, permitted a choice between maintaining a claim, however unrealisable, to Northern Ireland by rejecting amendments to Articles 2 and 3 of the constitution, or downgrading unity to a mere aspiration. Voters in Northern Ireland were permitted a choice between the GFA or an unspecified alternative in the event of rejection. Effectively, this choice was between partition with devolved power-sharing government or partition with direct British rule.

Yet, in the Irish Republic, when questioned in the European Values Study (1999–2000) shortly after the GFA referendum on the constitutional preference of the island of Ireland the most favoured preference was for a united Ireland, with 54 per cent support. Second preference was for an independent Northern Ireland with 32 per cent and lastly the retention of Northern Ireland within the UK with only 10 per cent.[33] Religious identification had an impact in terms of the level of support for each constitutional preference but all (Catholic, Protestant and non-affiliated) viewed them in the same preferred order. This trend on constitutional preference is considered to be relatively constant over time.[34] Despite opinion polls demonstrating a united Ireland as the number one constitutional preference in the Republic of Ireland this option has never been put to the people. Therefore, the GFA was not an exercise in self-determination, but rather the opportunity for expression of support to an agreement that would give Northern Ireland an element of autonomy within a UK structure and would give northern nationalists a role within the polity. For obvious practical reasons, the British and Irish governments were not prepared to put the option of an independent Ireland to an electoral test. This is *not* to suggest that there would have been an overall majority for an independent, united Ireland had those governments ever dared put such an option. Support for unity appears soft; much may depend on how the question is asked, sympathy for the idea appears conditional upon a lack of political or economic cost (e.g. in terms of taxation), there might be few takers for unity in a referendum, as distinct from an opinion poll. Nonetheless, the point is simply this: the GFA referendum was an endorsement mechanism for a particular constitutional arrangement to which no alternative was offered to the electorate; whilst the endorsement was overwhelming, that does not constitute full constitutional 'self-determination'.

A key question is whether the possession of a mandate can be expressed only through electoral support, or, can groups such as RSF and the 32CSM function in alternative arenas that grant them an element of representative legitimacy? Firstly, however it is necessary to consider the extent and success of dissident electoral endeavours. For RSF the sacrosanct policy of abstention has shaped the nature of their electoral endeavours. The policy followed by RSF to stay out of Leinster House, Stormont and Westminster – in the inconceivable event of the party attracting sufficient support to exercise its abstentionist credentials – is not based on their rejection of parliamentary politics *per se*. Rather the rejection of these institutions is based on their 'partitionist' nature. RSF consider the present constitutional arrangements to be a result of a betrayal of the All-Ireland Republic of 1916 and the First (thirty-two county) Dáil, and of the forced imposition of partition.[35] Whilst partition remains, abstention is viewed by the organisation as an uncompromising cornerstone of Irish republicanism. In addition, RSF have been consistent in the position that fusing militarism with constitutional politics is a contradiction; for them it is not seen as possible to be both a revolutionary and a reformist. In explaining this position Ó Brádaigh has often used the metaphor that it is impossible to ride two horses at the same time, the revolutionary and constitutional steeds. The feat cannot be performed because they are two horses going in opposite directions.[36] Far removed from the bicephalous characteristics of Provisional Sinn Féin post 1986 (increasingly constitutional yet still preaching armed revolution), for RSF, it is impossible to adopt contradictory approaches.

That RSF have not shifted their position on the policy of abstention provides them with a sense of exceptionalism and pride in not having compromised their stance whilst others have radically altered their policies. Those who have compromised are therefore portrayed as functioning within and supporting a system that reinforces partition. As Party President Des Dalton explained:

> You don't work the system, the system works you. Ultimately, once you accept that and once you accept the parameters of the state you accept everything that accompanies that ... We have never dallied in any way with constitutional politics, to a greater, lesser extent we have maintained our position ... and our analysis of our relationship with the state has remained constant over those years and I think it has been justified in the out playing of events with others who have been tempted to go on another route. I think that has been justified.[37]

Such an obdurate attachment to abstention centres upon the pure and unchanging republican interpretation offered by RSF. Whilst some would claim this has made them static and rigid, RSF take pride in their consistency and loyalty whilst others, in their view, have conceded.

Having only broken away from Sinn Féin in 1997–98 the 32CSM had no issue with the 1986 dropping of abstention to Leinster House. Today the 32CSM do not participate in institutions for reasons other than the obvious fact that they would not get elected, although they attempt to ignore their rejection, claiming that their 'mandate will not be measured by gerrymandered votes ... For us the ballot box means more than just numbers.'[38] Despite not standing candidates as an organisation they have recently however shown their approval for members to stand as independents. A prominent 32CSM member, Gary Donnelly, stood as an Independent Republican, in the 2011 local elections, garnering 11 per cent of the vote (612 votes) in Cityside in Derry, a low, but not negligible figure and one which fell only 19 votes short of winning a seat.[39] Donnelly was a former member of Sinn Féin who took an active role in election campaigns during the early 1980s and later left the party around the time of the GFA. Donnelly is now a prominent member of the 32CSM, often being the individual to represent the organisation in media appearances. He was imprisoned in August 2010 for committing an offence under terrorism legislation,[40] and in September 2011 was arrested in connection with the 2006 murder of Denis Donaldson but was then released the next day without charge.[41] The issues raised by Donnelly during the 2011 Council Election campaign reflected the 32CSM local agendas, including rates of pay for local workers, challenging anti-social behaviour (specifically drugs), the conduct of the PSNI and the treatment of 'political prisoners'.[42] When explaining why he decided to run for local election, Donnelly emphasised that it was not simply an independent decision:

> We decided to use the council elections as a platform to highlight a number of issues like British policing and the prison issues. As well as that the social issues that would affect the everyday lives of people in our community … There was a lot of people saying they wanted something different, they wanted to vote but none of the parties that were there represented that republican grass roots opinions and ideals.[43]

An additional motivating factor to run for local election was the disdain felt towards 'Derry-Londonderry' being awarded the UK City of Culture. Derry-Londonderry was named the first UK City of Culture in 2010. The aim of the initiative administered by the Department of Culture, Media and Sport was to bring significant social and economic benefits for the area. The 32CSM campaigned against the title on the grounds that it aimed to normalise British rule in a majority nationalist area. In keeping with the cultural theme, the 32CSM even launched a poster competition for people to submit designs that could be used in the 'Anti–British (UK) City of Culture Campaign' and be displayed around the area. Donnelly explained the opposition felt towards the UK title:

> It makes a mockery of every night that was spent in prison, every stone that was ever thrown in opposition, every drop of blood that was ever spilt on both sides. It makes it just a complete and utter mockery of that almost 800 years of struggle against British imperialism. Are we now expected to fully embrace the UK tag and sing and dance on the streets? The actual UK City of Culture programme has quickly descended into chaos … It is a farce. There is nothing that benefits working-class areas. It will benefit some hoteliers. There is no benefit in parts like the Creggan, the Bogside.[44]

After the local election campaign in 2011 Donnelly refused to shake hands with Martin McGuinness outside the polling station on the grounds that he had 'abandoned the republican community', and believed that McGuinness's gesture, 'was just a publicity stunt for the cameras, there is no other reason and it would probably have been used to discredit myself amongst republicans'.[45]

It is possible that Donnelly's bid for election signifies the beginning of more 32CSM members standing as independents. However, there is reluctance from the group to express a clear electoral strategy, the preference being to utilise elections for a tactical reasons. As Donnelly explains, 'I think electoralism can be used as a tactic, it isn't a principle … I can see some elections being used for getting your message out for tactical purpose.'[46]

In May 2014 Donnelly stood again as an independent candidate in local elections. In an attempt to present an alternative to the mainstream political parties, Donnelly's election literature did not break away from the community activism and local representation emphasised within his previous campaign. This time not only was Donnelly elected on the first count, he also topped the poll in Moor DEA with 1,154 votes; three other independents were also elected to Derry-Strabane Council.[47] Within a week of the local elections Donnelly refused to condemn a dissident bomb attack on the Everglades Hotel in Derry, targeted for hosting a recruitment event for the PSNI.[48]

As an organisation the 32CSM does not seek legitimacy through representation in the current political institutions. Such a point was exemplified when asking 32CSM member Michael Gallagher whether the organisation's goals can be achieved through political mechanisms:

> Republican goals cannot be achieved through political mechanisms as they stand in Ireland, i.e. there is a denial of democracy in Ireland. There is no democracy in this country ... I have no business for political mechanism as British machinery. My personal opinion is that there is going to be some sort of military solution to the problem.[49]

For the 32CSM the pursuit of a political mandate through the electoral arena is outmatched by the need for the continuation of an armed campaign. As John Murphy, a 32CSM member in Cork explains:

> The 32 County Sovereignty Movement can have thousands of members, if that was the case Britain wouldn't take any notice but if they thought for a moment that there was twenty members of the IRA successfully attacking British forces they would look up and take notice ... So, I think then people recognise ... you needn't have a vote to have a successful movement.[50]

The 32CSM therefore do not view constitutional politics as the arena that can ascribe them legitimacy. For them there is far more emphasis on gaining a mandate through 'community activism' and what they term creating an interface between themselves and the people.[51] Whilst the 32CSM are clear in their dismissal of an electoral mandate and their desire to prove the possession of democratic legitimacy through community representation they fail to present an obvious strategy in how this can be demonstrated. They state their wish to 'define and secure such a mandate as a tangible expression of sovereign democracy envisaged by the 1916 Proclamation. The mandate must be defined in terms of its democratic integrity and not simply in terms of electoral percentages.'[52] Despite wishing to possess a mandate as a 'tangible' expression, they are derided by constitutional politicians for failing to demonstrate evidence that they are capable of achieving serious backing. Whilst the electoral success of the 32CSM members does not yet stretch beyond local politics, the 2014 Council Elections demonstrated the level of electoral support that prominent individuals within specific areas are able to attract. It therefore becomes harder to reject certain groups on the grounds that they have no community support or mandate.

Despite refusing to take seats within Stormont, Leinster House and Westminster, Republican Sinn Féin candidates do participate in local elections in the Irish Republic. The abstentionist principle is not applied to local government assemblies, because 'they do not claim sovereignty over the territory they administer. It is therefore possible to participate in these bodies without prejudicing the right of Ireland to freedom and unity'.[53] Therefore, if elected (a very rare occurrence), RSF candidates do participate on councils. RSF candidates have been unable to stand on their party label in local elections north of the border due to the introduction of the 'Elected Authorities (Northern Ireland) Act' in 1989. Under the Act candidates had to pledge their support to certain conditions, such as declaring they would not support terrorism, before they were permitted to contest in elections. The declaration read as follows:

> I declare that, if elected, I will not by word or deed express support for or approval of – (a) any organisation that is for the time being a proscribed organisation specified in Schedule 2 to the Northern Ireland (Emergency Provisions) Act 1978: or (b) acts of terrorism (that is to say, violence for political ends) connected with the affairs of Northern Ireland.[54]

Because RSF refused to sign such a document that declared they did not approve the use of armed struggle, their nomination papers were refused, making them ineligible to stand. Therefore, RSF were left to contest elections only in the South.

In 2009 RSF fielded nine candidates in Irish local council elections, candidates having to stand as independents as the organisation is not registered as a political party. Throughout the campaign RSF promoted Éire Nua and Saol Nua as the alternatives to the failed free market capitalism of the twenty-six county establishment.[55] RSF were successful in one area, Tomás Ó Currain winning a seat in Galway County Council with 1,387 votes, or 8.4 per cent.[56] Following this solitary win Ó Currain was described, without irony, as RSF's 'most prominent elected candidate'.[57]

The last Northern Ireland Assembly election contested by RSF was in March 2007 where candidates were registered as 'Independents' in response to the Elected Authorities Act. In February of that year RSF announced they would field candidates in eleven of the eighteen constituencies in the forthcoming Stormont elections on an abstentionist ticket but eventually only six party members contested seats.[58] RSF's showing was negligible, polling a paltry total of 3,880 votes or 0.6 per cent of the votes across all the Northern Ireland constituencies.[59] At the same election Sinn Féin received 180,573 votes, 26.2 per cent of the overall total.[60] Such disparity demonstrates the inability of RSF to mount a meaningful electoral challenge to Sinn Féin.[61] It was clear from the rhetoric surrounding the RSF campaign that opposing Sinn Féin and the current political dispensation was the main intention, as demonstrated by Michael McManus, candidate for Fermanagh South Tyrone:

> Those who shamefully use the honorable [sic] name of Sinn Féin … have no right to call themselves Republicans. I appeal to the Republican people of this historic constituency to reject British rule, reject the RUC [sic] and send a clear message to the crown that we will neither be bought or broken.[62]

The main aim is to provide a political challenge rather than offer serious electoral rivalry, and RSF fails to register an electoral impact at local or assembly level either side of the border, whilst Sinn Féin remains on an upward trajectory, albeit at a slower pace than the spectacular gains of the early 2000s and amid greater nationalist abstention. Both RSF and the 32CSM are more concerned with other campaigns such as rights for political prisoners. However, this focus cannot disguise the lack of support, blamed by the Party President, Des Dalton, upon the media's unwillingness to air republican alternative perspectives:

> Whilst the media were at times quite willing to give a window there to say we are opposed to this … We were never given the opportunity to present our alternative. This is what we believe [is a] step forward; this is the opportunity to have a debate about the kind of Ireland we want. I even experienced that myself in media inter-views where you would be asked about your attitude to armed struggle and so on, at times, the media interviewer, when you start talking about things like Éire Nua and the vision of the kind of Ireland you would like to see they tend to dismiss that and are not really interested in that at the time. They just want to move on and talk about rejectionists if you like.[63]

What is important for RSF is not a mandate represented by electoral support but a mandate from history. This is reflected in the preservation of Tom Maguire's 'last political will and testament'.[64] Tom Maguire was a member of the army executive within the IRA and the last surviving member of the First Dáil. During the 1969–70 split Ó Brádaigh and fellow republican leader Dáithí Ó Conaill secured Maguire's recognition of the Provisional IRA as the lawful successor to the previous Army Council. Again after the 1986 split the side that would go on to form RSF sought Maguire's approval to make the Continuity IRA the legiti-mate successors. Maguire approved whilst simultaneously rejecting the same request from the Adams delegation. For RSF such a symbolic act is invaluable in terms of providing historical legitimacy. Geraldine Taylor of RSF explained its importance:

> Throughout the history of the republican movement, there is [was] always some-body from the First Dáil Éireann … to recognise they were the caretakers of the republican movement. In 1969 when the split took place with the sticks and that, they wanted to go political, the Provos were founded then and Tom Maguire recognised them as the legitimate government of the republic. In 1986 when the split took place again, the same Provies went back to this man and he chased them. Republican Sinn Féin is the legitimate government of the republic. We were the caretakers. Now Tom Maguire has died. But these other groups do not have this history that we have. We are the republican movement. They aren't.[65]

For Taylor, history and republicanism form a symbiotic relationship where one cannot exist without the other. The precedence given to history and tradition can be clearly identified in RSF's newspaper, *Saoirse*, where more coverage is

dedicated to history and commemorations than current events or direct political expression of the organisation.[66] As a result, it is unsurprising that RSF have
attained a 'Dad's Army' stereotype.[67] Joe Barr, a younger member of the 32CSM
in Derry, was a previous member of RSF and left due to what he describes as the
group's lack of productivity:

> I was with Republican Sinn Féin probably for about two years I would say but …
> they don't do anything. There was nothing to do apart from we would have a
> meeting once a month and they would give me ten *Saoirse* to sell … That's all it
> was, 'there you go, see you3 next month. Don't forget to bring that ten pounds'.
> I think there was one commemoration I went to and that was it.[68]

Beyond using electoral performance as a judgement of support, the Northern
Ireland General Election Survey in 2010 was a rare measurement of public
opinion on dissident groups. It aimed to 'analyse whether there are particular
categories of the Northern Ireland population, identifiable via demographic
and attitudinal exploration, which offer a modicum of sympathy to dissident
Republicanism'.[69] One of the key questions within the survey relating to dissident groups enquired about the level of sympathy ('a lot', 'a little', or 'none')
with

> the reasons why some Republican groups (such as the Real IRA and Continuity
> IRA) and often called 'dissident Republicans' continue to use violence, even if you
> don't condone the violence itself.[70]

The figures that emerged were seen as surprisingly high and gained a considerable amount of media attention.[71]An overall figure of 8.2 per cent of respondents stated that they have sympathy for the reasons why some republican
groups continue to use violence, but within the nationalist community, this
figure constituted 14 per cent. This approximated to almost one-third of those
self-identifying as nationalists as distinct from merely being from a nationalist
community background (using previous census labelling).[72] However, it is also
important to put these quantities into perspective. In the same survey only 24
per cent of people identified themselves as nationalist[73] (low nationalist self-
identification (only 20 per cent) is also confirmed in the 2010 Northern Ireland
Life and Times Survey).[74] Therefore those who demonstrated sympathy for
republican groups which continue to use violence amounted to one-third of less
than one-quarter of the population.

The extensiveness of dissident sympathy was nonetheless perhaps higher than
might have been anticipated, yet the figures of sympathy for dissident groups did
not markedly differ from two earlier, largely unnoticed, BBC Northern Ireland
Hearts and Minds polls conducted in 2002 and 2006. These indicated combined
support for RSF and 32CSM of 7.1 per cent.[75] The 2010 Northern Ireland election study question asked about the level of 'sympathy' for dissidents, a much

softer term than 'support' and the results therefore do not assume a substantial amount of backing for dissident violence. Sympathy for the reasons behind dissident violence, which could include simply that there is no united Ireland, is some distance removed from outright support. The findings do, however, challenge the mainstream narrative that dissident groups elicit no regard whatsoever within the nationalist community. It may be more accurate to assert that they attract a very low, but not negligible, quantity of sympathy.

In addition, it is usually the case survey respondents tend to produce answers perceived as socially acceptable. For example, during the troubles there was a constant under reporting of Sinn Féin electoral support due to the party's links with the PIRA; a trend coined as the 'shy Shinners' syndrome.[76] Given the 'socially acceptable' conditioning of answers, it is *possible* that the 2010 results on attitudes to 'dissidents' could under-report sympathy, although this is mere conjecture and the limited electoral evidence suggests otherwise. The 2010 General Election Survey may have indicated that the picture frequently painted by the media and mainstream politicians that these groups are 'a tiny minority with little support' and made up of 'marginalised, disaffected young people'[77] perhaps needs a little qualification. RSF President Dalton commented:

> It is vital for people like Republican Sinn Féin to give that voice, and represent that strand of revolutionary republicanism because it is very much painted that there was this 99.9 per cent of people who have signed up to this [Good Friday Agreement], this is not the case. There are you know, and I think even Professor Jonathan Tonge's study on that showed, there still remains that core … who would from a greater to a lesser extent uphold revolutionary republicanism … that base of republicanism remains there … it is important, that strand of republicanism continues to be voiced and we see that as our primary duty.[78]

Despite usually downplaying the need to indicate a contemporary electoral mandate and instead emphasising their legitimacy as coming from history, Dalton is keen to highlight a survey that does hint at some backing.

The dissident critique of Provisional Sinn Féin

> They sold out their republican principles, ideals and everything else. Now and again you will hear, 'Oh we will get you a united Ireland' but they are not really concerned about there being a united Ireland.[79]

'Dissident' republicans are frequently considered purely in 'rejectionist' terms. Their actions are viewed as a negative reaction to the peace process. It is necessary to explore further the dissident critique of the current Sinn Féin position to reveal what specific aspects they focus on and whether the groups emphasise different features, and if so, why? Given these critiques, why has Sinn Féin been so successful in maintaining considerable unity within the organisation?

The dissident critique of Sinn Féin tends to centre on their acceptance of partitionist institutions, the GFA and PIRA's decommissioning, and endorsement of policing. Whilst both RSF and the 32CSM utilise these acts to demonstrate the 'sell-out' of republican principles there are distinct differences. The 32CSM and RSF agree that Sinn Féin has abandoned republican principles. However, in detailing this abandonment they highlight different aspects in order to expose this betrayal. RSF's Dalton recounts the steps of Sinn Féin's submissions:

> The first big step was obviously recognising Leinster House. People like Ruairí Ó Brádaigh warned of the consequence of this. They were all you know 'Ruairí is out of touch and he is bringing an old analysis to an all new situation', and it just doesn't add up. Then the first Provisional ceasefire came in and then they were decommissioning. Then ultimately they signed up to the acceptance of the unionist veto. Where in that situation they effectively recognised that Ireland isn't a nation in the unitary sense. You are accepting that there is the six county state with a legitimacy and so on.[80]

For RSF, Sinn Féin removed their claims to the republican tradition by agreeing to take seats in Leinster House. Yet RSF has struggled to articulate an alternative. The party is considered in relation to its opposition to mainstream politics and Sinn Féin's full absorption into 'partitionist' institutions. It is difficult for RSF and other groups to project their own opinions. Ultimately, as Taylor explains, the actions and language of Sinn Féin have a direct impact on other republican organisations:

> It means that the struggles are harder to achieve now that it was years ago because of the sell out by the Provos. It is most difficult for republicans because former republicans are now part and parcel of administering British rule … So it is more difficult now that it was years ago.[81]

Due to the frequent portrayal of Sinn Féin as the archetypal form of republicanism, other groups' fidelity to the ideology is often considered in relation to what Sinn Féin represent. This has obviously had a damaging effect on RSF by inhibiting their scope to represent the enduring and perpetual republican tradition. Dalton describes the impact of the Sinn Féin agenda on RSF:

> Now in 2011 it's not a particularly easy time to be a republican. Now when I say republican, I mean, a lot of people use that label I would mean republican in the traditional sense of that word and what it means, what it really means, which is a revolutionary tradition … they [Sinn Féin] subvert the revolution in the name of the revolution if you like. And that is what they have been doing; they have been invoking the republican in the name of the republic. Because as I say, they are using all the right language, they obviously come from a background of having been activists themselves and so on. For a lot of people they would still view them as representing republicanism. So if they hear a contra argument to that it is quite confusing.[82]

For RSF, who are described as demonstrating a 'commitment to an unchanging, almost theological version of Irish republicanism',[83] the critique of Sinn Féin is focused on their removal of principles justifying the label 'republican'. RSF are frequently presented as an organisation that has little to offer beyond their rejection of the Sinn Féin agenda. They do not have the means to generate public interest based on their own aims and objectives. Instead they are only offered a window of opportunity if it is in relation to their links to paramilitaries or their opposition to Sinn Féin. They have been placed in a rejectionist 'box' where they are given very few occasions to express anything else beyond the narrow topics that can rally human interest outside the parameters of the RSF membership.

For the 32CSM, whilst their critique of the Sinn Féin position questions the extent to which the organisation can still be considered republican, it is based more on the U-turns made by the organisation in relation to 'armed struggle', a position typified in the assertion of one member; 'I mean to me personally, just to be a republican, even just to be considered a republican the first thing you have to do is recognise the right to bear arms against a repressive force.'[84]

It is unsurprising that members of the 32CSM portray an almost symbiotic relationship between armed struggle and republicanism considering the timing of their departure. The 32CSM members that split from Sinn Féin did so at a time when the continuation of a military capacity was being seriously threatened. Considering they had already accepted the 1986 downgrading of abstention, their departure was based less on constitutional issues and more on the future of an armed capability.

A key aspect of the 32CSM critique consists of highlighting supposed hypocrisy from Sinn Féin in denouncing the continued use of armed struggle. Shortly after McGuinness's 'traitors to the island of Ireland'[85] comments in 2009, the 32CSM highlighted the U-turns made by Sinn Féin by posting video clips from the 1980s of McGuinness claiming that armed struggle will be the ultimate yielder of a united Ireland, as he stated 'We don't believe that winning elections and winning any amount of votes will bring freedom. At the end of the day it will be the cutting edge of the IRA which will bring freedom.'[86] John Murphy, from the 32CSM in Cork outlines the contradiction of the Sinn Féin position on denouncing armed struggle:

> Well basically, you talk about irony. You might often see *Youtube* clips from the seventies and eighties with things the likes of Adams and McGuinness have said and turned things totally on their head. There is actually an ironic clip of Martin McGuiness telling a reporter that no amount of votes for Sinn Féin will bring Irish freedom, at the end of the day it will be the cutting edge of the IRA that will bring freedom. These were his words and now I think they got tired, individuals, but I don't think they had a right to make decisions then for the rest of the movement. I

have never lived in the six counties but I can imagine, you know, every day fighting a war, politics in your face. But I don't think they had the right to talk for everyone and draw the movement down that road.[87]

Considering such a reassessment on the part of McGuinness in relation to the role of the IRA and the position of armed struggle, it is unsurprising that the 32CSM utilise such U-turns to demonstrate the duplicity of the Sinn Féin position. When questioned about the denunciation of armed tactics by former members of the PIRA, a member of the 32CSM responded with the following:

> I would say it was just hypocrisy, it's just hypocrisy. It's people who have had enough, who have been compromised and decided … to try and take the movement whatever direction while they have an easy life for themselves. I don't believe that for one minute people like Martin McGuinness or Gerry Adams have the desire for peace at their heart … Personally, Martin McGuinness, for me would have been cold blooded, he would have been ruthless … A lot of people went to their graves, particularly in the eighties, fighting for an Irish Republic, and he was at the helm of the movement, the military and political movement.[88]

RSF also considers the denunciation of 'armed struggle' as a betrayal, but as an inevitable consequence of the compromises that preceded such condemnation. Geraldine Taylor argues:

> The very foundation which the republican movement was founded on is still intact and that is the situation that we see now. The Provos went further and further down that slippery slope, which we knew they were going to do. Recognise Stormont, they do recognise Westminster, make no mistake in that. They have offices over there, the only thing they haven't done is take their seats. They surrendered all their weapons, they surrendered them and no army that has been victorious has ever surrendered their weapons. Those weapons were acquired by the freedom fighters of Ireland, they didn't just belong to the Provies, yet the Provies just handed them over. Now they are part and parcel of administering British rule.[89]

Despite these claims of dissident republicans, Sinn Féin has remained remarkably united whilst going through such profound transition. Considering the republican movement's propensity to splinter it was not surprising that dissent would emerge (the only surprise perhaps was that MI5 claimed to be surprised). The scale of Sinn Féin change was far greater than the number of departures, whilst the party demonstrated its capacity to attract new backing. The relative unity of Sinn Féin has been the result of a long-term strategy which began in the 1970s. In order to avoid major blocs of opposition forming and causing a serious threat to the continuity of the movement the strategy had to be a long-term project. Dalton uses the following analogy to describe the gradual implementation of change:

Those who were unhappy with it were being siphoned off piece by piece by piece so that ultimately there was no major bloc of opposition left. I think that, from their point of view, was quite clever and it was a long strategy and it was well thought out. I know that the analogy that Adams used around that time in the eighties, this project was like a bus from Derry to Cork. The bus would stop, some people would get off and other people would get on. By the time the bus arrives in Cork you might have a whole new set of people on the bus but the driver was still the same. You can see an element of that. I think that has been the genius of what Adams has done, that he has managed to do that. What he has done, is that he looked at the various schisms along the way, the various splits, and he learnt the lessons from those. Particularly what the Workers Party did. They attempted to do it all in one block. He certainly wasn't going to do that.[90]

Dalton recognises the inherent characteristic of the republican movement to split but credits Adams with the limited departures in comparison with the scale of change. Whilst he pays tribute to Adams for an adroit and well-planned strategy, Dalton's reference also alludes to the result of such a transition being a hollowed-out entity, represented by the shell of a vehicle devoid of a consistent ideology and a membership that are only on board for the ride.

There is another thread of republicanism that espouses more of a social-ist element within its politics. In addition to groups that emerged from the Provisionals, the label of dissident has been used to describe those left-wing groups that emerged post GFA and those that emerged from earlier splits in the movement before 1969. Both of these republican strands contain groups that are keen to promote themselves as being socialist revolutionary as well as republican organisations.

The socialist revolutionary thread of republicanism

Through the twentieth century republicans have, to varying degrees, espoused a social radical tendency. Some have been careful to stress that the priorities of the struggle for Irish freedom need to remain with the national question. As Jack Bennett made clear, 'It may be considered valid in today's conditions to set some form of socialism as an ultimate objective – so long as socialism is not made a pre-condition for achieving national freedom.'[91] This has at times conflicted with a form of Irish republicanism which has been more convinced in its political and social analysis of providing a remedy to the Irish national ques-tion, espousing the view of 1916 Marxist rebel James Connolly that 'the cause of Labour is the cause of Ireland. The cause of Ireland is the cause of Labour. They cannot be dissedered.'[92] On this analysis, a united Ireland and establishing a socialist republic are inextricably linked. The organisations that retain a social-ist interpretation of Irish republicanism are groups such as the Irish Republican Socialist Party (IRSP) and éirígí. Despite neither now being linked to paramilitary groups, both are commonly labelled 'dissidents' for their rejection of the Good Friday Agreement.

The Irish republican socialist movement, or the 'Irps', emerged from the Official wing of the republican movement in the years after the split with the Provisionals in 1969. In 1972 the Officials called a ceasefire. Several senior figures, most notably Seamus Costello, retained the belief in needing traditional 'physical force' Irish republicanism whilst promoting a socialist political programme. Costello clashed with the Officials' leadership and eventually formed a breakaway group, the Irish Republican Socialist Party (IRSP) and led their militant wing the Irish National Liberation Army (INLA). Costello was elected chairman of the IRSP and became the INLA's first Chief of Staff.[93] The IRSP, formed in 1974, brought together many socialist and republican fighters.[94] Therefore, the new grouping aimed to combine a left-wing struggle with pursuing an armed struggle through the INLA.

Whilst the tensions within republicanism around the late 1960s and early 1970s were to some extent the result of antagonism towards socialism and working-class politics it should not be reduced to a left–right division. Rather than seeking reform in the North through a socialist programme and a redefinition of power relations, the Provisionals' immediate priorities were of communal defence and Catholic protection. Fra Halligan, member of IRSP Ard Chomhairle (national executive) and long-term member, argues that the division between the Officials and the Provisionals was based upon the latter's desire to use force as a means of defending northern nationalist communities whilst the Officials possessed an element that advocated reform within a socialist dimension:

> The politics, there was no politics. It was devoid of any politics [in the Provisionals]. The Official IRA and their leadership, who went on to become the Workers Party, yes there was politics being talked then and people saying why haven't we achieved our aims or our objectives through a different fashion. But it was too early and we believe it was far too raw to do that.[95]

The IRSP declares itself a revolutionary socialist organisation standing in the tradition of James Connolly.[96] The aim of the IRSP is to bring together as many of the working class as possible – Protestant and Catholic – in a broad front and 'to end imperialist rule in Ireland, and establish a thirty two county democratic socialist republic with the working class in control of the means of production, distribution and exchange'.[97] For Halligan, the socialist aspect of his beliefs takes prominence over his republican values:

> To me now, my republicanism has a small 'r' and the socialism has a very large 'S' … If all these societies, the 32CSC, RNU, these 1916 societies that seem to be springing up, if they were to come together, what would they be coming together for? What would be their intention? I didn't join the republican movement at all in my life. I joined the republican socialist movement.[98]

Whilst the IRSP are no longer aligned with an organisation pursuing physical force republicanism, they are considered to be dissidents based on their rejection of the Good Friday Agreement. Their analysis was that the GFA would copper-fasten the division of Ireland and institutionalise sectarianism, and that as republicans it was not possible to accept the Agreement on the grounds that it would be accepting partition:

> The causes of the conflict have never been addressed ... The good folk up on the hill at Stormont, will look after everything. If Martin [McGuinness] and Peter [Robinson] are running about hand in hand that doesn't make any difference to the Falls Road or South Armagh or Derry or wherever. Basically what you are seeing here from what they would call the dissidents, we would call them 'dissenters', is really a core of republicanism, you can't accept Stormont and the partition of your country.[99]

Despite the IRSP's denunciation of armed struggle in the current context, they still recognise that the negative connotations connected to the label of 'dissident' are hard to escape, especially given their past associations with the INLA and their current stance against the GFA. Such being the case, the connotation is that those groups who are anti-Agreement are also anti-peace, despite announcing that the 'war' is over. An IRSP member expressed it thus: 'the problem was that two elements were deliberately linked – the Good Friday Agreement and peace. If you weren't fully behind what was in the Agreement, it was made to look as if you must be for a continuation of the war: indeed, there must be something wrong with you.'[100] Even though the IRSP emerged from a split in the socialist arm of Irish republicanism, distinct from the Provisional wing, their republicanism is still considered in relation to what Sinn Féin represent:

> Martin McGuinness would stand up and say 'I am a republican and I am very proud to be one.' There would be a big chorus of 'no you are not Martin'. For me it doesn't matter. Martin was involved for an awful long time. I would see Martin now and his party as constitutional nationalist. I have told them that. They have argued with me, but what does it matter? I was never a man to wear a badge. Are you trying to convince yourself because you are not convincing anyone else?[101]

The rigid label of dissident therefore does not allow for an alternative interpretation of republicanism, in this case an interpretation that rejects the legitimacy of armed struggle yet refuses to agree to the terms of the GFA. At no time have the IRSP directly split from the Provisional movement, yet they are placed into the dissident box, a label that is based on their ideological departure as opposed to the result of a physical split or division in the movement's membership.

A left-wing dimension to republican politics remains divisive. Post GFA saw the emergence of the group éirígí who describe themselves as a socialist Irish republican political party, committed to ending British occupation of the six counties and establishing a thirty-two county democratic socialist republic. The nearest translation for the name éirígí is 'rise up' or 'arise' and is taken from the socialist and trade unionist James Larkin's famous quote: 'The great appear great because you are on your knees – let us rise.'[102] Éirígí was founded in Dublin by former Sinn Féin activists who had become disillusioned by the direction of the party in April 2006. Éirígí chairperson, Brian Leeson, a former Sinn Féin Ard Chomhairle member, left over 'their [Sinn Féin's] gradual abandonment of the core national position on the national question' and their 'their gradual movement away from the correct left socialist position'.[103] Leeson was accompanied by other former Sinn Féin activists in opposition to the changes within the party, especially around the time Sinn Féin's endorsement of policing became increasingly inevitable.

Éirígí stresses the centrality of socialism and the working-class struggle in answering the national question, arguing that the campaign for a united Ireland and class action cannot be separated. Believing that electoral politics alone cannot successfully bring change to Irish people and society, éirígí promotes active campaigning on a range of political, economic and social issues and encourages participation as a means to empower and mobilise the working class.[104] Éirígí has been involved in a range of campaigns. One of the first was 'Reclaim the Republic', launched in May 2006, to mark the ninetieth anniversary of the 1916 Rising. This involved the distribution of 60,000 colour copies of the 1916 Proclamation nationwide, with the aim of encouraging people to visibly display the poster with pride.[105] A number of individuals were asked to contribute to a collection of writings on the theme of 'What The Proclamation Means To Me'. The contributors came from a variety of backgrounds including the arts, journalism, trade unionism, and political and community activism. It appeared from the outset that éirígí was intent on marrying the core historical ideals and thinking of the republican tradition with 'a revolutionary current that has distinguished itself historically from the predominant conservative nationalist tendency'.[106] By associating itself with the pinnacle of republican scripture, the 1916 Proclamation, éirígí attempted to identify itself as a leftist revolutionary party with its roots firmly in the republican tradition.

Other campaigns include, 'We only want the Earth!', protesting over the Dublin government handing over the rights to all Irish oil and gas explorations to a host of domestic and foreign private energy companies. In addition the organisation ran the 'Different Name Same Aim' campaign against policing in Northern Ireland. Éirígí distributed leaflets and displayed banners to highlight that despite policing reform the PSNI remain a sectarian force who are still carrying out an anti-republican agenda. The battle against supposed 'political policing' is a key part of éirígí's campaign for a British withdrawal.[107] They also protested against the British Queen's visit to Ireland in 2011.

Despite its youth, éirígí appears to offer organisational coherence with an emphasis on grass-roots political campaigning. The IMC described éirígí as a grouping based on revolutionary socialist principles, 'with a focus on aggressive protest activities', but had 'no information to suggest that it is involved in para-military activity'.[108] Éirígí's niche area is revolutionary socialist and anti-GFA, yet, unlike the IRSP, it is not tainted by former links to any paramilitary grouping.

The fringes of local electoral politics

Both the IRSP and éirígí have recently stood candidates in local elections and intend to pursue this path in the future. In reference to electoral politics how-ever, the IRSP makes the claim that 'we don't want to be politicians, we are radi-cal community activists, we are not politicians'.[109] Unlike Republican Sinn Féin, the IRSP does not uphold abstentionism as being fundamental to republicanism and adopts a more pragmatic approach towards electoralism and participation. The founding statement of the party in 1974 stated, 'The Irish Republican Socialist Party is not an abstentionist Party, and will decide its attitude towards the contesting of any particular election, on the basis of a thorough analysis of the conditions prevailing at the time.'[110]

In May 2011, for the first time in thirty years, the IRSP stood in elections, contesting five local wards. The best performance was in Strabane with 3.8 per cent of the votes, the least amount of votes being in the Lower Falls with 0.6 per cent.[111] Paul Gallagher, standing in Strabane, missed out on securing a seat by one vote whilst the IRSP overall were the party with the highest number of votes not to get a seat.[112] The IRSP demonstrates the multifaceted nature of 'dis-sident' Irish republicanism. With the party's clear emphasis upon socialism as the republican core, it rejects armed struggle yet remains against the Good Friday Agreement, and stands in local elections but claims not to believe that there is a 'parliamentary road to socialism in Ireland'.[113] Such a combination of character-istics is recognised by the party itself as potentially 'contradictory in its nature. We are involved in an ex-prisoners group and we are involved in peace building and reconciliation. Then we are highly critical of the GFA.'[114] The result is a curious mix of republicanism, socialism, community activism and pragmatism within a political party.

At the éirígí Ard Fheis in May 2007, the decision was taken to move from being a campaign group to become a political party. In 2009 the group adopted a written constitution outlining the 'inherent weaknesses of the current elec-toral process'[115] whilst maintaining a sense of realism by accepting the need to embrace this 'process' and the centrality of existing political institutions. Éirígí continues to fuse socialist politics with the national question, arguing that its philosophy is based 'on the firm belief that the people of Ireland, and indeed, the wider world, have the fundamental and inalienable right to economic, political and national self-determination and independence'.[116]

Éirígí stood in the 2011 Assembly Elections on a radical social and economic agenda and as an alternative to the SDLP and Sinn Féin, claiming to provide an opposition to the government's fiscal cuts. Éirígí claimed its decision to contest this election was to protest against governmental cuts to public services. John McCusker,[117] éirígí's West Belfast chairman and candidate in Lower Falls for Belfast City Council, stated that éirígí was 'providing a platform whereby a radical voice could be given for this community that somebody that was not part of implementing the cuts or agreeing the cuts could give some kind of credible voice against it'.[118] Another éirígí candidate, standing in the Upper Falls, was Pádraic Mac Coitir, an active trade unionist and ex-prisoner.[119] The organisation gained 11.3 per cent of the vote in the Upper Falls and 6.6 per cent in the Lower Falls.[120] Although these results demonstrate the existence of pockets of support, this may also be confined to the small areas contested by éirígí.

Conclusion

Exploring further the origins of several dissident groups has revealed the multifaceted nature of modern day Irish republicanism. The groups explored here in this chapter all emerged at different times, for different reasons and from different branches of Irish republican lineage. They all express differences in their interpretation of republicanism and demonstrate different approaches to electoral politics.

The mainstream emphasis upon mandates has dictated that the political relevance of such groups can be expressed only through electoral politics. According to this analysis, which is commonly expressed by politicians and the mainstream media, the groups mentioned in this chapter fail to pass the criteria and clearly lack the democratic mandate required for serious consideration. However, for those who are members or support these groups, demonstrating an electoral backing is by no means a primary concern.

Despite being placed under the same banner of 'dissidents', these groups all have their own niche on the republican spectrum. Each of the four groups promotes a different interpretation of the tradition. RSF, who consider their 'mandate' as a product of the past, are rooted in an unyielding politics of 1916–19. The 32CSM are more pragmatic in their political approach in terms of acceptance of the twenty-six county state and being cognisant of the need for campaigns of contemporary relevance, yet still demonstrate a reluctance to stand candidates in elections, an aversion partly derived from the likelihood of abject failure and partly due to the group's inherent faith in militarism as a necessary and justifiable tactic. Instead of promoting an electoral strategy, the 32CSM express the need for an armed campaign, central to the republican strategy. The IRSP, however, are keen to move away from their association with paramilitarism and instead push forward a socialist agenda. They still appear to be a group in transition, eager to build on their support base and develop more of an electoral strategy. Éirígí on the other hand have never been linked with a paramilitary organisation. Because those members who left Sinn Féin and went on to join éirígí did so after acceptance of the GFA and PIRA decommissioning, it is possible to assume that their departure was not on the basis of maintaining armed republicanism. They therefore have the benefit of starting a new organisa- tion with a 'clean slate', aiding the impression that they are a genuinely novel republican socialist organisation. The next chapter, which explores the strategies, campaigns and future challenges of various republican groups, will assess further the dissident standpoint.

Despite the differences in these groups' origins they are still referred to with the collective label of 'dissidents', overlooking heterogeneity within the broad republican movement. Whilst the 32CSM and RSF emerged directly from the Provisional branch of republicanism, the IRSP emerged out of the split in the Official movement, éirígí, whilst containing some former members of Sinn Féin, emerged eight years after the signing of the GFA. The dissident label is uti- lised mainly in reference to departure from Sinn Féin's avowed republicanism, which has become elevated to the template for all others. Therefore, the term 'dissident' represents Sinn Féin's ability to take ownership of the republican franchise.

Notes

1 M. McGovern, '"The Old Days are over": Irish Republicanism, the Peace Process and the Discourse of Equality', *Terrorism and Political Violence* 16, no. 3 (2004), p. 638.

2 *Irish Times*, 'Dissident groups have no mandate for violent campaign, says Tánaiste', 27 April 2011.

3 *Belfast Telegraph*, 'Our message to bombers: an open letter to dissidents', 21 January 2012.

4 *RTE News*, 'Eamon Gilmore "disgusted" by Real IRA threats', 29 April 2011. See also, *Belfast Telegraph*, 'Real IRA will not win: McGuinness', 26 April 2011.

5 See *News Letter*, 'Sinn Féin chief switches tactics', 1 July 2008.

6 *An Phoblacht*, 'Uncomfortable conversations are key to reconciliation', 5 March 2012.

7 *Ibid*.

8 C. Hueckel, 'Sinn Féin without the IRA: Legitimacy or Loss of Popular Support', *Osprey Journal of Ideas and Inquiry* 31, no. 6 (2007), pp. 4–5.

9 *BBC News*, 'IRA statement in full', 28 July 2005.

10 See J. Tonge, '"No-one likes us; we don't care": "Dissident" Irish Republicans and Mandates', *Political Quarterly* 83, no. 2 (2012), p. 219.

11 See R. White, *Ruairí Ó Brádaigh: The Life and Politics of an Irish Revolutionary* (Bloomington, Indiana University Press, 2006).

12 *Ibid*.

13 Geraldine Taylor, interview with author, Belfast, 21 October 2011. As of 2014, Taylor was no longer a member of RSF.

14 32CSM, 'Background' (n.d.), www.derry32csm.com, accessed 28 November 2011.
15 *Ibid.*
16 In 1998, there were two Ard Fheisanna. One was held in April, another in May. The 32CSC were barred from both.
17 M. Frampton, *Legion of the Rearguard: Dissident Irish Republicanism* (Dublin, Irish Academic Press, 2011), p. 98.
18 The 32CSM, 'Background' (n.d.), www.derry32csm.com, accessed 28 November 2011.
19 The PIRA were not present at the GFA discussions. Sinn Féin may have been there but there was never any acceptance that they were representing the PIRA. All they were asked to do was use any influence possible to engage paramilitaries in the decommissioning process. This meant that Sinn Féin could no longer support any form of armed activity by the PIRA.
20 32CSM, 'Background' (n.d.), www.derry32csm.com, accessed 28 November 2011.
21 Interview with Bernadette Sands McKevitt, Radio Free Eireann, 32CSM, 30 December 1997.
22 Michael Gallagher, interview with author, Derry, 29 January 2010.
23 In the 2011 Assembly elections 32CSM-affiliated Garry Donnelly stood as an Independent candidate and polled 612 votes, placing him fifth.
24 32CSM, 'Background' (n.d.), www.derry32csm.com, accessed 28 November 2011.
25 Frampton, *Legion of the Rearguard*, p. 100.
26 For further discussion on legislative restrictions and reporting of RIRA activity, see S. A. Whiting '"The Discourse of Defence": "Dissident" Irish Republicanism and the "Propaganda War"', *Terrorism and Political Violence* 24, no. 3 (2012), pp. 483–503.
27 *Belfast Telegraph*, 'Real IRA will not win: Martin McGuinness', 26 April 2011.
28 *BBC News*, 'BBC Hearts and Minds Poll: detail', 17 October 2002.
29 *BBC Hearts and Minds Poll 2006*, available at Conflict Archive in Northern Ireland, www.cain.ulst.ac.uk/issues/politics/polls.htm#02, accessed 12 May 2012.
30 *Irish Times*, 'Dissident groups have no mandate for violent campaign says Tanaiste', 27 April 2011.
31 Sinn Féin won 73 of the 105 seats in Dáil Éireann at the 1918 Irish General Election.
32 Gerry Adams, Presidential Address to Sinn Féin Ard Fheis, Dublin, May 1998, available at www.cain.ulst.ac.uk/events/peace/docs/ga10598.htm.
33 European Values Study, 1999–2000, in, T. Fahey, B. Hayes and R. Sinnott, *Conflict and Consensus: A Study of Values and Attitudes in the Republic of Ireland and Northern Ireland* (Dublin, Institute of Public Administration, 2005).
34 See Fahey, Hayes and Sinnott, *Conflict and Consensus*, pp. 87–113.
35 Presidential Address of Ruairí Ó Brádaigh, Republican Sinn Féin, 93rd Ard Fheis, Dublin, 9 November 1997.
36 D. Sharrock and M. Davenport, *Man of War, Man of Peace* (Basingstoke, Macmillan, 1997), pp. 421–422.
37 Des Dalton, interview with author, Dublin, 21 October 2011.

38 32CSM, 32 Country Sovereignty Movement New Year Statement, 1 January 2010, www.derry32csm.com/2010/01/32csm-new-year-statement-2010.html.

39 Elections results available at www.ark.ac.uk/elections/lgderry.htm, accessed 17 July 2012.

40 *BBC News*, '32CSM man charged under terrorism legislation', 20 August 2010.

41 *RTE News*, 'Dissident released over Donaldson murder', 12 September 2011.

42 May 2011 Council Election, Election Communication Literature, www.irishelectionliterature.wordpress.com, accessed 2 February 2012.

43 Gary Donnelly, interview with author, Derry, 16 April 2013.

44 *Ibid.*

45 *Ibid.*

46 *Ibid.*

47 *Belfast Telegraph*, 'Republican dissident elected to Derry and Strabane Council as SDLP loses dominance', 26 May 2014.

48 *Derry Journal*, 'Donnelly reacts to bomb', 30 May 2014.

49 Michael Gallagher, interview with author, Derry, 29 January 2010.

50 John Murphy, interview with author, Cork, 2 March 2011.

51 See *Derry Journal*, '32CSM vow to "provide leadership"', 5 January 2010.

52 32CSM, 'Dismantling Partition' (n.d.), www.32csm.info, accessed 2 August 2010.

53 Republican Sinn Féin Poblachtach, *Elections and Abstention* (Dublin, Republican Sinn Fein, 2000).

54 'Elected Authorities (Northern Ireland) Act 1989 – Chapter 3', Opsi.gov.uk, accessed 2 February 2012.

55 *Saoirse*, 'Local Election Manifesto 2009', May 2009.

56 *Irish Times*, 8 June 2009.

57 *Irish Republican News*, 7 June 2009.

58 *Saoirse*, February 2007.

59 See ARK (Access Research Knowledge): Northern Ireland Elections, www.ark.ac.uk/elections, accessed 15 February 2012.

60 *Ibid.*

61 M. Frampton, *Legion of the Rearguard*, p. 69.

62 *Saoirse*, March 2007.

63 Des Dalton, interview with author, Dublin, 21 October 2011.

64 White, *Ruairí Ó Brádaigh*, p. 327.

65 Geraldine Taylor, interview with author, Belfast, 21 October 2011.

66 See chapter 6 for an analysis of the contents of *Saoirse*.

67 See Frampton, *Legion of the Rearguard*, p. 69.

68 Joe Barr, interview with author, Derry, 8 March 2010.

69 J. Evans and J. Tonge, 'Menace without Mandate? Is There Any Sympathy for Dissident Irish Republicanism in Northern Ireland?', *Terrorism and Political Violence* 24, no. 1 (2012), p. 62.

70 *Ibid.*, p. 69.

71 See as one example, *Londonderry Sentinel*, 'Up to 30 percent supporting dissidents', 14 October 2010.

72 ESRC 2010 Northern Ireland General Election Survey, results available at www.

esds.ac.uk/findingData/snDescription.asp?sn=6553 and at www.liv.ac.uk/politics/staff-pages/ESRCSurvey/index.htm, accessed 4 March 2012.

73 *Ibid.*
74 Northern Ireland Life and Times Survey, 2010, available at www.ark.ac.uk/nilt/2010/Political_Attitudes/UNINATID.html, accessed 12 May 2012.
75 BBC Hearts and Minds Survey, available at www.cain.ulst.ac.uk/issues/politics/polls.htm#02, accessed 12 May 2012.
76 See F. Cochrane and J. Tonge, 'Old Extremism or New Moderate Centrism? The 2001 Election in Northern Ireland', in L. Bennie, C. Rallings, J. Tonge and P. Webb (eds), *British Elections and Parties Review, Volume 12: 2001 General Election* (London, Frank Cass, 2002), p. 57.
77 Column Eastwood, Mayor of Derry, quoted in *Irish Post*, 15 October 2010.
78 Des Dalton, interview with author, Dublin, 21 October 2011.
79 Geraldine Taylor, interview with author, Belfast, 21 October 2011.
80 Des Dalton, interview with author, Dublin, 21 October 2011.
81 Geraldine Taylor, interview with author, Belfast, 21 October 2011.
82 Des Dalton, interview with author, Dublin, 21 October 2011.
83 Frampton, *Legion of the Rearguard*, p. 59.
84 John Murphy, interview with author, Cork, 2 March 2011.
85 *News Letter*, 'Murderers are traitors to Ireland – McGuinness', 10 March 2009.
86 Martin McGuinness quoted at, www.derry32csm.com/2009/08/cutting-edge-of-ira-will-bring-freedom.html?z#!/2009/08/cutting-edge-of-ira-will-bring-freedom.html, accessed 16 March 2012.
87 John Murphy, interview with author, Cork, 2 March 2011.
88 Member of 32CSM, interview with author.
89 Geraldine Taylor, interview with author, Belfast, 21 October 2011.
90 Des Dalton, interview with author, Dublin, 21 October 2011.
91 J. Bennett, 'The Northern Conflict and British Power', *Irish Sovereignty Movement Pamphlet*, no. 1,973 cited in M. L. R Smith, *Fighting for Ireland? The Military Strategy of the Irish Republican Movement* (London, Routledge, 1995), p. 22.
92 James Connolly, cited in Éirígí, 'From Socialism Alone Can the Salvation of Ireland Come' (n.d.), www.eirigi.org/pdfs/socialism.pdf, accessed, 26 June 2012.
93 M. Hall (ed.), *Republicanism in Transition: (1) The Need for a Debate* (Belfast, Island Publications, 2011), p. 5.
94 IRSP, *Republican Socialist Programme for Ireland* (Belfast, IRSP, n.d.), p. 3.
95 Fra Halligan, interview with author, Belfast, 1 May 2012.
96 IRSP representative, in Hall (ed.), *Republicanism in Transition*, p. 5.
97 IRSP, *Republican Socialist Programme for Ireland*, p. 4.
98 Fra Halligan, interview with author, Belfast, 1 May 2012.
99 IRSP member A, interview with author, Belfast, 2 June 2012.
100 IRSP member B, interview with author, Belfast, 2 June 2012.
101 Fra Halligan, interview with author, Belfast, 1 May 2012.
102 Éirígí, 'For a Socialist Republic' (n.d.), www.eirigi.org.about_us/faq.htm, accessed 15 December 2009.

103 Brian Leeson, interview with the author, Dublin, 24 June 2009, cited in Frampton, *Legion of the Rearguard*, p. 230.

104 See Éirígí, 'New Year Statement', 2 January 2010, www.eirigi.org/latest/latest010110.html, accessed 2 January 2010.

105 Éirígí, 'Reclaim the Republic', poster (n.d.), www.eirigi.org/pdfs/campaigns/reclaim_republic_campaign.pdf, accessed 17 July 2012.

106 Éirígí, 'For a Socialist Republic' (n.d.), www.eirigi.org.about_us/faq.htm, accessed 15 December 2009.

107 See Éirígí, 'Republican Newry Says No to the PSNI', 14 February 2010, www.eirigi.org/latest/latest140210print.html, accessed 15 February 2010.

108 *Twentieth Report of the Independent Monitoring Commission* (London, The Stationery Office, 2010), p. 9.

109 IRSP representative, in M. Hall (ed.), *Republicanism in Transition: (1) The Need for a Debate*, p. 5.

110 IRSP, *Founding Statement of the IRSP* (Dublin, IRSP, 1974), www.irsp.ie/Background/history/founding.html, accessed 21 June 2012.

111 For full results see ARK: Northern Ireland Elections, www.ark.ac.uk/elections/fa11.htm, accessed 21 June 2012.

112 IRSP, *Republican Socialist Programme for Ireland*, p. 6.

113 Fra Halligan, interview with author, Belfast, 1 May 2012.

114 *Bunreacht eirigi*, p. 1, available at www.eirigi.org/pdfs/eirigi_Constitution.pdf, accessed 1 November 2011.

115 *Ibid.*

116 *Ibid.*

117 For more information and campaign literature see www.eirigi.org/pdfs/poblacht_na_noibrithe/Poblacht_na_nOibrithe_apr11_jmc.pdf.

118 Slugger O'Toole, 'Catching up with éirígí's John McCusker – starting "a community fight back"', available at www.sluggerotoole.com/2011/04/16/catching-up-with-eirigi-john-mccusker/, accessed 16 April 2011.

119 For more information and campaign literature see www.eirigi.org/pdfs/poblacht_na_noibrithe/Poblacht_na_nOibrithe_apr11_pmc.pdf.

120 For full results see ARK: Northern Ireland Elections, www.ark.ac.uk/elections/fa11.htm, accessed 21 June 2012.

5

Continuity or dissidence? Dissident republican strategies and campaigns

Exploring the origins of various dissident republican groups is important in assessing the catalysts behind their formation. In order to explore their contemporary political outlook and strategic rationale (assuming this might be identified), it is necessary to assess the avowed goals and objectives of each group and how each considers these might somehow be attained. It is also necessary to assess what, if any, political resources or advantages might be available to each group. In the previous chapter, the dissident critique of the Provisional movement was considered. However, it is also imperative to question whether, beyond this critique, dissidents are capable of presenting a viable alternative to Sinn Féin policies. It is easy for dissident groups to criticise the constitutional path taken by Sinn Féin, but do they themselves possess a convincing substitute? How do various groups feel towards the creation of a 'broad front' and what are the challenges for these organisations? These questions need to be addressed in order to consider what threat dissidents pose to Sinn Féin's possession of the republican franchise and to assess the potential longevity of militant republicanism.

Strategies for Irish unity amongst dissident organisations

Éire Nua (New Ireland) is the RSF policy document that outlines their proposed vision for a united Ireland. Despite existing in previous formats, the programme was given a revamp by Ruairí Ó Brádaigh and Dáithí Ó Conaíll and then formally launched as a Provisional policy in 1971. It was then updated again in 1972 to apply the idea of federalism to the vision of a unified Irish state.[1] Éire Nua proposed to redraw the Irish state by establishing a unified four province federal structure. The four provinces of Ulster, Connacht, Munster and Leinster would all have their own self-governing parliament. The system proposed a three-tiered political system that would bring with it a complete reordering of governmental structures at federal, provincial and local level. The idea is that through a federalist structure maximum devolution can be transferred to the lower levels of governmental organisation to create strong regional local councils. It would also give unionists in the North a slight majority.[2] RSF contends that, 'a federal system, with strong regional and local government, will make it possible for unionists and nationalists to co-operate in the common interest, pooling the talents of all and working together to build a new and prosperous Ireland'.[3] Therefore, the primary concern of Éire Nua is for the creation of a secular decentralised Ireland that protects the rights and traditions of all communities, although the removal of the Union would, by definition, remove the core of unionism, notwithstanding a strong 'unionist' presence in a nine county northern legislature.

The federal policy caused tension within the Provisional movement throughout the 1970s. The northern contingent was unconvinced by a proposal whereby unionists would retain a majority in an Ulster parliament. With northerners increasingly controlling the IRA Army Council, Éire Nua caused a division between Sinn Féin and IRA policy. The policy therefore became part of the wider power struggle that emerged within the Provisionals by the end of the 1970s.[4]

It is unsurprising, given previous allegiances to Éire Nua, that federalism was placed at the centre of the RSF strategy after the 1986 division. RSF continue to promote it as the only document which proposes an alternative to the 'failed arrangement' under the Good Friday Agreement, the key criticism being that the peace process provided the consolidation of English rule in Ireland and ultimately the denial of Irish sovereignty.[5] As described by Geraldine Taylor, RSF have continued commitment to Éire Nua:

> That is why we are trying with our policy document. We even went over to Downing Street a lot of years ago and handed in our policy document to try and move towards a united Ireland but they didn't respond at all. We have also sent them to unionist politicians and everything else. No feedback on them at all, but we intend to get it updated and we intend on doing the same thing again. To call on them and to talk about … we are prepared to go anywhere to discuss this document and any queries any of them have. It is the only document which is out there.[6]

RSF are unable to stir interest for Éire Nua outside their own parameters. Whilst the plan indicates a genuine willingness to offer autonomy to the unionist community, unionists will clearly not accept a federal Ireland, given its severance of British sovereignty. In addition, despite being reformatted for relevance within a twenty-first century context, Éire Nua is criticised for being regressive and outdated, a relic of a romantic, agrarian (there is little indication of industrial policy) vision of an Ireland of a bygone age, and bereft of serious cognisance of the existence of two nations on the same island. Frampton notes RSF's consistency in that 'what had been judged appropriate to 1971 was held to be no less appropriate for the post 2000 world'.[7]

In 1991 RSF began drafting a new social and economic programme for the organisation. Soal Nua called for an economic system that would put human interests and development before the interests of finance and concern for profit, viewing 'conventional economics as an unsustainable discipline which must be subordinated to social, environmental, ethical and spiritual values'.[8] The document attacks 'free-rein transitional capitalism [which] is a denial of true democracy, is outside any democratic control, is predatory and dehumanising'.[9] Similar to most RSF political thought, Soal Nua is very idealistic in the sense that it projects a rather mythical vision of a desired Ireland, drawing upon a nostalgic version of pre-capitalist Ireland for inspiration. Rather than providing a prescriptive document to remedy the ills of modern day capitalism, RSF offer a romanticised ideal. It is indicative of the party's isolation, however, that even amid an acute crisis of capitalism within Ireland the party has made scant impact.

The 32CSM have created several policy documents that address issues such as Irish democracy, republican unity, dismantling partition and the politics of policing. Most intriguing of these documents is the group's submission to the United Nations in April 1998, resubmitted in 2001. The intention of the submission was to promote internationally the contention that British sovereignty over Northern Ireland is illegal, a 'colonial' claim breaching political, economic and social rights.[10] The submission argued that the denial of Ireland's national sovereignty contravenes the mandate provided by the last all-Ireland elections in 1918 and the subsequent establishment of an all-island Republic.

The submission was an unusual construction with its focus ranging from an in-depth nostalgic republican historical analysis to the assertion of rights of sovereignty in international law. The majority of the submission's focus is upon historical background with the inclusion of arguments from the Nobel Peace Prize winner and Irish politician Sean MacBride, emphasising the rights of self-determination and Irish sovereignty:

> Ireland's right to sovereignty, independence and unity are inalienable and indefensible. It is for the Irish people as a whole to determine the future status of Ireland. Neither Britain nor a small minority selected by Britain has any right to partition the ancient island of Ireland, nor to determine its future as a sovereign nation.[11]

The stated aim of the submission was to investigate the breaches of UN covenants and request an appropriate ruling:

> we respectfully request the United Nations Commission on Human Rights strongly urge the Government of Britain to comply immediately and unconditionally with its international obligations and respect the democratic wishes and that most fundamental and non-negotiable right of the Irish people, the basic right to self-determination. [12]

Despite making the above 'request', the overall practical intention of the UN submission was unclear, other than as profile-raiser for the 32CSM which might at least put Britain on the defensive over its claim to Northern Ireland and emphasise that this claim remained contested regardless of the contents of the GFA.

Beyond pleas to the UN, the political strategy for the resolution of the Anglo-Irish conflict, *Irish Democracy: A Framework for Unity*, was launched in 2005. The 32CSM intended this to prove the veracity of their own position as well as provide a template for discussion and debate. Within the document they separately addressed the British government, the Irish government and unionists.[13] Overall, the document reflects the organisation's opposition to the Good Friday Agreement, viewing Sinn Féin's support for the deal as preventing the realisation of national sovereignty, whilst also portraying the current political arrangements as a denial of democracy to the Irish people. Predictably, the GFA was criticised as ignoring the historical basis of the political problem:

> The 32 County Sovereignty Movement's objections to the political process which culminated in the signing of the Good Friday Agreement lay in the fact that the cause of the conflict between our two nations, the violation of Irish sovereignty, was not to be addressed by the process but was used to be a precondition for entry in to negotiations in that those wishing to take part had to concede that no such violation existed.[14]

For the 32CSM, conflict resolution within the current context will never be successful. The organisation views constitutional change as the catalyst in creating the political and ideological circumstances in which 'empowerment can be facilitated.'[15] The current arrangements are considered deficient and redundant in terms of providing the basis of conflict resolution due to the fact that their existence is a denial of democracy to the Irish people. The 32CSM asserts that the violation of Irish sovereignty has not been addressed. The organisation also criticises Sinn Féin for entering talks based upon the acceptance of the Mitchell Principles of non-violence, which were to lead to IRA decommissioning, without making discussions of British sovereignty an equal pre-condition for talks. The Mitchell Principles committed participants to democratic and exclusively peaceful means of resolving political issues and to the total disarmament of all paramilitary organisations, with such disarmament verifiable to the satisfaction of an independent commission. They required participants to renounce, and to oppose any effort in the same direction by others, the use of force, or threats to use force, to influence the course or the outcome of all-party negotiations. Moreover, the Mitchell Principles removed vetoes over the outcome of talks. All parties had to agree to abide by the terms of any agreement reached in all-party negotiations, and to resort to democratic and exclusively peaceful methods in trying to alter any aspect of that outcome with which they may disagree; and to urge that 'punishment' killings and beatings stop and to take effective steps to prevent such actions.[16] These principles, which were pre-conditions to entering negotiations, thus amounted to a repudiation of armed struggle and a commitment to peaceful methods regardless of outcomes. For the 32CSM, such movement in advance of the removal of British sovereignty was entirely unacceptable.

Notwithstanding supremely optimistic forays to the UN, the 32CSM, unlike RSF, appears more willing to apply an element of pragmatism to its approach in calling on the need for debate and consultation with other republican groups and individuals (Sinn Féin are no longer considered by the 32CSM as republican). In an attempt to separate itself from RSF, the 32CSM aimed the criticisms of exclusivity and isolation in their direction, arguing that there are 'those who interpreted principles in an overtly restrictive way severely restricting our ability to propagate the practical benefits for people which these principles are meant to deliver'.[17] In contrast to RSF, the 32CSM recognises the need to maintain ideological principles which also allow for the practical pursuit of politics. As an example, it is not interested in RSF's arcane contestation of the legitimacy of Leinster House. Thus, 32CSM Publicity Officer Ciaran Boyle contended:

> If you put Republican Sinn Féin in the context of now, they have become dinosaurs. They have got principles but there's a thin line between principles and arrogance … You sort of have to progress and move with the times … people change, their mind-sets change and things about you change.[18]

Thus, the 32CSM appear more tolerant of alternative interpretations and are more welcoming of debate, although the militarism of the organisation and association with the RIRA, notwithstanding ritual denials, tend to obscure the more flexible aspects of the organisation's outlook. Yet, similar to RSF, the language utilised and the arguments of the 32CSM offer clarity of ideological dogma, but imprecision concerning how the organisation intends to realise ideas and objectives. The lexicon used often encourages this ambiguity, via, for example, use of terms such as 'empowerment'. Whilst these documents allow one to gain a deeper understanding of the organisation as a whole with regard to ideas and opinion, they do not provide a clear and distinct outline of each organisation's intended strategy. Dissidents tend to offer critical analysis rather than prescription (beyond 'Brits Out' mantras) and *A Framework for Unity* fails to provide much more than a political critique.[19]

Broad fronts versus isolation

With the emergence of more groups opposing the Sinn Féin agenda since the Good Friday Agreement, 'dissident' republicanism has become highly fragmented. Such a diverse and disparate picture might seem illogical considering the relatively small nature of each group. It is therefore understandable why there has been a consistent level of debate around the creation of a so-called 'broad front'. Beyond the obvious numerical advantages of bringing groups together it is unclear what would be the practical arrangements of a 'broad front'. For example, would it mean cross-group leadership? Does it constitute just the sharing of resources? Or, does it require the supporting of similar causes such as the political prisoner campaigns? What is clear is that some groups are far keener to promote unity amongst and between groups than are other organisations.

RSF have remained opposed to the idea of uniting the various strands of dissident republicanism in a broad front that can together contest the direction of Sinn Féin and the peace process. RSF have re-affirmed they do not intend to become a part of any other republican grouping that does not completely share their vision of an Irish republic, disdaining other groups which stayed with Provisional Sinn Féin post 1986 for the downgrading of republican principles through the removal of abstention in respect of Leinster House. For RSF, their republicanism represents the unbroken and continued tradition:

> From the point of view of Republican Sinn Féin we would see ourselves as Sinn Féin, we celebrated our centenary in 2005 and so on. When Ruairí Ó Brádaigh and Dáithí Ó Conaíll left over Leinster House in the Ard Fheis in 1986 they brought with them the constitution of Sinn Féin intact and reconvened in the West Country Hotel as the Sinn Féin organisation. The use of the word continuity is very important in it. We are very aware of that historic continuity and an unbroken link right back. So we would see ourselves from that point of view as representing that strand of revolutionary republicanism which is unbroken.[20]

The emphasis within RSF of the organisation as *the* embodiment of the republican tradition is drawn from their unbroken tradition and continuity in the face of concession. RSF celebrate that they have not been tempted by the potential electoral rewards of constitutionalism. RSF are proud of remaining loyal, where others have strayed. For this reason the party's President, Des Dalton, insists that he could only work with those who were in total alignment with RSF policies and beliefs. He criticises other groups for refusing to say,

> 'look we got it wrong in '86, our analysis was wrong, but rather than establishing another organisation we accept that there is a republican movement there, let's try and build that and let's try and work on that'. Instead of that [these groups claim] 'we are going to try and justify ourselves, that we were right ... we are just going to set up another organisation'. If you like, the ideology is not there. The ideological base is not there because you can't just wish away all the other stuff.[21]

Therefore, if individuals did wish to move over to RSF, such a transfer would clearly involve some form of acceptance that RSF were right in 1986 and onwards and 'they' were wrong.

The 32CSM is far less hostile to co-operation, being less bound by republican self-ascribed 'purity'.[22] It is not uncommon for the 32CSM to join forces with the Republican Network for Unity (RNU) and Irish Republican Socialist Party (IRSP) at political rallies, meetings and debates. The reasoning behind their support for the creation of a broad front is that together groups can be stronger and develop influence. As distinct from RSF's need to address the past in order to ascertain, 'who was right, and who was wrong', the 32CSM adopt a broader approach more embracing of all anti-GFA republicans. This point is demonstrated in the following *Sovereign Nation* editorial:

> 2004 must mark the year of republican unity and previous dissensions must be consigned to the rubbish bin of history. As we all know to our cost, the republican movement is unmatched anywhere for its propensity to fragment and fractionalize … The 32 County Sovereignty Movement is intent on promoting unity amongst ALL republicans.[23]

Here the 32CSM are demonstrating that their continuation with Sinn Féin post 1986 should be resigned to irrelevance in terms of demonstrating their dedication to republican principles. Unlike RSF, the 32CSM argue that it is unnecessary for them to justify their loyalty to Sinn Féin up until 1997. Additionally, in agreeing to consign history to the 'rubbish bin' of the past, the 32CSM are reaching out to disaffected Sinn Féin followers. Such a statement demonstrates to the grass-roots that they could move across and join the critics of Sinn Féin without having to justify their previous continued support for the organisation.

By pushing forward a socialist agenda ahead of a republican analysis the IRSP are interested in a different kind of broad front, one bringing together the working class and trade unionists:

> At the end of the day the IRSP is committed to a 32–county socialist workers' republic – that is our goal, we haven't diluted that for thirty-six years and are not going to now … We don't want to achieve it in isolation because we know we can't. We want to bring together as much of the working class as we can – Protestant and Catholic – into a broad front.[24]

The IRSP are not as sceptical of the broad front idea as RSF but there is still reluctance. The difficulty behind the creation of a broad front seems to be based upon their intent to move away from their previous association with an armed group. When asked about the IRSP's views on a united front, party representative Fra Halligan responded in a cautious manner, sceptical of the purpose and motives of the other republican groups:

> There is also a more sinister element to it as well. If that car bomb in Newry had made its way to the centre for example. When it goes off it has a life of its own, it is indiscriminate. It is going to kill kids and old people. So you are saying to yourself well if you want to come together and that is your object, then we would be saying, 'well, no thank you'. If you are going to come together to come to the streets and protest about what is happening today then we will be with you every step of the way.[25]

The creation of a broad front has the obvious appeal of presenting unity amongst those republican groups who oppose the arrangements of the GFA and the direction of Sinn Féin. Whilst they are typically described as small factions with little, or no, support, a united opposition to the political status quo would be harder to ignore. The 32CSM and the IRSP both acknowledge the need for discussion and claim to welcome debate on the future direction of Irish republicanism. RSF on the other hand, are more interested in their own interpretation, and new members embracing that position, than providing space for discussion or debate.

Republican Network for Unity

Another group that is keen to promote unity amongst republican factions is the Republican Network for Unity (RNU). Originally formed in opposition to Sinn Féin's endorsement of the policing in 2007, RNU emerged out of the former pressure group known as 'Ex-POW's and Concerned Republicans against RUC/ PSNI & MI5'. At the Wolfe Tone memorial in Bodenstown, it was announced that the former pressure group had 'served its purpose when constitutional nationalism betrayed the Republic by endorsing the British Crown forces. Today, RNU, having contributed greatly to the process of wider republican re-alignment, establishes itself as an entity in its own right.'[26] Therefore, RNU's opposition to the path taken by Sinn Féin was based upon the perceived failure of Adams's party to challenge the 'British war machine', symbolised by the building of a large new MI5 headquarters in Belfast.[27]

RNU are not a political party and state they do not have any immediate plans to stand in elections. They do however adopt a pragmatic approach towards electoral politics by acknowledging that it could be a possible avenue to be explored in the future.[28] Many of the members are former 'political prisoners' and ex-combatants with well-known high-profile republicans such as Carl Reilly, Martin Óg Meehan and Tony Catney. Some of these figures are recurrently linked in the media to armed groups such as ONH and the RIRA, claims vehemently denied.[29]

Although the bulk of former prisoners associated with RNU are from outside Belfast (drawn in disproportionately large numbers from Tyrone) the group has become particularly active in West and North Belfast. RNU are very active within the Greater Ardoyne Residents Collective (GARC), an organisation committed to organising peaceful opposition to the Orange Order parades marching through republican areas. RNU are often mistakenly described as an umbrella organisation for other dissident groups to come together. They refute being the driving force behind the creation of a dissident republican united front, but they do encourage the coming together of republican groups especially over the rights of republican prisoners and opposition to the PSNI.[30] RNU state, 'we recognise that Unity is strength ... for this reason we urge solidarity between all Revolutionary and progressive forces in Ireland. We strongly value the prospect of future unity between disparate republican organisations in particular, however we are an entity in our own right, and contrary to popular opinion are not an umbrella group.'[31]

Such an interpretation of republican unity is very much in line with the adage of 'together we are stronger'. For groups that adopt a more pragmatic approach, such as the 32CSM and RNU, there appears to be a more relaxed and practical interpretation towards the coming together of the various dissident groups, especially in relation to prisoner campaigns.

Republican prisoner campaigns

Despite the GFA the rights of republican prisoners remains an active and powerful subject, centred around their status as being politically motivated, distinct from common criminals. The republican interpretation of the conflict considers the British state as an oppressive and aggressive actor. Some republicans are therefore involved in reactionary violence where imprisonment is an unfortunate repercussion in their fight for civil rights and self-determination. Today, republican dissident groups remain highly active in campaigning for the rights of political prisoners. There is also a strategic rationale, as the imprisonment and treatment of Irish republicans by a 'foreign state' is one of the few potential providers of sympathy for dissidents.

Many of the prisoner campaigns have rested on defining the motivation behind certain actions. Such a definition depends upon the interpretation of a prisoners' actions being 'purely political', not ordinarily criminal. Therefore, awarding the label of 'political prisoner' involves some judgement about what acts can be considered as politically motivated. The past actions of the British state in categorising the status of republican prisoners proved to be emotive and contentious.

'Special category status' existed in 1969, *de facto* treatment as prisoners of war. Under such status prisoners did not have to work whilst they were in prison and were allowed to wear their own clothing as well as have other privileges such as additional food and tobacco. To a backdrop of increasing paramilitary activity, in 1971 the decision was made by the British government to bring back internment. Authorities were given the power to detain suspected terrorists without trial. Between 1971 and 1975, 2,060 republicans and 109 loyalists were detained.[32] The right of trial by jury was suspended for certain offences, where instead the court consisted of a single judge, a 'Diplock Court'. In 1975, the Gardiner Report suggested that anyone convicted of terrorist offences was to be treated in the same manner as ordinary prisoners, including wearing prison issue uniform and doing prison work.[33] This change brought with it a re-categorisation of the status of paramilitary prisoners, henceforth treated as ordinary criminals. The policy was subsequently endorsed by the Conservative government from 1979 onward, Prime Minister Margaret Thatcher declaring: 'We are not prepared to consider special category status for certain groups of people serving sentences for crime. Crime is crime, it is not political.'[34] Such change provoked considerable local resistance as well as significant international condemnation. The re-categorisation of prisoner status by the British government was met with (eventually) vigorous campaigns from the republican community, both within and outside prison walls, which, by the 1980s, increased support for the IRA and, as it entered electoral mode, Sinn Féin.[35]

In response to the government's ending of special category status, republicans refused to wear prison uniform opting instead for prison issue blankets, which evolved into a 'dirty protest'. It is estimated that by 1978, 300–400 republican prisoners engaged in this form of protest.[36] In addition, by 1981 a second wave of hunger strikes began, led by Bobby Sands. After sixty-six days on hunger strike Sands passed away. His death produced a negative reaction against the British state internationally and an estimated 100,000 people attended his funeral.[37] Following Sands' death nine more hunger strikers died. The protests, with respect to the political status of republican prisoners, had a profound impact, leading directly to 'the political development of Sinn Féin and this was ultimately to transform the nature of Irish Republicanism'.[38]

Along with decommissioning and demobilisation of paramilitary groups, demilitarisation and policing reform, prisoner releases presented a significant hurdle in negotiations for the GFA.[39] It was agreed that under the terms of the deal qualifying paramilitary prisoners, from those organisations remaining on ceasefire, were to be released from prison within two years. The provisions for the release of prisoners in Northern Ireland and the Republic allowed for the exclusion of those groups opposed to the peace process and those still engaged in armed action.[40] Therefore, those on the republican side who were initially excluded from early release were the INLA (although this changed), CIRA and the RIRA. By 2008, 449 prisoners had been released (196 loyalists, 241 republican and 12 non-aligned) under the provisions of the 1998 Agreement. These numbers joined the thousands of former prisoners who had already served their time; estimates calculate the overall number of those imprisoned to be about 15,000 republicans and 5,000–10,000 loyalists.[41]

There is existing material on the fate of politically motivated prisoners after their release, which looks at the impact of imprisonment, and the role of individuals in conflict transformation and reconciliation from both the republican and loyalist community.[42] However, there is a void in the literature when it comes to considering those current 'political prisoners' who refused to accept the 'carrot' provided by the GFA of prisoner release and those who subsequently have been imprisoned for dissident republican activities. 'POW' ('Prisoner of War') campaigns, pickets and demonstrations make up a great deal of the literature and publications produced by dissident groups.[43] Prisoner rights are still a major part of the republican campaign. For example, the newspapers of RSF and the 32CSM contain statements and articles from CABHAIR[44] and the IRPWA (Irish Republican Prisoners Welfare Association) respectively, asking for donations, reporting on conditions and supplying information about upcoming demonstrations. RNU have a POW department named Cogús[45] campaigning on issues of prison conditions and have called for the donation of books to Maghaberry, whilst the IRSP also have their own organisation, Teach na Fáilte.

Promoting the current prisoner campaign is an important aspect of dissident propaganda. For dissidents there are several beneficial reasons in promoting the campaign for republican prisoners. Firstly, highlighting alleged poor treatment of republican prisoners contradicts the claims of normalisation in Northern Ireland. In May 2011, republican prisoners in Maghaberry prison began a 'dirty protest', using similar tactics to those used by PIRA prisoners in the 1970s and 1980s. Prisoners protested over strip searches, lock-up times and freedom of movement. There are frequent reports within dissident newspapers describing the treatment of republican prisoners as degrading and inhuman.[46] 32CSM member Gary Donnelly explained the nature of the protests:

> It is about forced strip searches and controlled movement and there was a prolonged protest. Prisoners decided to come off the protest to give the establishment time to get sorted in an act of good faith and they have just had it repeatedly thrown back in their face.[47]

Such coverage claims that despite the signing of the GFA life has not changed for some republicans. Reports of the republican prisoner campaigns also provides an opportunity to challenge Sinn Féin, questioning the ability and willingness of Sinn Féin to act on this issue. As Carl Reilly, national chairperson of RNU, states, there are individuals in Stormont administering power who are former prisoners and ex-combatants: 'From their own experience they should understand that these men are suffering.'[48] However, it should also be noted that whilst the prisoner campaign is featured highly in the publications of dissident organisations these issues do not manage to seep into the mainstream news as important matters.

Secondly, being such an emotive subject, the prisoner issue has the potential to mobilise a broader range of support. Highlighting the condition of prisoners and their campaign is likely to appeal to human interest. This has especially been the case with the imprisonment of Marian Price. Famous for her role in the bombing of the Old Bailey in London in 1973, Price was released on licence in 1980 after serving seven years. This licence was revoked in May 2011 as Price was charged with supporting an illegal organisation after holding a speech for a masked individual to read at a 32CSM Easter rally. In June 2012, the Northern Ireland Prison Service confirmed Price had been moved from Hydebank Prison to hospital after increasing concern over her health.[49] Her situation is described (not just by dissident republicans) as a form of internment without trial.[50] Another active campaign is for the release of Martin Corey. Corey was released in 1992 on licence for the murder of two RUC officers. His licence was revoked in

2010 on the basis of evidence from 'closed material'.[51] Such campaigns attempt to encompass a broad range of support beyond political difference. As a member of the 'Release Martin Corey' committee stated, 'People don't have to agree with Martin Corey's politics to see what is happening to him is wrong.'[52] The subject of prisoner release is promoted as a human rights issue broader than an exclusively republican campaign.

Sinn Féin has felt obliged to respond to dissident pressure for prisoner releases and better conditions (although mainly only in respect of the Price and Corey cases), given that the party supports law and order and, by definition, has to now back the incarceration of 'militarist' republicans engaged in attacks upon the police or Army. For dissident groups, some of the largest demonstrations have been in aid of prisoner campaigns. As a subject the treatment of prisoners issue has the potential to mobilise support and raise awareness on a humane level. Sinn Féin recognises the possible danger in such campaigns gaining traction, challenging its own republican narrative, and thus has been anxious to portray itself as active on the Price and Corey issues. It is obliged to respond to these situations yet the difficulty for Sinn Féin in adopting such a selective approach is that it highlights that the party believes that all other dissident republicans deserve to be in jail, a logical consequence of the party's decision to support policing in 2007.

Finally, promoting the prisoner issue associates groups with the fight for a united Ireland. The subject of prisoner treatment is imbued with great historical significance, being an issue of importance at key moments such as the Easter Rising, the Civil War and the 1956–62 Border Campaign.[53]

Such moments have a poignant position in Irish republican history.[54] In late 2012, a prison officer was killed for the first time in Northern Ireland for almost twenty years. David Black, who worked in Maghaberry Prison, was shot from an adjacent vehicle whilst driving between Portadown and Lurgan on the M1 motorway. The paramilitary group formed by a merger between various dissident organisations took responsibility for the attack claiming their motive was to protect and defend republican prisoners. Whilst discussing the attack on David Black, Gary Donnelly expressed the inevitability and historical continuity of such incidents:

> One prison officer has lost his life over this recently and there is absolutely no need for it. None whatsoever ... David Black didn't have to die. History will tell you if you treat prisoners like that they, their organisations on the outside, will take some type of action. We have been through all of this before. However, the establishment seems content in turning the clock back.[55]

By replaying tactics of the past dissident groups are attempting to directly associate themselves with a continuing struggle. The campaign for political prisoners provides an opportunity for dissident groups, when faced with the accusations of being traitors to republicanism, to present themselves as being part of a continuing struggle for the republican cause with considerable antecedents.

Future challenges

It is unsurprising that there are those within the republican movement who reject the need for a political mandate in order to challenge the status quo. The claims of possessing a mandate that emerge more from historical determinism than from the current context are similar to the Provisionals' arguments from 1970 to 1981. Violence was then also articulated as a historical right of the people of Ireland to resist their British oppressors, a position not dissimilar to that of today's dissidents.[56] However, the context within which republicanism functions has been utterly transformed by the Good Friday Agreement. The actions of the PIRA may not ever have been met with mass approval yet the response to their actions was rarely met with the scale of condemnation that followed the RIRA's 1998 Omagh bombing.

This is not to say that armed action during the troubles was never met with disapproval from the republican community, La Mon, Enniskillen and Warrington being three of several examples. Today, however, the protest seems to be broader in scope. The universal reaction against Omagh in 1998 seemed to demonstrate how the North was no longer 'unfinished business', or merely the difference between anti-partitionist Fianna Fáil and anti-partitionists through armed Provisionalism; republicans post the GFA now had a stake in the North. The protest about violent activity post 1998 was therefore not so much about the numbers involved in the demonstration, but because, in a changed context, those involved appeared broader in scope. Today, the support for Sinn Féin's constitutional role continues to grow as their electoral success increases. It is no longer enough for groups to proclaim resistance to the British state as their *raison d'être*. They now also have the task of convincing people of their positioning as opposed to the popular desire to bring about an end to the armed conflict.

Accused of wanting to protect the memory of past generations as opposed to seeking a mandate from the living, RSF are aware of the narrow description given to them and express the need to broaden the narrow stereotype that they have been awarded:

> I think our biggest challenge if you like is getting that message out there and getting past the narrow box which we have been placed in. [Be] Given the opportunity to articulate that we actually have a vision of the kind of Ireland, it is not simply a 'Brits out' organisation. We actually have something that is much more profound than that, much deeper than that. We have a vision for an Ireland and it is one that is very clearly thought out and set out there as well. But I think that would be a strength that we have to bring to a new, young generation.[57]

Whilst keen to broaden their reach, RSF still view their representation of the revolutionary republican tradition as the true faith essential to the organisation's existence. Insiders see their organisation's consistency of rejectionism as a virtue, not a handicap:

> Again, I think we are one of the only true revolutionary organisations that are out there ... Rather than tinkering on the edge of the system, we are the people who are saying the whole system is rotten. Things need to change. There has to be fundamental radical change. I think that is what we have to say to a new generation and I think for a lot of young people who are looking for something new, something fresh, something radical, I think we bring that. We bring that fresh new message. I think that to an extent that is ultimately one of the strengths that we have.[58]

A more downbeat assessment of recruitment possibilities is offered by the 32CSM. Asked 'what is there to attract younger members', Michael Gallagher responded:

> There is nothing attractive about being a republican. To be honest with you, it's a life of hardship and misery. People try and romanticise it, but to be honest with you the republican movement in Ireland has never been short of recruits ... And that will always be the case and it's been proven over eight centuries ... What attracts people to it – attract might be the wrong word, because there is nothing attractive about it, but why? There are always people in Irish Republicanism in the pursuit of justice, in the pursuit of democracy in this country.[59]

Such an answer presents a picture of resistance and self-sacrifice. Other 32CSM members responded that the best recruitment possibilities are still provided via antipathy to state forces, a common theme being that nothing has changed in terms of policing:

> Resistance, the police. We can put recruitment posters out but the police around the town do the recruitment for us. It's still a sectarian police force, it's still the RUC.[60]
>
> My friends are starting to ask now. What is the movement? What are yous all about? The thing that attracted me was just watching Irish men being abused in the street, young children being abused. People can't walk through town without hands up, without friggin' guns pointed at them. Their houses are being raided daily and I thought no.[61]
>
> I can tell you, there is nothing romantic about it. It is nothing but hardship. You become a social leper, you lose work, you lose friends. So people might think there is this big romantic story, but I can assure you, it is not ... To be fair if I am meeting someone that wants to join for the first time I give them the worst scenarios. I tell them about the harassment, I won't draw someone in under false pretences. You know I tell them exactly what is involved.[62]

The 32CSM and RSF are often met with the accusation of lacking popular support, but resistance to the current arrangements or demonstrating unwavering allegiance to the republican tradition is of more importance than acquiring an electoral mandate. It may be a challenge for these groups to attain further members but whilst the desire for resistance to the status quo or for the affiliation to historical determinism remains, so dissident groups may endure, albeit on a small scale.

Conclusion

In an attempt to explore further the politics of dissident groups rather than merely military aspects, this chapter has focused on strategy, broad fronts and campaigns. There is a need to consider what these republican groups have to offer. Do they provide a serious threat to Sinn Féin in any way and to what extent? Presenting a critique of the mainstream republican movement is the easy part. The problem for dissidents comes in advancing a credible alternative strategy.

The dilemma for dissident groups is that whilst a significant proportion of their campaign involves critiquing the direction of Sinn Féin, they do not back it up with a clear and workable alternative. The policy documents *Éire Nua* and *Irish Democracy: A Framework for Unity* serve as a rebuttal to accusation of dissidents not attempting to present their own strategy, yet neither provide a viable alternative. Dissidents fail to explain, or even address, how abstention or continuing armed struggle might work when these strategies failed to achieve a united Ireland from 1920 until the 1990s. There is no guarantee that the current 'third phase' of participation will bring the intended result either, but the costs are less and the political rewards greater. Therefore, from a political perspective, dissident groups ostensibly serve little purpose other than to annoy Sinn Féin by highlighting the party's U-turns and hypocrisies.

The negatives facing dissidents are ultimately their lack of support and the feeling amongst most nationalists that Sinn Féin presents the only credible political vehicle for republicanism. This is a credit to the party's ability to remain relatively unified despite the scale of transition. Other damaging aspects are the unremittingly negative media coverage surrounding dissident groups, which are uniformly portrayed as fixated with violence (the legacy of Omagh remains strong) and as a blight upon communities (although dissidents also of course live within those communities). Dissidents are seen as out of time and out of step with political transition.

Where dissidents may be able to register an impact is on localised issues such as prisoner campaigns, parades, anti-social concerns, historical lineage and lack of economic progress. Therefore, whilst forming and presenting a critique of Sinn Féin is important to the dissident strategy they also need to locate their own niche on the republican spectrum and publicise this as what they are about. Republican groups in Northern Ireland are able to grab attention using violence, but not so much in reference to their politics. The following chapter will focus on the military aspects of the dissident campaign.

Notes

1 R. White, *Ruairí Ó Brádaigh: The Life and Politics of an Irish Revolutionary* (Bloomington, Indiana University Press, 2006), p. 165.
2 Republican Sinn Féin representative in M. Hall (ed.), *Republicanism in Transition: (1) The Need for a Debate* (Belfast, Island Publications, 2011), pp. 9–10.
3 Republican Sinn Féin Poblachtach, *Éire Nua: A New Democracy* (Dublin, Republican Sinn Féin, 2000).
4 E. Moloney, *A Secret History of the IRA* (London, Penguin, 2002), p. 183.
5 Republican Sinn Féin Poblachtach, *Éire Nua*, pp. 11–12.
6 Geraldine Taylor, interview with author, Belfast, 21 October 2011.
7 M. Frampton, *Legion of the Rearguard: Dissident Irish Republicanism* (Dublin, Irish Academic Press, 2011), p. 61.
8 Republican Sinn Féin Poblachtach, *Saol Nua: A New Way of Life* (Dublin, Republican Sinn Fein, 2004), p. 2.
9 *Ibid.*, p. 2.
10 32CSM, *United Nations Submission* (1998), www.32csm.info, accessed 2 August 2010.
11 Sean MacBride, cited *ibid.*
12 32CSM, *United Nations Submission* (1998), www.32csm.info, accessed 2 August 2010.
13 32CSM, *Irish Democracy: A Framework for Unity* (2005), www.32csm.info, accessed 2 August 2010.
14 32CSM, *Preparing an Irish Democracy* (n.d.), www.32csm.info, accessed 2 August 2010.
15 *Ibid.*
16 British and Irish governments' document on UDP participation at talks, 26 January 1998, available at Conflict Archive in Northern Ireland (CAIN), www.cain.ulst.ac.uk/events/peace/docs/bi26198.htm, accessed 6 August 2012.
17 *Ibid.*
18 Ciaran Boyle, interview with author, Derry, 8 March 2010.
19 32CSM, *Irish Democracy: A Framework for Unity* (2005), www.32csm.info, accessed 2 August 2010.
20 Des Dalton, interview with author, Dublin, 21 October 2011.
21 *Ibid.*
22 32CSM, *Dismantling Partition* (n.d.), www.32csm.info, accessed 2 August 2010.
23 *Sovereign Nation*, February–March 2006.
24 IRSP representative, in, Hall (ed.), *Republicanism in Transition: (1) The Need for a Debate*, p. 5.
25 Fra Halligan, interview with author, Belfast, 1 May 2012. The quotation makes reference to a 600 pound car bomb that was discovered by police in an abandoned van in Newry, close to the Irish border in April 2012.
26 Republican Network for Unity, Bodenstown Address, 2007, www.republicannetwork.ie, accessed 26 April 2012.
27 See also H. Patterson, 'Beyond the "Micro-Group": The Dissident Republican Challenge', in P. M. Currie and M. Taylor (eds), *Dissident Irish Republicanism* (London, Continuum, 2011), pp. 78–79.

28 RNU representative A, interview with author, Belfast, 1 May 2012.
29 See *Belfast Telegraph*, 6 October 2011; 9 August 2011.
30 RNU representative B, interview with author, Belfast, 1 May 2012.
31 Republican Network for Unity, *About Us*, www.republicannetwork.ie, accessed 24 July 2012.
32 G. Hogan and C. Walker, *Political Violence and the Law in Ireland* (Manchester, Manchester University Press, 1989), p. 94.
33 See Great Britain Parliament, *Report of a Committee to Consider, in the Context of Civil Liberties and Human Rights, Measures to Deal with Terrorism in Northern Ireland* [Gardiner Report] (London, HMSO, 1975).
34 P. Taylor, *Behind the Mask: The IRA and Sinn Fein* (New York, TV Books, 1998), p. 282.
35 See F. Stuart Ross, *Smashing H Block* (Liverpool, Liverpool University Press, 2011).
36 P. Shirlow and K. McEvoy, *Beyond the Wire: Former Prisoners and Conflict Transformation in Northern Ireland* (Pluto Press, London, 2008), p. 38.
37 P. Taylor, *Provos: The IRA and Sinn Fein* (London, Bloomsbury, 1997), p. 282.
38 Shirlow and McEvoy, *Beyond the Wire*, p. 39.
39 *Ibid.*, p. 4.
40 K. McEvoy, 'Prisoners, the Agreement, and the Political Character of the Northern Ireland Conflict', *Fordham International Law Journal* 22, no. 4, (1998), p. 1,561.
41 Shirlow and McEvoy, *Beyond the Wire*, p. 2.
42 See P. Shirlow, J. Tonge, J. McAuley and C. McGlynn, *Abandoning Historical Conflict? Former Political Prisoners and Reconciliation in Northern Ireland* (Manchester University Press, Manchester, 2010); McEvoy, 'Prisoners, the Agreement, and the Political Character', pp. 1,539–1,576.
43 Within *Saoirse* and *Sovereign Nation* prisoner campaigns made up 7.8 per cent and 9.9 per cent respectively of the newspapers' coverage. See S. A. Whiting, '"The Discourse of Defence": "Dissident" Irish Republicanism and the "Propaganda War"', *Terrorism and Political Violence* 24, no. 3 (2012), pp. 483–503.
44 Cabhair translates to 'assistance'.
45 Cogús translates to 'conscience'.
46 See *Sovereign Nation*, April–May 2011, pp. 1, 12; *Saoirse*, February 2004, p. 3.
47 Gary Donnelly, interview with author, Derry, 16 April 2013.
48 B. Rowan, 'Is There a Key to Unlock the Dissident Protest in Maghaberry?', 18 December 2011, available at www.eamonnmallie.com/2011/12/is-there-a-key-to-unlock-the-dissident-protest-in-maghaberry-by-brian-rowan, accessed 26 July 2012.
49 *UTV News*, 'Marian Price moved to hospital', 22 June 2012, available at www.u.tv/News/Marian-Price-moved-to-hospital/0552df8e-e579–4e16–b9ad-4b84a4912d86.
50 A letter discussing the violation of human and civil rights of Price was signed by numerous community activists, politicians and academics, see *Irish Times*, 'Detention of Marian Price', 17 July 2012, available at www.irishtimes.com/newspaper/letters/2012/0717/1224320253375.html.
51 *BBC News Northern Ireland*, 'Martin Corey must remain in jail ahead of appeal', 10 July 2012, available at www.bbc.co.uk/news/uk-northern-ireland-18787982.

52 Cait Trainor in *Belfast Telegraph*, 'Campaign to push for release of dissident republican', 25 July 2012.

53 See for background of republican prison campaigns, McEvoy, 'Prisoners, the Agreement, and the Political Character', pp. 1,539–1,576.

54 See G. Sweeney, 'Self-Immolation in Ireland: Hunger Strikes and Political Confrontation', *Anthropology Today* 9, no. 5 (1993), p. 14.

55 Gary Donnelly, interview with author, Derry, 16 April 2013.

56 See J. Tonge, '"No-one likes us; we don't care": "Dissident" Irish Republicans and Mandates', *Political Quarterly* 83, no. 2 (2012), pp. 219–226.

57 Des Dalton, interview with author, Dublin, 21 October 2011.

58 *Ibid.*

59 Michael Gallagher, interview with author, Derry, 29 January 2010.

60 Ciaran Boyle, interview with author, Derry, 8 March 2010.

61 Joe Barr, interview with author, Derry, 8 March 2010.

62 John Murphy, interview with author, Cork, 2 March 2011.

6

Militarism as a component of dissident republicanism

> There is no republican violence. Republicanism is a non-violent phenomenon that merely strives to implement the rights of an oppressed people – the right to freedom from British rule is denied by … British military policies and propaganda. Violence in Ireland is a British thing, resistance to that violence, to ensure an end to violence once and for all is an Irish response.[1]

The actions of the Provisional IRA (PIRA) earned them the label of 'the most ruthless terrorist army in the world'.[2] It is therefore unsurprising that the PIRA campaign has attracted much academic attention. Such accounts include historical narratives, investigations into strategy and tactics and examination of the balance between the military and political arms of the Provisional movement.[3] The decommissioning and exit of the Provisional IRA tends to be seen (in the media most obviously) as the neat closing of a historical era, despite the evidence from most global peace processes of continuing violence long beyond ceasefire agreements and peace deals, accompanied by the emergence of new violent 'spoiler groups'.

However, armed groups are still in evidence in Northern Ireland. From April 2011 to March 2012 the Police Service of Northern Ireland (PSNI) recorded 67 shootings and 56 bombings related to the security situation.[4] From 2005, when the Provisional IRA 'went away' until March 2012 there was a total of 528 shootings and 375 bombings, the vast bulk perpetrated by republican dissidents.[5] Militant republican groups that continue to advocate the legitimacy of armed struggle such as Óglaigh na hÉireann (ONH), Continuity IRA (CIRA) and Real IRA (RIRA), operate far below the capabilities of the PIRA, but have developed a limited campaign of violence. This has been mainly at a low level with a few glaring exceptions, the most obvious being the worst atrocity ever in Northern Ireland when the RIRA killed 29 civilians, plus a small number of killings of British Army and PSNI officers and that of a Territorial Army volunteer. Therefore, whilst the Northern Irish peace process is praised for its delivery of a much more peaceful security situation and its political inclusivity, there remains the presence of those who refuse to reject the utility of violence as a *modus operandi* and join an exclusively political process.

This chapter will focus on the origins and strategies of various armed republican factions that emerged before and after the GFA. Analysis will focus on the nature of the threat posed by dissidents as well as communal difference in the perception of this threat and the repercussions this may have for community relations. Critical evaluation will also be given to the historical relevance of armed struggle within the republican tradition.

The origins of armed dissent

Accompanying the GFA was optimism that physical force republicanism might be consigned to history. Much analysis focused on the evolution of the Provisional movement into constitutionalism, followed by assessment of the relegation of armed tactics and the eventual disbandment of the PIRA. Considering the republican propensity to split, especially around the position of armed struggle, there was surprisingly little attention awarded to the possibility of other groups continuing in the militant tradition. The capacity of the PIRA far outweighed that of any other republican faction at the time and it was assumed that it had a near-monopoly on republican force. It was also assumed that the PIRA held the capability of 'dealing' with splinter groups – 'internal housekeeping' as it was described by the Secretary of State at the time of the GFA, Mo Mowlam. Thus although republican splits were evident in 1986 and 1997, eventually leading to the formations of the Continuity and Real IRA, the significance of those splits was not necessarily fully realised at the time.

The threat from dissident groups has remained a consistent backdrop to the transformed constitutional arrangements. In evidence to the House of Commons, Chief Constable of the PSNI from 2002 to 2009 Sir Hugh Orde stated, 'Without question, the intensity has increased. The determination of the main groups, Continuity IRA and Real IRA, is clear by the evidence of the level of attacks and variety of attacks.'[6] Director General of MI5, Jonathan Evans, admitted having an initial evaluation that as time elapsed and the new constitutional arrangements took root, the dissident threat would decline. Yet by 2010, Evans acknowledged:

> we [secret services] have seen a persistent rise in terrorist activity and ambition in Northern Ireland over the last three years. Perhaps we were giving insufficient weight to the pattern of history over the last hundred years which shows that whenever the main body of Irish republicanism has reached a political accommodation and rejoined constitutional politics, a hardliner rejectionist group would fragment off and continue with the so called 'armed struggle'.[7]

There existed a gap in the knowledge of policy makers and security services in understanding these groups. Recently, however, more research on armed dissident republican groups has begun to emerge.[8] Dissident groups are also referred to in the literature as 'ultras'[9] and violent dissident republicans (VDRs).[10] This chapter will focus mainly on the following: the decommissioning of the Irish National Liberation Army (INLA), and the continued use of armed struggle by CIRA, RIRA, ONH and Republican Action Against Drugs (RAAD). This account is not intended to provide insight into the inner working of these covert organisations, but rather to provide an outline into the nature of their activity, aims and objectives and to place them in a historical context.

Dormant dissidence: the case of the Irish National Liberation Army (INLA)

An organisation that remains associated with the label 'dissident' is the Irish Republican Socialist Party (IRSP), despite their armed wing, the INLA, having decommissioned. The IRSP opposes the GFA but declines to back violence, believing it has no utility and no support. The INLA carried out the car bomb attack that killed Conservative politician Airey Neave in March 1979 and also took responsibility for the bombing at the Droppin' Well Bar in County Derry in 1982 that killed eleven soldiers and six civilians. In one of its final acts, in 1997, the organisation killed Billy Wright, leader of the loyalist 'dissident group' the Loyalist Volunteer Force (LVF), inside the Maze Prison. The INLA were described as being ruthless and responsible for the most 'dreadful spectacles' of the troubles.[11]

After a 24-year campaign, the INLA called a ceasefire in August 1998[12] and one year later stated that 'There is no political or moral argument to justify a resumption of the campaign.'[13] In October 2009, INLA confirmed its armed struggle was over and argued that the group's aims would best be advanced through exclusively peaceful political struggle. Despite this announcement and no evidence to suggest that the INLA had been involved in subsequent terrorist activity, the Independent Monitoring Commission (IMC) stated in 2009 that it was still 'a threat' and that it was no less capable of violence than it had been in the recent past and 'remained deeply involved in serious crime, notably extortion'.[14]

Fra Halligan of the IRSP is quite clear in expressing his belief that there is no justification of the continued use of armed struggle:

> What we are saying is that conditions don't exist any longer for armed struggle. The jails are full of young lads facing ten or twenty years. The graveyard could be full of them again and we are saying just hold on. Sit down and talk. Explore, 'is there not a different road to take?'
>
> They do explore that with us but there is a diehard pure republican tradition or tendency out there and that is tunnel vision, and that is my personal belief. It doesn't leave any room for discussion or dialogue … I don't believe that Massereene or Ronan Kerr or Stephen Carroll in Craigavon moved anything one iota.[15]

The IRSP proclaim that 'there is no militarist road to socialism',[16] yet they remain anti-Good Friday Agreement on the basis that it 'copper fastened partition'. Despite the INLA having decommissioned, the IRSP are still labelled as dissidents. Such a label therefore does not take into account the differences between the anti-GFA groups that may or may not engage in military action. The term 'dissident' has been used to describe groups that emerged before and after the GFA, those who focus on community-based action and local concerns, and those who see the benefits of a broad front and those who do not.

Continuing armed struggle

The oldest of anti-GFA armed republican groups, the CIRA was formed long before the climax of the peace process. It emerged as the military wing of RSF, but did not become active until 1994. The group announced their arrival via the newspaper *Saoirse* in February 1994 by releasing a statement and pictures of a 'firing party' in commemoration of the last surviving member elected to the Second Dáil, Tom Maguire.[17] This also coincided with the 75th Anniversary of the First (All Ireland) Dáil Éireann. Such symbolism was a deliberate attempt to directly associate the organisation with Óglaigh na hÉireann as its descendants, or the Irish Republican Army.[18] From the outset, the CIRA presented themselves as traditionally minded and from the same lineage as their political wing, RSF.

In July 1996 the CIRA committed its first attack, detonating a 250 pound car bomb outside a hotel in County Fermanagh. Other attacks followed in Belfast and Derry that same year. The CIRA was accused of playing a role in the 1998 Omagh bombing along with the RIRA (see below).[19] Unlike the RIRA, the CIRA did not declare a ceasefire and vowed to continue a campaign of attacks, including the targeting of the police.[20] The CIRA claimed responsibility for the murder of Constable Stephen Carroll in March 2009 in Craigavon, the first killing of a PSNI officer.

The response from Sinn Féin's Martin McGuinness to this attack and the Real IRA's killing of two British soldiers two days earlier (see below) was to label the perpetrators as 'traitors to the island of Ireland'.[21] The use of the term 'traitor' by McGuinness, on the basis of the lack of mandate for dissidents and the support for the Good Friday Agreement expressed by Irish people was logical yet startling.[22] It positioned Sinn Féin firmly within the constitutional arena (the party's initial statement had merely described the killings of the soldiers as 'wrong' and 'counter-productive') and implied somehow that a previous national mandate for PIRA violence had existed, causing anger amongst dissidents and even some unease within remaining hardline elements within Sinn Féin – the next edition of *An Phoblacht* made no reference to the 'traitors' comment.[23]

By the end of 2009, the IMC reported that the CIRA sought to enhance its capabilities by increasing its numbers through recruitment and stepping-up efforts to train members, including the use and manufacture of explosive devices.[24] The CIRA therefore remains determined to maintain opposition to the political dispensation via the use of violence. The group regards the changes to policing as cosmetic, demonstrated by its political associates (despite denials) RSF's continued use of the old 'RUC' label to describe the PSNI.

In 2010 there were reports of factionalism within the CIRA. A group of CIRA members claimed a new Army Council had been elected, which was described as 'more militant and more Northern based'.[25] In an interview to the *Irish Times* the new, younger CIRA breakaway group described those they had moved away from as the 'old guard' and 'pensioner' leadership.[26] In response a statement released to the newspaper *Saoirse* stated how the demands of the breakaway faction had been refused by the original CIRA leadership who claimed to have dismissed members, including two who previously held senior positions. The statement also claimed that the Army Council was intact and in control whilst warning against others using its name.[27] There was clearly frustration amongst some younger members of the CIRA who appeared keener to promote co-operation with other organisations and labelled the 'old guard' as 'tired, weary, old men who are refusing to hand over the reins'.[28]

The emergence of the Real IRA (RIRA) followed the PIRA's 1997 reinstate-ment of its ceasefire declared three years earlier and fractured in 1996. The PIRA Quartermaster General, Michael McKevitt, resigned and led a breakaway group. McKevitt's wife, Bernadette Sands-McKevitt, the younger sister of Bobby Sands, along with former PIRA volunteer Marian Price, also demonstrated sup-port for the breakaway faction, accompanied by a few other significant former Provisionals.[29] Carrying such republican credentials the breakaway faction had the potential to prove a serious irritant to Sinn Féin. The armed faction that opposed the ceasefire labelled itself Óglaigh na hÉireann. The group later became labelled the Real IRA, when during a road block in South Armagh, 'a few of the lads were making a propaganda video and having a bit of a laugh, telling people that they were the "real" IRA … it's just a soundbite … the group has always been Óglaigh na hÉireann'.[30]

The paramilitary group emerged in parallel with the 32 County Sovereignty Movement. The 32CSM publish statements from the RIRA and report on their activity. Members accept that there is a military track pursued in parallel to a more political, community-based agenda.[31] A 32CSM member explained the relationship when asked about the dynamics between the political front and the RIRA:

It runs alongside the political element. You can't have an armed group and just have an armed group. You have to have political thinking beside it. I'm not saying that the 32 County Sovereignty Movement are the Real IRA, or hand in hand, but we support them and they support what we think.[32]

From late 1997, the RIRA began (without using the title) to plant large bombs in towns. In August 1998 the RIRA opposition to the PIRA ceasefire was made graphically evident by the Omagh bomb, inadequate warnings contributing to a death toll of twenty-nine civilians. In a decisive break, Sinn Féin condemned the bombing, Gerry Adams stating, 'I have condemned it without equivocation. This appalling act was carried out by those opposed to the peace process.'[33] Three days after the Omagh tragedy the RIRA released two statements. The first argued that they had given sufficient warning about the location of the bomb (directions that they claim had then been mistakenly followed and resulted in more harm than intended) and offered apologies to the civilians.[34] The second statement announced a suspension of military operations.[35] Omagh demonstrated the harmful and self-defeating nature of such tactics.

The hiatus of RIRA activity did not last, despite private meetings between the RIRA's part-founder, Martin McKevitt, and the Fianna Fáil government's envoy, Martin Mansergh. In January 2000, the RIRA released a statement via the 32CSM, under the banner of Óglaigh na hÉireann, 'In every generation the Irish people have rejected and challenged Britain's claim to interfere in Ireland's affairs.'[36] This statement was followed up by several incidents, including a bomb explosion underneath Hammersmith Bridge in London. Considering the blast came four years after the PIRA had failed in an attempt to bomb the same bridge, this incident announced the RIRA had returned and Britain could be targeted via the use of similar tactics. In March 2001, the RIRA detonated a car bomb outside the BBC studios in West London and in August the same year carried out a similar action in Ealing Broadway, also in West London.[37]

This was the last time the RIRA launched attacks in Britain, although the desire may remain. As a republican prisoner claimed, 'One bomb in England is worth a thousand in Ireland.'[38] Despite the threat level of a dissident republican attack on the British mainland being raised by the Home Office from 'substantial' to 'severe' in March 2010, at present, the RIRA have failed to prove a capacity to carry out such attacks.[39]

In the decade from 2000 to 2010, the RIRA carried out a sporadic campaign.[40] On 6 March 2009, Chief Constable of the PSNI, Sir Hugh Orde, announced that the threat posed by dissident republicans had reached 'critical level' and was at its highest since 2002.[41] A day later Sappers Mark Quinsey and Patrick Azimkar were killed in a gun attack at the Massereene army barracks. The attack was later claimed by the RIRA.[42] A year later the RIRA claimed responsibility for the bomb attack at MI5 headquarters in Holywood, April 2010. The group may be unable to launch a successful campaign on the British mainland, but they have proved an ability to target high-profile locations, such as army barracks and the secret service headquarters in Northern Ireland. Other targets have included PSNI stations and individual members of the police service. The RIRA have also targeted locations involved in Derry's hosting of the UK City of Culture in 2013 an event viewed as reinforcing Derry's role within the UK.[43]

Since the RIRA's inception, there has been collaboration between the different militant groupings.[44] This was formalised at the end of July 2012 when several republican factions announced they had come together within a unified structure under a single leadership via a statement released to the *Guardian* newspaper.[45] Those republican factions that joined together were the RIRA, RAAD and a coalition of disparate republican groups and are referred to in the media as the 'New IRA'. The groups collectively referred to themselves as the Army Council of the IRA and pledged to pursue a campaign targeting police officers and soldiers, declaring:

> In recent years the establishment of a free and independent Ireland has suffered setbacks due to the failure among the leadership of Irish nationalism and fractures within republicanism…the Irish people have been sold a phoney peace, rubber-stamped by a token legislature in Stormont.[46]

This dissident faction is aware it does not have the capacity to maintain a sustained campaign, stating, 'To go at it full steam would increase momentum short term, but we believe ultimately would fail within a very short period of time.'[47] The actions of the new IRA grouping have been characterised by the calculated shooting of the prison officer David Black in late 2012 as well as the shooting of Kevin Kearney in October 2013, in Alexandra Park, North Belfast. The character of armed republicanism therefore has been sporadic and infrequent yet precise and calculated in its targets.

In reference to dissident groups, Frampton observes that 'the boundaries across these entities often appeared fluid: it was not always easy to tell where one ended and another began'.[48] This is especially true for the RIRA and RAAD. Therefore, is the announcement of a fusion of dissident groupings anything new? Does the announcement of a new coalition represent simply a rebranding exercise or publicity stunt? One of the other groups involved in this announcement is RAAD, an organisation whose actions in seeking community control mean they are often described as being a vigilante group.[49]

The struggle for community control

Republican dissidence has also involved a struggle for community control, a battle for legitimacy in working-class nationalist areas once dominated by the PIRA. Public support for dissident activity is essential for the groups' survival and effectiveness. Throughout the troubles both republican and loyalist paramilitaries provided an alternative to the criminal justice system enforced by the state and employed their own system of punishment as a form of social and political control. In order to maintain dominance and create discipline within the ranks during a period of transition and reform after the GFA, the rate of punishment attacks, as well as the scale of their brutality, increased in comparison to the pre-1997 ceasefire period.[50] This violence takes the form of verbal warnings, exile, physical beatings and shootings for crimes that are criminal (drug dealing) or political (informing) in nature.[51] Beyond the physical aspect of such campaigns these acts are also utilised as a form of community control. However, there is a danger such punishments could be seen as excessive and alienate the perpetrators from the targeted community. To counter the possibility of alienation it is possible to observe the use of 'defensive' propaganda, a strategy that justifies violent actions whilst reducing the loss of support.

> [To] minimise the loss of support that results from such actions, elaborate campaigns are constructed that detail the alleged activities of the target and thus create the conditions in which the republican movement can engage in an act of community repression under the guise of community policing.[52]

Such tactics remain an important aspect of the dissident campaign within working-class communities. John Murphy, a 32CSM member in Cork claimed:

> So, I think that even in the working-class areas such as Cork and Dublin the IRA have taken it upon themselves to execute drug dealers and that went down very well with the people. So, I think then people recognise … you needn't have a vote to have a successful movement.[53]

Similar tactics are also utilised by the armed group RAAD, formed in 2008 and operating mainly in Derry, where activity is greatest in the nationalist/republican areas of the Creggan and the Bogside.[54] RAAD have been accused of building up or playing on hysteria concerning the spread and use of drugs in the local community. In their first interview, in the *Derry Journal* a year after their formation, the group stated:

> Our objectives are very simple. We are determined to rid the local community of these individuals. We view them as career criminals whose activities have ruined the lives of so many young people in the past and we're not prepared to tolerate that any longer.[55]

RAAD has warned numerous young men, accused of drug dealing, to leave the city or face the consequences. From April 2011 to March 2012 there were 33 paramilitary-style shootings, all attributed to republicans, as have been the vast majority of all such shootings since 2007.[56] It is alleged from 2009 to 2012 around 200 men have been forced to flee their homes in the area whilst there have been 85 punishment-style shootings.[57] The group has been responsible for one death. In February 2012 Andrew Allen, from Derry, was shot in Buncrana,

Donegal. Allen had been forced out of Derry after warnings from the group who accused him of being involved in the selling of drugs.

The RAAD campaign is designed to spread concern about the use of drugs within the local community and as a result provide sympathy for the group's actions, in that they are pro-active in the fight against such a threat to the area. The group state:

> There is absolutely no political agenda within our organisation ... Our only aim is to eliminate drug dealers from our society and put an end to them destroying our community. Our only concern is to end the threat posed by the supply of both illegal and prescription drugs, a threat which has already claimed the lives of a number of young people, ruined other lives and torn many families apart. There is no political agenda whatsoever within our organisation.[58]

By making the drugs issue the focal point of their campaign, RAAD also aim to highlight the inaction of others. The group is clear in stating that it does not intend to challenge the peace process on a political level, but is rather contesting Sinn Féin and the police in terms of their standing in the community and their ability to deal with local concerns. A younger member of the 32CSM commented on this inaction when discussing a recent incident where RAAD had shot a seventeen-year-old in the Derry Waterside area. The victim was accused by RAAD of being 'heavily involved' in anti-social behaviour in the district and was subsequently shot in both legs after four men forced their way into his home.[59] The 32CSM member expressed the 'inevitability' of such events occurring:

> Obviously it was terrible he had to get shot in the leg or his mother and father had to watch. But even people have been shot and their brothers and sisters would associate with us and say well they deserved it. It's wrong. I would rather have an Irish police force that could take people to the courts but we don't. We have the militia. They are not Irish they are British.[60]

Such events attempt to usurp the PSNI and Sinn Féin in 'protecting' communities. Therefore, whilst exerting community control by explicitly targeting 'anti-social behaviour', RAAD are simultaneously attempting to undermine the police and their position in the community. Before the announcement of their merger in the 'New' IRA, RAAD increasingly targeted security forces, including the throwing of blast bombs at PSNI vehicles.[61]

The changing nature of armed republicanism: the 'new wave'

In early 2006 the IMC noted the presence of a group in the Strabane area. This group had labelled themselves as Óglaigh na hÉireann (ONH), which translates to Soldiers of Ireland, and was believed to have splintered from the CIRA.[62] The group were responsible for several attacks including those against PSNI officers, members of the District Policing Partnership (DPP) and Strabane PSNI station.[63] The title of ONH was used by the PIRA in the past, but more recently the name had been used by a faction of the RIRA.[64]

It was this faction of the RIRA that emerged in 2005, and claimed to have recruited members from across the spectrum of groups, such as ex-PIRA, INLA and RIRA.[65] This faction has been involved in several attacks upon police officers. In October 2009, a bomb exploded under the car of a female partner of a PSNI dog handler in East Belfast. The target was intended to be her partner.[66] In January 2010 the group claimed responsibility for a car bombing near Randalstown. The target was Constable Peadar Heffron, who was an Irish language specialist for the PSNI and captain of the PSNI GAA team.[67] Heffron sustained critical injuries and as a result had his leg amputated. These targets were deliberate and based on the victims' association to the security forces. After these incidents, 10,000 mirrors were distributed to officers and civilians employed by the police to check under their vehicles.[68]

As a response to the PIRA cessation of 'armed struggle', there appeared a 'new wave' of militant republicanism that seemed harder to define, more fluid in its membership and more sporadic in its attacks. The 'new wave' of armed republican activity from 2007 onwards was connected to Sinn Féin's decision to support the PSNI, the final leg of its constitutional journey in Northern Ireland. It brought some new members (and expertise) to the dissident groups and helped bring closer co-operation in terms of membership, resources and know-how. The attack at Massereene barracks in 2009, which resulted in the death of two British soldiers, indicated a pooling of resources in terms of guns, bullets and gunmen.[69] It is therefore necessary to question whether dissidents pose more of a threat now they are pooling their resources, or does it just confirm what was already known, that the membership between some military groups is flexible and pragmatically fluid?

Whilst the announcement of a merger in July 2012 between certain groups formalised structures, the arrangement represented little new. However, it did highlight the changing nature of armed dissident republicanism. Even combined, the groups do not possess the capacity to pursue a sustained campaign, yet this limited capacity is acknowledged internally. Michael Gallagher from the 32CSM observes:

> Armed republicanism, i.e. the IRA campaign can resist British rule in Ireland. Now forcing a British withdrawal? I can't see it happening. But it can make it uncomfortable in Ireland, you know, resist … People decided to resist and armed republicanism is an option.[70]

Despite having limited capacity, by engaging in sporadic attacks, groups such as the RIRA, RAAD, ONH and CIRA are at least capable of challenging normalisation. Within the modern context armed republicanism is unable to pursue a sustained campaign or pose a direct threat to the current status quo, but it can attempt to destabilise it through sporadic attacks. A republican prisoner commented on this nature of a campaign, 'They pop up, do something, and disappear again. That's why it's so good.'[71] It would therefore be unwise for the security services to attempt to understand these groups purely in terms of their capacity to fight their way to a standstill or in a belief they can create British withdrawal. Rather, militant republicanism's short- and medium-term goals are to resist current political arrangements and stop Northern Ireland embedding as an entirely secure, peaceful and normalised political entity. A 32CSM member articulated the hope that the limited campaign could be further developed:

> Well at the moment they think we are criminals … What we have to do [is] create a revolutionary movement and align everyone in the country to that mindset, that occupation is wrong. Especially as the status quo at the minute is that it is OK to have two states and it's wonderful. That's why the IRA are shooting people and resisting.[72]

When asked further about what armed republicanism can achieve that unarmed republicanism cannot, resistance was again key to this rationale:

> To me from my personal point of view unarmed republicanism is pointless because of the British. You could have 10,000 people tomorrow on a march and no-one would take us on. But when you blow up a courthouse or you shoot a member of the armed forces they have to react. They have to react because everyone starts looking in and saying what is going on. You can have as many pickets as you want but on their own, it's nothing, they are not going to achieve anything … You have to stand up to the mark; do you know what I mean? Resist.[73]

Whilst violent dissident republicanism is often discredited for lacking capacity and support[74] there is realism amongst these groups in terms of what they can and cannot achieve. For them, like many republican generations before, resistance is viewed as more alluring than what they state as the alternative, surrender. As a republican prisoner put it:

> Well for me armed republicanism can get the point across. I think that people see you as more willing to resist. Whereas unarmed republicanism to me is a surrender. As, 'well then OK, we will just do as we are told'. Whereas armed republicanism says 'we are here, we are ready to fight'.[75]

Whilst there is realism that the dissident armed campaign cannot 'fight the Brits out of Ireland', there is also the presence of romanticism in attempting to resist the current arrangements.

Keeping the flame alive

Rather than marking their foundations within the recent republican divisions, dissident groups tend to draw their credence from the republican tradition and claims to being the IRA. The continued use of violence is presented by dissident groups as a continuation of the Irish revolutionary military tradition with its history in the Easter Rising and the War of Independence (hence the confusion over the title of Óglaigh na hÉireann, which has been used by various groups including the PIRA). Armed groups portray their existence as continuation of the armed tradition as opposed to a struggle that is detached from the historical continuity of the IRA. Such continuity offers credibility, allowing dissidents to employ the credence attached to the claim of being the IRA, reinforced by a long historical tradition.

As a result, there exists an element of wanting to 'keep the flame alive' with the continued use of violence by dissident republicanism. This aspect focuses again on remembrance and history, especially in terms of remembering those generations that lost their lives fighting for Irish freedom. Such an interpretation suggests that by surrendering weapons and ending an armed campaign for less than a united Ireland is treacherous, a betrayal not only of republican principles but of the previous generations of the republican dead. A member of RSF articulated such sentiment:

> Well you think of those men and women who aspired to getting their country free and it is important to remember all that. It was a hard slog and a lot of them paid the price with their lives and everything else and will do in the future until we acquire a united Ireland. I mean the unfortunate thing about it is that there is a price to pay; there always will be a price to pay.[76]

Such a statement typifies the use of martyrdom within modern day republicanism, especially within RSF. Retelling the hardship suffered by republicans has the potential to legitimise actions through the prism of the past, emphasising the need for endurance and keeping the flame alive no matter what the odds are against them. Therefore, a dominant theme for militant dissident republicanism is that of no compromise. Whilst this theme of historical continuity runs through all dissident groups, it is represented in varying degrees. Those who broke away in 1986 are far more likely to stress the historical significance of an armed campaign, even regularly claiming, via detailed features in *Saoirse*, that Operation Harvest, the failed 1956–62 Border Campaign, did have utility in keeping the struggle alive. The 32CSM, aligned with the RIRA, focuses on the centrality of armed struggle and the right to bear arms as a republican principle. As the following statement from a 32CSM member demonstrates, the right to pursue an armed campaign is central to republican principles:

I mean they [Sinn Féin] have totally turned their back on republican principles. I mean to me personally, just to be a republican, even just to be considered a republican the first thing you have to do is recognise the right to bear arms against a repressive force. It doesn't matter if it is a sustained campaign, but the first thing you have to do is recognise the right to bear arms against an oppressive force … individuals need to have the right to protect themselves against the British forces where and when the opportunity arises.[77]

Here it is acts such as the decommissioning of weapons and being unable to form a defence against a 'repressive force' that are betrayals. RSF's Des Dalton claims that, whatever differences exist between groups, 'resistance' may always exist in some degree to British rule in Northern Ireland:

Whether Republican Sinn Féin was saying this or not, if Republican Sinn Féin went out of existence in the morning it wouldn't change the fact that there would be a section of people there who were not prepared to accept British rule. I think history has shown that, I think in every generation as long as there is British rule in Ireland there is always going to be a section who are prepared to resist that.[78]

Public perceptions of the dissident republican threat

Dissident groups are commonly referred to as small, insignificant and possessing an intent to disrupt the peace that outweighs their capacity.[79] Their threat is often judged in terms of numbers and capacity. The result is the downplaying of any tactics or purpose. Thus Sinn Féin's Gerry Kelly, in a typical assertion, insists that 'they have no strategy and their aims are as clear as mud'.[80] Yet parallel to the downplaying of the dissident republican armed capacity was the raising of the threat level of a dissident attack from 'substantial' to 'severe' and MI5 allocating a growing proportion of its resources to the threat.[81] It is logical to assess the threat of armed dissident republicanism by the modest physical force capabilities of the groups themselves. However, it is reductionist to judge the problems posed by political violence solely by the depth and use of armed force. Rather than focusing on capacity to measure threat level, it should be seen that it is the kind of threat that terrorism poses that makes it terrorising.[82] In other words, the threat of a group should not necessarily be measured merely by their direct capacity and ability to strike at will, but also by the perception of that threat.

In broader research evaluating the nature of political violence, the perceived threat level differs depending on various factors, the most important of which is whether group objectives can be contained and the threat reduced. As Zarakol notes, 'claims to legitimacy that can be accommodated within the modern state system's ordering principles are the least ontologically threatening'.[83] Consequently, the threat is greater when the current arrangements cannot accommodate the group's objectives. According to such an analysis a change in the political system is not necessarily enough to secure the end of terrorist activity. Thus Wilkinson asserted that: 'In political terms the Good Friday Agreement created a unique opportunity to build a lasting peace ... But, sadly, politics is not enough to secure the end of terrorist conflicts. It is important to recognize that the new agreement was only a document.'[84]

Unionists continue to hold an image of the 'IRA bogeyman', always present in the psyche throughout the history of the northern state, even though the major armed conflict of 1970–97 might be seen as an era of exceptionalism, a deviation from a more peaceful norm. In the 2010 Northern Ireland General Election Survey, the perceived threat from dissidents was seen as much greater by the Protestant community.[85] A majority (53 per cent) of Protestants believed the dissidents constituted a major threat; only 17 per cent of Catholics thought likewise. Few in both communities thought the dissidents offered 'no threat'.[86] Whilst dissident violence will not achieve a united Ireland in terms of sending the 'Brits home', it is also about perception. In creating a perceived threat, dissidents have the potential to prevent the impression of Northern Ireland being a normalised, consolidated state. Therefore, in response to the rhetoric that 'violence will not work', and that 'armed struggle will not achieve a united Ireland', dissidents are aware they are not going to fight the British Army 'into the sea' but they can pose a *perceived* threat, whilst the asymmetry in threat perception is potentially damaging for community relations

Conclusion

The scale of change within Sinn Féin and enforced dismemberment of the PIRA meant that it was inevitable that dissent would emerge; the surprise lies in the lack of anticipation. A broad spectrum of small groups have emerged resistant to compromise, still maintaining, against much evidence, that an armed campaign possesses some utility. Armed republicanism does not have the domestic or international support (ideological, financial or political) it possessed during the PIRA campaign, capacity and volunteers are much more limited and the range of attack narrow. However, groups have demonstrated an ability to adapt to these restrictions where attacks are more likely to be localised and targets are specific. Despite the low level of campaign, all groups that engage in armed struggle have to attempt to justify and rationalise their actions. The use of force within communities is framed as a form of protection. Groups such as RAAD that emphasise the need for community control by targeting specific individuals, are able to highlight the inadequacy of the state, whose legitimacy is any case rejected, in responding to issues such as drug dealing and anti-social behaviour.

It is also possible to explore the rationalisation of force in terms historical precedence. Historical aspects such as the credence attached to the name of IRA and the desire to keep the flame of armed republicanism alive play a significant role within the rationalisation of dissident activity. The mainstream discourse attempts to condemn the actions of groups such as ONH, CIRA, RIRA and RAAD by claiming they have no mandate in reference to their lack of public support. However, whilst this might damage the broader public perception of dissident groups, such arguments about lacking a mandate are somewhat futile in preventing the continuation of armed struggle by some groups. These groups take their legitimacy from the refuge of the past and republican history. For them, republicanism does not, and never has, needed a mandate from the living.

Notes

1 Tarlach McConnell, interview with author, Portlaoise Prison, 8 March 2010.
2 J. Adams, R. Morgan and A. Bambridge, *Ambush: The War Between the SAS and the IRA* (London, Pan Books, 1998), p. 21. The claim is highly contentious however. The LTTE (Tamil Tigers) in Sri Lanka, for example, was classed by many states as a 'terrorist group' and used a far higher level of violence than the IRA, even possessing its own naval and air units.
3 See for example, R. English, *Armed Struggle: A History of the IRA* (Basingstoke, Macmillan, 2003); J. Augusteijn, 'Political Violence and Democracy: An Analysis of the Tensions within Irish Republican Strategy, 1914–2002', *Irish Political Studies* 18, no. 1 (2003), pp. 1–26; J. Bowyer Bell, *The Secret Army: The IRA* (Oxon, Transaction Publishers, 2003); M. L. R. Smith, *Fighting for Ireland?: The Military Strategy of the Irish Republican Movement* (London, Routledge, 1995); M. O'Doherty, *The Trouble with Guns* (Belfast, Blackstaff Press, 1998); A. Richards, 'Terrorist Groups and Political Fronts: The IRA, Sinn Féin, the Peace Process and Democracy', *Terrorism and Political Violence* 13, no. 4 (2001), pp. 72–89; M. Von Tagen Page and M. L. R. Smith, 'War By Other Means: The Problem of Political Control in Irish Republican Strategy', *Armed Forces and Society* 27, no. 1 (2000), pp. 79–104; R. Munck, 'Irish Republicanism: Containment or New Departure', in A. O'Day (ed.), *Terrorism Laboratory: The Case of Northern Ireland* (Aldershot, Dartmouth Publishing, 1995); K. Rafter, *Sinn Féin 1905–2005: In the Shadow of Gunmen* (Dublin, Gill and Macmillan, 2005); T. Shanahan, *The Provisional Irish Republican Army and the Morality of Terrorism* (Edinburgh, Edinburgh University Press, 2009); E. Moloney, *A Secret History of the IRA* (London, Penguin, 2002).
4 Police Service of Northern Ireland, *Police Recorded Security Situation Statistics: Annual Report Covering the Period 1st April 2011 – 31st March 2012* (Belfast, Northern Ireland Statistics and Research Agency, May 2012).
5 *Ibid.*
6 Oral Evidence of Chief Constable Sir Hugh Orde OBE, Assistant Chief Constable Judith Gillespie and Chief Inspector Sam Cordner, House of Commons Northern Ireland Select Committee (HC 1174–i), 5 November 2008, available at www.parliament.the-stationery-office.co.uk/pa/cm200708/cmselect/cmniaf/c1174–i/c117402.htm.

7   *Daily Telegraph*, 'Jonathan Evans' terrorism speech', 17 September 2010.

8   J. Tonge, '"They haven't gone away you know". Irish Republican "Dissidents" and "Armed Struggle", *Terrorism and Political Violence* 16, no. 3 (2004), pp. 671–693; J. Evans and J. Tonge, 'Menace without Mandate? Is There Any Sympathy for Dissident Irish Republicanism in Northern Ireland?' *Terrorism and Political Violence* 24, no. 1 (2012), pp. 61–78; M. Frampton, *Legion of the Rearguard: Dissident Irish Republicanism* (Dublin, Irish Academic Press, 2011); J. Horgan and J. Morrison, 'Here to Stay? The Rising Threat of Violent Dissident Republicanism in Northern Ireland', *Terrorism and Political Violence* 23, no. 4 (2011), pp. 642–669; A. Sanders, *Inside the IRA: Dissident Republicans and the War for Legitimacy* (Edinburgh, Edinburgh University Press, 2011); R. White, 'Structural Identity Theory and the Post Recruitment Activism of Irish Republicans: Persistence, Splits, and Dissidents in Social Movement Organizations', *Social Problems* 57, no. 3 (2010), pp. 341–370; A. McIntyre, 'Of Myths and Men: Dissent within Republicanism and Loyalism', in A. Edwards and S. Bloomer (eds), *Transforming the Peace Process in Northern Ireland: From Terrorism to Democratic Politics* (Dublin, Irish Academic Press, 2008), pp. 114–132.

9   Tonge, '"They haven't gone away you know"', pp. 671–693.

10 Horgan and Morrison, 'Here to Stay?', pp. 642–669.

11 Bowyer Bell, *The Secret Army*, p. 535.

12 *BBC News*, 'UK and Ireland welcome INLA ceasefire', 23 August 1998.

13 *BBC News*, 'INLA declares war is over', 8 August 1999.

14 *Twenty-Second Report of the Independent Monitoring Commission* (London, The Stationery Office, 2009), p. 9.

15 Fra Halligan, interview with author, Belfast, 1 May 2012.

16 IRSP, Republican Socialist Programme for Ireland (Belfast, IRSP, n.d.), p. 6.

17 *Saoirse*, February 1994.

18 For further discussion on the republican legitimacy associated with Tom Maguire see chapter 4.

19 *Independent*, 'Omagh bomb legal victory: the men behind worst atrocity of the Troubles', 9 June 2009.

20 *Irish Times*, 'The Continuity IRA pledges attacks', 12 December 1998.

21 *News Letter*, 'Murderers are traitors to Ireland – McGuinness', 10 March 2009.

22 For further discussion on McGuinness' use of the word 'traitor' in this speech see S. A. Whiting, '"The Discourse of Defence": "Dissident" Irish Republicanism and the "Propaganda War"', *Terrorism and Political Violence* 24, no. 3 (2012), pp. 483–503.

23 See *An Phoblacht*, 12 March 2009.

24 *Twenty-Second Report of the Independent Monitoring Commission* (London, The Stationery Office, 2010), p. 9.

25 *Irish Times*, 'CIRA leaders deny ousting claim', 7 July 2010.

26 *Irish Times*, 'Militant faction claims it has taken over leadership of the CIRA', 28 July 2010.

27 *Saoirse*, 'Army Council intact and in control', June 2010.

28 *Irish Times*, 'Militant faction claims it has taken over leadership of the CIRA', 28 July 2010.

29 Frampton, *Legion of the Rearguard*, pp. 98–100.

30 32CSM member, Dublin, 26 March 2010, cited in Sanders, *Inside the IRA*, p. 209.
31 See chapter 4 for more insight into the balance between politics and armed struggle for the 32CSM.
32 32CSM member, interview with author, Derry.
33 Gerry Adams, Keynote Statement on the Current State of the Peace Process, 1 September 1998, Conflict Archive in Northern Ireland (CAIN), available at www.cain.ulst.ac.uk/events/peace/docs/ga1998.htm, accessed 9 August 2012.
34 *Irish News*, 'First Statement issued by the "real" IRA', 18 August 1998, www.cain.ulst.ac.uk/events/peace/docs/rira18898a.htm, accessed 9 August 2012.
35 *Irish News*, 'Second Statement issued by the "real" IRA', 18 August 1998, www.cain.ulst.ac.uk/events/peace/docs/rira18898b.htm, accessed 9 August 2012.
36 *Sovereign Nation*, 'For immediate release: statement by Óglaigh na hÉireann', 1 January 2000.
37 *BBC News*, 'Bomb Blast outside BBC', 4 March 2001.
38 Independent Republican Prisoner A, Portlaoise Prison, 16 July 2010.
39 See *BBC News*, 'Irish terror attack a "strong possibility"', 25 September 2010.
40 For timeline of armed activity, see appendix of Frampton, *Legion of the Rearguard*.
41 M. Frampton, *The Return of the Militants: Violent Dissident Republicanism. A Policy Report for The International Centre for the Study of Radicalisation and Political Violence* (London, ICRS, 2010), p. 43.
42 Henry McDonald, *Guardian*, 'Real IRA claims murder of soldiers in Northern Ireland', 8 May 2009.
43 *Guardian*, 'Real IRA blamed for Derry bomb', 13 October 2011, available at www.guardian.co.uk/uk/2011/oct/13/bomb-explodes-derry-northern-ireland.
44 Frampton, Legion of the Rearguard, p. 93.
45 *Guardian*, 'Republican dissidents join forces to form a new IRA', 26 July 2012.
46 *Guardian*, 'New IRA: full statement by the dissident "Army Council"', 26 July 2012.
47 Brian Rowan in the *Belfast Telegraph*, 'Dissidents: interview with terror splinter group', 3 November 2010.
48 Frampton, *Legion of the Rearguard*, p. 246.
49 See for example, *Belfast Telegraph*, 'Fears mount after police uncover RAAD weapons', 16 July 2012.
50 N. Jarman, 'From War to Peace? Changing Patterns of Violence in Northern Ireland, 1990–2003', *Terrorism and Political Violence* 16, no. 3 (2004), pp. 420–438.
51 See A. Silke, 'Rebel's Dilemma: The Changing Relationship between the IRA, Sinn Féin and Paramilitary Vigilantism in Northern Ireland', *Terrorism and Political Violence*, 11, no. 1 (1999), pp. 55–93.
52 K. Sarma, 'Defensive Propaganda and the IRA: Political Control in Republican Communities', *Studies in Conflict and Terrorism* 30, no. 12 (2007), p. 1,074.
53 John Murphy, interview with author, Cork, 2 March 2011.
54 See Frampton, *The Return of the Militants: Violent Dissident Republicanism*.
55 *Derry Journal*, 'Only way to eradicate drugs scourge is to remove the dealers', 18 August 2009.
56 Police Service of Northern Ireland, *Police Recorded Security Situation Statistics: Annual Report covering the period 1st April 2011 – 31st March 2012.*

57 See John Lindsay, quoted in the *Guardian*, 'Derry: fear and republican vigilantes stalk new city of culture', 13 May 2012; *RTÉ News: Prime Time*, 'Shooting by appointment', 22 May 2012; *BBC News*, 'Two men in custody after major PSNI operation against RAAD', 13 July 2012.

58 *Derry Journal*, 'Only way to eradicate drugs scourge is to remove the dealers', 18 August 2009.

59 *Derry Journal*, 'RAAD Claim Waterside Gun Attack', 19 October 2009.

60 Joe Barr, interview with author, Derry, 8 March 2010.

61 *Derry Journal*, 'RAAD Targets PSNI Vehicle', 13 August 2012.

62 *Sixteenth Report of the Independent Monitoring Commission* (London, The Stationery Office, 2005), p. 14.

63 *Seventeenth Report of the Independent Monitoring Commission* (London, The Stationery Office, 2007), p. 9.

64 See P. M. Currie and M. Taylor (eds), *Dissident Irish Republicanism* (London, Continuum, 2011), pp. 14–15; *Twenty-Second Report of the Independent Monitoring Commission*, p. 7. By 2009 the IMC announced it would no longer use the name ONH to refer to the Strabane-based group.

65 B. Rowan, in *Belfast Telegraph*, 'Dissidents: interview with terror splinter group', 3 November 2010.

66 *Belfast Telegraph*, 'Bomb allegedly was the work of dissidents', 21 October 2009, available at www.belfasttelegraph.co.uk/community-telegraph/east-belfast/bomb-allegedly-was-the-work-of-dissidents-14537754.html, accessed 29 August 2012.

67 *BBC News*, 'Injured officer Peadar Heffron regains consciousness', 24 January 2010, www.news.bbc.co.uk/1/hi/northern_ireland/8477845.stm, accessed 29 August 2012.

68 *Telegraph*, 'Oglaigh na hEireann profile: police issued with bomb mirrors to counter splinter group', 4 April 2010.

69 See Brian Rowan, *Guardian*, 'Analysis: coalition of terror may talk big but it cannot deliver', 31 July 2012.

70 Michael Gallagher, interview with author, Derry, 29 January 2010.

71 Independent Republican Prisoner A, interview with author, Portlaoise Prison, 16 July 2010.

72 32CSM member, interview with author.

73 Ibid.

74 Sinn Féin, 'Dissidents behind destruction at New Lodge bonfire', 9 August 2012, available at www.sinnfein.ie/contents/23927, accessed 31 August 2012.

75 Independent Republican Prisoner A, interview with author, Portlaoise Prison, 16 July 2010.

76 RSF member, interview with author, Belfast, 21 October 2011.

77 32CSM member, interview with author.

78 Des Dalton, interview with author, Dublin, 21 October 2011.

79 See Jon Tonge, cited in the *Scotsman*, 'Peter Geoghegan: New IRA same old stance', 1 August 2012; Andrew Sanders, cited in *Daily Telegraph*, 'A handshake for peace, but discord in Northern Ireland remains', 29 June 2012.

80 Gerry Kelly, cited in *An Phoblacht*, '"Dissidents" cannot achieve a united Ireland, says Sinn Féin's Gerry Kelly', 27 July 2012.

81 See *The Economist*, 'The curse of the conflict junkies', 2 December 2010.
82 A. Zarakol, 'What Makes Terrorism Modern? Terrorism, Legitimacy, and the International System', *Review of International Studies* 37, no. 5 (2011), pp. 2,311–2,336.
83 *Ibid.*, p. 2,315.
84 P. Wilkinson, 'Politics, Diplomacy and Peace Processes: Pathways Out of Terrorism?', *Terrorism and Political Violence* 11, no. 4 (1999), p. 71.
85 See chapter 4 for further discussion of the survey findings, results available at www.liv.ac.uk/politics/staff-pages/ESRCSurvey/index.htm, accessed 4 March 2012.
86 J. Tonge, M. Braniff, T. Hennessey, J. W. McAuley and S. A. Whiting, *The Democratic Unionist Party: From Protest to Power* (Oxford, Oxford University Press, 2014).

7

Spoiling the peace?

Northern Ireland is often presented as a model of conflict management in terms of its DDR (Disarmament, Demobilisation and Reintegration) processes and its political progress, a rare example of a functioning consociation.[1] Yet dissent over the terms and conditions of a peace agreement is a common feature within any peace settlement. As Darby explains:

> Disaffection within paramilitary organisations is perhaps the most obvious threat to peace processes. Such organisations are rarely monoliths presented by their opponents; rather they are complex organisms performing a variety of functions and providing an umbrella for different interests.[2]

Those who use violence to undermine negotiated peace, often referred to as 'spoilers', can be identified in almost all peace processes. There is a tendency to draw on international comparisons when discussing the Northern Irish model of peace negotiations, particularly when considering how parties in conflict elsewhere can be brought into the political process and abandon their weapons. What features less in those international comparisons is the emergence of spoiler groups, dissenting from the emergent political consensus and reverting to more 'traditional' modes of operation. Despite the obvious successes of its peace process and the understandable determination of local politicians and press to construct a positive narrative, Northern Ireland has not been an area of exceptionalism. Spoilers were present even before the Good Friday Agreement was signed. Given the claims to historical longevity and to ownership of the IRA title the emergence of spoiler groups was arguably even more likely in the Northern Irish case than in other conflicts.

This chapter will discuss how these groups attempt to justify the continuation of armed struggle in spite of the peace process. It will do this by discussing the perceived utility of violence, drawing partly on existing theories of dissident groups or 'spoilers'. This is in order to answer what role armed struggle, in its limited form, might play for dissidents. Secondly, attention will turn to considering the contextual variables and 'root causes' of violence such as the impact of the economy and state counter measures.

Contextualising movement from violence: the spoiler debate

The post-GFA context now finds Northern Ireland the subject of inspiration for peace processes in other conflict areas, most especially, but far from exclusively, the Basque region. President Obama paid tribute to the peace process during a visit to the Republic of Ireland, stating how the reconciliation in the North provided hope to other areas, demonstrating that peace is attainable even in unlikely places, such the Middle East.[3] As an example of the attempts at peace process policy transfer, in 2007 Martin McGuinness and the DUP's Jeffrey Donaldson attended talks in Finland with Iraqi politicians to discuss principles of inclusivity and non-violence. The recommendations made are described as containing clear comparisons to the Mitchell Principles on non-violence, which set the context for negotiations towards the Good Friday Agreement.[4] In addition, directly after the signing of the GFA a cross-party delegation of Northern Irish politicians held talks in Spain on whether their experiences could be adapted to resolve the Basque conflict. In October 2011, the Basque separatist group ETA called a ceasefire a few days after a conference attended by Northern Irish politicians urging them to lay down their weapons.[5]

In the search for solutions to conflict elsewhere Northern Ireland is often presented as a successful model for others to follow, especially in terms of negotiating with paramilitaries to put down their weapons. Inclusion in the peace talks served as a carrot to incentivise co-operation, the abandonment of violence and the continuation of peaceful means. Providing a space for paramilitaries at the negotiating table is vital to any peace process. As O'Kane argues, 'key to successful inclusion can be identifying the players in the violent groups who may be more moderate than the wider group they belong to and therefore potential partners for peace. Groups are not homogenous.'[6] Such a point highlights the importance of inclusion in reference to 'violent groups', but also underlines the problem that these groups are not necessarily politically or ideologically cohesive. There is a need to consider those who do not necessarily agree with the compromises attached to any peace process and how this shapes dissident groups in Northern Ireland.

When violence ends, the policy agenda shifts rapidly from military containment towards addressing a new set of problems beyond principles of non-violence. These include incorporating ex-paramilitaries in political negotiations, and how to handle such sensitive issues as amnesties, political prisoners, the decommissioning of weapons and the policing of divided societies.[7] These sensitive issues within a negotiated settlement often produce leaders or factions who are unsatisfied with the outcome. As Stedman notes, 'Even the best designed settlements must be prepared for violence from leaders and organisations who decide that the kind of peace in question is not in their interest.'[8] Indeed violence 'precedes peace processes and continues as an unavoidable background during them'.[9]

Peace processes create spoilers who perceive their political interests as being undermined by accommodations falling short of traditional goals. Having invested heavily in armed struggle, there may be a desire to continue this path. Stedman identifies spoilers as being inside or outside the process. An inside spoiler 'signs a peace agreement, signals a willingness to implement a settlement, and yet fails to fulfil key obligations to the agreement'.[10] Inside spoilers utilise strategies of stealth and are willing to keep the peace process going as long as it is beneficial to them. Outside spoilers use strategies of violence and are 'outside parties who are excluded from a peace process or excluded themselves'.[11]

The utility of spoiler theories is to allow comparisons between conflict areas to 'evaluate the appropriateness and effectiveness of different strategies of spoiler management'.[12] The literature on spoiler groups and spoiler management focuses on creating a typology for categorising the different actors based on their motivations and tactics. Spoiler management is therefore set in context, asking important questions such as: How might preventative action be taken? How have these renegade groups emerged? Are there strong structural determinants? What do they want to achieve?

However, what is distinct in terms of the spoiler debate in relation to dissident republicanism is the lack of consideration for the historical determinism used as a justificatory force that drives militant groups. Considering the scale of change within Sinn Féin and the historical propensity for the republican movement to split, it was inevitable that during the Northern Irish peace process dissent would emerge. For the majority within Sinn Féin and the PIRA, agreeing to the GFA represented the evolution of tactical considerations and a natural development in order to adjust to contextual realities.[13] However, for others this revision went too far and indicated the desertion of principles that are fundamental to republicanism as an ideology.[14] It signified a betrayal of previous generations who lost their lives fighting for Irish freedom. The works of Stedman and of Darby and Mac Ginty are useful in explaining opposition to peace processes and resistance to accommodation. Spoiler group theories provide useful criteria in managing the risk of spoilers emerging; such as high inclusivity, strong leadership and coercion to deter or alter unacceptable spoiler behaviour.[15] The inevitability of spoilers is recognised in all peace processes, but such groups may be containable.

Spoiler theories require considerable contextual adjustment for the Northern Irish case, which had an additional obstacle for negotiators. Republicanism has a long tradition of armed struggle that other groups involved in peace negotiations elsewhere may not possess to such a degree. Other organisations such as the Tamil Tigers, ETA and Hamas all have traditions and offer a historical narrative of their own struggles, but none can base their creation as far back as the IRA, whose own antecedents arguably can be traced back to 1798. In addition, spoiler theories assume a fresh challenge to peace. The Northern Irish case relies upon historical myth-making as justification for armed struggle and determination to acquire rights of ownership to a famous 'brand name' – the IRA. Such historical validation is highlighted in the following comment from a 32CSM member:

> People only listen to the likes of Adams and that saying that they [dissidents] have no support. The IRA, it never needed the acknowledgement from people … The leaders of 1916, they were spat on by the people of Dublin as they were marched through the streets with Dublin people waving Union Jacks in their face. The IRA is always legitimate as long as there is a British occupation in this country. That can never be taken. People say it's boring, it's the same old spiel. It is the same old spiel, but it is the same old situation.[16]

The memory evoked by republican movements is appropriated to shape a sense of belonging, carve out an identity and legitimise the present.[17] Often these symbols, situations of remembrance and commemoration, become distorted as a new political or ideological setting urges a new emphasis or different interpretation of this narrative. As a result, remembering has the potential to reveal a conception of the present, as the past is selected and redefined to fit the current context. There is a danger that the over-indulgence in history interprets republicanism as impervious to contextual influences, and fails to respond adequately to changed material conditions or political circumstances. However, to ignore the importance of history completely would obscure any possibility of understanding the forces behind the phenomenon of dissent within Irish republicanism. History and remembrance have a justificatory service and need to be seen in this sense; a useful tool in which to frame and justify actions and beliefs.

A key purpose of the politics of war memory is to strengthen the bonds between those inside the organisation whilst connecting to departed comrades. It also has the potential to glorify the sacrifice of past republican militants. Militant dissident groups today therefore define the hardship suffered by republicans throughout history as martyrdom. The commemoration of such endurance has the potential to maintain support via emotional rhetoric and supposed 'lessons of history' for continuing armed struggle. Commemorations provide a highly emotive tool for younger generations or new members. As a result, suffering or imprisonment is not necessarily viewed as a defeat but as a continuing phase of the struggle.

History provides useful lessons and rhetoric to justify the continuation of armed struggle despite the peace process. A mandate for such action is therefore justified as likely to be received retrospectively. The 'spoiler debate' does not account for the historical determinism underpinning republicanism; yet this is not to assume the irrelevance of contextual realities such as the nature and tactics of the security forces, public opprobrium, or economics. This chapter will continue to discuss these contextual factors and the evolving state security response.

Cycle of violence: action and response

In order to consider the reasoning and justifications behind the continued use of violence by some republican factions it is necessary to explore the situation 'on the ground', including the nature of the state's security response to dissident republicanism in Northern Ireland. Studies exploring the state response to political challenges in the form of dissent and rebellious insurgency find that when an authority is challenged by violence, it engages in some form of repressive action often responding with force.[18] This serves as a stimulus to the mobilisation of its challengers leading to a fresh armed response which in turn provides further provocation for state action. This cyclical state–violent actor dynamic has been presented as a cycle of crisis and response (see figure 2).

The result of this cyclical trend is therefore the perpetuation of action and reaction, as is the case in Northern Ireland. Dalton, from RSF contextualises this dynamic below:

> Our history if you like is a cycle of conflict. It is a cycle of resistance followed by repression, followed by an attempt at pacification be it the various agreements that we have had going right back to 1921 and even before that whereby there have been attempts made to pacify a sizeable section of the population. What more than often happens is that the cycle just begins and repeats itself again, it just continues on.[19]

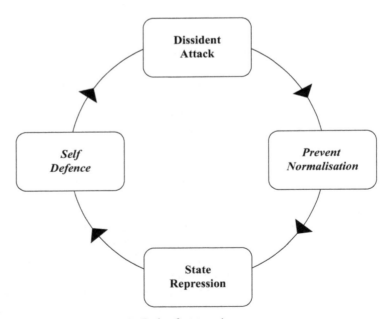

2 Cycle of crisis and response

It is a cycle of violence where each side blames the other for the crisis which leads to their response. The fundamental downfall of the crisis response model is the indeterminable question of which side represents the crisis and which the response. Whilst this model may not be able to determine the catalyst of the conflict it does prove useful when considering the impact of certain government policy and how the state attempts to conclude cycles of violence.[20]

Much of the debate focusing on how states should respond to armed groups centres around whether coercive or conciliatory policies should be pursued in response to violence. The logic in using coercive tactics is that the use of harsh policies to punish armed groups would deter future acts. The overarching rationale with this approach is that when states respond aggressively they develop a reputation for being tough on terrorism and deter further violence; whilst those states that do not respond forcefully are seen as giving in to demands, and develop a reputation for being weak.[21]

Alternatively, states can adopt a more conciliatory approach by focusing on the root causes of violence in an effort to reduce the 'incentives' to use terrorism. This approach accepts that certain conditions such as poverty, political grievance, social inequality and exclusion encourage armed activity where failure to understand these conditions may result in unsuccessful counter-terrorism policies.[22] Whilst hostile state responses may perpetuate the cycle of violence the aim of addressing these causal factors is to remove any underlying justification for resisting the authority of the state.

The economics of peace

The issue of causality between economic performance and terrorism is multifaceted. For example, whilst terrorism may have a negative influence on inward investment, economic factors may also play an important part in explaining the causes of terrorism. Economic activity is affected by the reduction in international trade and investment, the disruption of tourism flows and the relocation of resources away from private investment.[23] Even in advanced western countries the uneven nature of economic growth is able to fuel social and political unrest.[24] Periods of downturn result in fewer economic opportunities and when collective frustration within communities or areas of society over economic discontent surfaces, political violence is more likely to emerge.[25] But how does socio-economic context impact 'dissident' groups? Economic stability and social mobility tend to suppress any appetite for militarism. According to such an analysis, in urban Catholic areas, where support for the PIRA and Sinn Féin traditionally emerged, 'dissident' groups can no longer capitalise on socio-economic inequalities, which prevents them gaining a strong foothold in such areas.

Whilst it is difficult to quantify the effects of the troubles on the Northern Irish economy the persistence of internal unrest disrupts the rate of social and economic change, distorting both employment and investment patterns as well as constraining the ambit of urban restructuring.[26] In societies of deep-rooted and protracted conflict external funding has the potential to initiate dialogue between communities and encourage new relationships. The intention of such funding is that economic assistance will create an environment conducive to peace building by providing the resources for the stimulation of constructive inter-group contact in an attempt to promote cross-community engagement, encourage local networks and reduce social marginalisation.

In theory, the benefits generated by external economic assistance from the supra-national institutions, such as the European Union, have the potential to be felt throughout civic society. However, economic uncertainty has demonstrated how peace dividends provide a fragile form of support in propping up the peace. There is a risk that the amount of funding going into post-conflict situations implies a proportionately sized result. Figures of spending may provide a super-ficial picture; the prospect of external funding encouraging peace building is one thing, whereas delivery of that peace is another. It is therefore important not to overestimate external economic aid having a positive and consistent impact across the whole of civic society. Whilst financial aid is undoubtedly important to peace building and reconciliation it is essential to view it as one component within a multi-track approach. Because of the emotional and symbolic roots of ethnic conflict, 'the provision of economic aid must be combined with other peace building approaches that nurture the transformation of relationships and structures through a process of reconciliation'.[27] Whilst financial aid from exter-nal sources facilitates peace building and reconciliation, it is essential to consider the effect of such funding.

Shirlow pursues this point by questioning the destination for dividends and whether funds are being directed to the most beneficial areas. He goes on to claim that in the past dividends have tended to bypass local communi-ties and be fed straight into private investment strategies, with the aim of economic growth becoming a catalyst for prosperity and the continuation of peace.[28] As a result, middle income and higher income groups have benefited the most from investment opportunities and economic investment, whilst low income groups are excluded from engaging in social mobility and employment opportunities:

> The illusion is one of progress, equality and social advancement. The reality, however, is of unjust class alignments and the perpetuation of the very social and reproductive relationships which produce, stimulate and engender social uneven-ness and a sense among those who are socially alienated that, whether there is peace or war, virtually nothing is going to change.[29]

Whilst job creation and the stimulation of enterprise are important they do not directly address the nature and meaning of ethnic conflict. Violence has remained an episodic feature of Northern Irish society since the GFA yet where 'meaningful work is undertaken with regard to discouraging criminality and membership of paramilitary organisations, funding is uneven and limited'.[30] Such points on the unevenness and allocation of resources question the potential for peace dividends to satisfy all parties involved and therefore aid post-conflict reconciliation.

The interaction between state, civil society and the economy is by no means straight forward. Whilst external economic aid has the potential to transform the context within which Northern Irish politics operates, it is also important to mention that the socio-economic reality for certain sectors of society may not have been touched by the positive effects of external funding. Whilst economic inequality between Catholics and Protestants has closed significantly since the early 1990s, there is still evidence to suggest that parity between the two communities has not yet been reached.[31]

The Northern Irish economy suffers from long-standing weaknesses, such as a swollen public sector, low employment and under-productivity alongside a weak private sector, none of which have been fully addressed via the peace process and its supposed economic dividend. As the UK government acknowledges:

> Northern Ireland is one of the UK's most disadvantaged regions on many measures. It has the lowest wages and one of the lowest labour productivity rates. It has a weak private sector, with strong dependence on the public sector. These weaknesses reflect a number of unique factors, not least the legacy of 30 years of conflict, the demographic structure and the peripheral location of Northern Ireland, as well as issues surrounding deprivation and rurality.[32]

Over 30 per cent of all Northern Ireland jobs are in the public sector compared to a UK average of around 21 per cent.[33] In 1992 this figure was 37 per cent; therefore the economy has managed to rebalance slightly.[34] The bloated public sector appeared ripe for pruning, as David Cameron appeared to hint at the start of the 2010 general election campaign.

Northern Ireland has the highest proportion of inactive people of working age at 28.4 per cent, which is 5 percentage points above the UK average.[35] During the recession, between 2007 and 2011, unemployment rates in Northern Ireland were broadly in line with the UK average. However, looking beyond the average statistics, it is possible to correlate the figures for social deprivation by ward with areas of rioting.[36] It is therefore not difficult to make connections between social disadvantage and political unrest.[37]

The key question is, has the economic downturn created a climate in which dissidents can prosper? The fear is that certain working-class nationalist communities will feel a growing alienation from Sinn Féin and the current status quo, to the extent of questioning, 'what benefits has the peace process brought?', and that such alienation might provide a fertile recruiting ground for paramilitaries.[38]

Ciaran Boyle from the 32CSM demonstrated such a point when asked what bearing the economic situation had on support for dissident republicans:

> the people who are more likely to be disillusioned are the ones who cannot get a job. They are the ones who are going to spread support. They are not going to go to pickets or protest, they will probably join the IRA. If people go for months and months and months without a job and their weans are starving – what are you going to think then? 'The problem is with the status quo.'
>
> There is no doubt that if the economy is bad then republicanism benefits. If people have their backs against the wall, if they have nothing to lose, then republicanism will be attractive because technically you have nothing to lose. It's the same in any context, in any struggle. Once the going gets tough people start to take action.[39]

Between 1992 and 2011 the gap in unemployment between the two communities in Northern Ireland fell from 9 per cent to 2 per cent, yet Protestants continue to have a higher rate of economic activity compared to the Catholic population (74 per cent to 70 per cent).[40] In addition, Catholic areas that bore the brunt of the troubles still feature highly in the top ten overall-deprivation measures.[41] Such remaining, yet markedly reduced communal disparity, has lead Jarman to warn that there exists

> recognition that the Belfast Agreement was not the panacea to Northern Ireland's Troubles and even if it is possible to establish and sustain a devolved, locally accountable administration, the problems of violence are going to remain, persist and even increase unless greater attention is paid to the causes of such violence and the activities that help to encourage it.[42]

In Northern Ireland there remains a correlation between socio-economic status and dissident sympathy in nationalist areas, with the working-class and unemployed most likely to offer sympathy.[43] Unless economic regeneration improves along with enhanced socio-economic prospects for lower income groups there is a risk that they will be unable to connect with the peace process, and as a result any accommodation amongst political elites would be based on insecure foundations.[44] Dissident sympathy is evident in pockets of working-class urban areas of north Belfast and in economically struggling border locations, although the solitary study of such sympathy suggests its ideological basis somewhat outweighs the effect of economic variables.[45] Whilst historical determinism plays a large role within republicanism, there is a need to place this within the boundaries of context. The difficulty for dissidents is that, unlike the PIRA, they cannot harness relative disadvantage as a major source of support. Despite Catholic unemployment remaining higher than that found amongst Protestants there has been a significant diminution of inter-communal economic differentials.

The British state response

Suppression of armed republicanism through legislation has been a consistent weapon in the government's arsenal against armed republicanism throughout history. The introduction of internment in the early 1970s and the Prevention of Terrorism Act in 1974 were responses to the increasing scale of paramilitary violence in Northern Ireland at the time. The legislation, which predominantly targeted Catholic communities, is described as producing a 'greater sense of alienation from the British state and ensured that a certain section of the community sought redress for the discriminatory practices of the state through methods outside the law'.[46] Therefore, rather than suppress the armed threat, the enacted legislation led to a growth in the membership of the PIRA and an intensified bombing campaign.

The implementation of legislation remains a consistent feature of the state's response to armed republicanism. More recently, the Terrorism Act (2000) was utilised in Northern Ireland to target dissident republican groups. This Act aimed to make temporary provisions for Northern Ireland in relation to the prosecution and punishment of certain offences, the preservation of peace and the maintenance of order. The Terrorism Act, which replaced the Prevention of Terrorism Act (1989), considered outdated, allowed Northern Ireland to continue using non-jury trials for certain offences and granted controversial stop and search powers. Stop and search powers of the Terrorism Act came under Section 44, which grants any uniformed police officer the powers to stop and search persons and vehicles without suspicion if the police are operating in a designated area under special authorisation.[47] This power has been criticised by human rights groups such as Liberty for being too broadly drafted and intimidating to those who do not pose a terrorist threat.[48] The European Court of Human Rights eventually ruled in

Table 2: Number of person and vehicle searches under Section 44 of the Terrorism Act

Period	No. of persons stopped and searched under TACT S44	No. of vehicles stopped and searched under TACT S44
2005	204	156
2006	948	791
2007	2,167	1,801
2008	6,922	6,016
2009	24,519	24,521

Source: Figures taken from M. McKibbin, Northern Ireland Terrorism Legislation: Annual Statistics 2009/10 (London, Northern Ireland Office, 2010).

January 2010 that the powers were a violation of human rights.[49] Authorisation
to use Section 44 stopped in Northern Ireland in July 2010.[50]

However, the stop and search powers were used at a rapidly increasing
rate during the time Section 44 was authorised, rising dramatically between
2005 and 2009. By 2009 over 34,760 persons in Northern Ireland had been
stopped and searched under Section 44 (see table 2). From February 2001
until March 2010, 309 charges were made under the whole of the Terrorism
Act.[51]

Considering the number of searches under Section 44 in comparison to the
low number of subsequent charges under the Terrorism Act, the efficiency and
purpose of such legislation is brought in to question. This point is especially
pertinent given that witnessing stop and search scenarios has been used as a justification and a motive for joining dissident groups, as a younger member of the
32CSM explained:

> I joined the 32 County Sovereignty Movement just watching people such as himself
> [Ciaran Boyle] walking through town [Derry], and I didn't even know who he was
> but they were being stopped three or four of them with their hands up and one of
> the members' daughter. She was being lifted off her baby seat and being searched
> and all. And I thought: I can't support that. This is British militia attacking Irish
> people on Ireland's soil.[52]

Deterrent policies introduced by the state and control measures such as the
Terrorism Act are not necessarily effective in restricting support for dissident
groups, especially if the rate at which such actions encourage individuals to join
organisations is greater than the numbers charged under the legislation.

In the Republic of Ireland, membership laws also provide a point of contention. For example, John Murphy, a member of Cork 32CSM, was arrested
in December 2003 along with four others and charged with membership of
the IRA. All were subsequently tried in a non-jury Special Criminal Court
(SCC) and were charged.[53] Murphy described this process as a modern form of
internment:

> Since 1998 there have been laws amended, like the membership laws in the 26
> counties which is basically a modern form of internment. Where they basically
> bring a republican before the court, it's a three judge court. You're not entitled to a
> jury and basically it is the words of a Chief Superintendent that convicts you added
> with small bits of evidence like republican books and CDs they find in your house.
> Literally ridiculous stuff like that.[54]

In May 2008 the Court of Criminal Appeal (CCA) found the SCC did not
have the jurisdiction to try and charge the five in question because they were not
charged 'forthwith' after being arrested.[55] Using the above two examples from
both sides of the border, such measures imposed by the state have potentially
fuelled support for dissident groups and provided legitimation for using violence

as a form of retaliation to state repression. Counter measures from the state can therefore be utilised by dissidents to represent state repression where any further dissident violence is framed as a reactionary form of self-defence, ultimately fuelling the action-response cycle (see figure 2).

The evolving security context in Northern Ireland

Much academic attention has been afforded to the evolving British state response towards the PIRA.[56] Throughout the course of the troubles the British state pursued policies of suppression, criminalisation and eventually accommodation. Structural developments within the security services, broad political support for policing and tactical change have altered the domestic context within which armed dissident republican groups operate today.

Firstly, in the post-GFA context, tactical changes within policing and demilitarisation mean that security deployment, operations and instillations in Northern Ireland have been substantially reduced. At the height of the troubles in 1972 the British government had deployed 43,000 troops in Northern Ireland.[57] In overall efforts to demilitarise Northern Ireland, a reduction of state military and security personnel occurred parallel to the decommissioning of weapons by the PIRA. In July 2007 the British Army ended its 38-year-long military operation in Northern Ireland. After this period a regular garrison of five thousand troops were to remain based in Northern Ireland.[58] Yet the military personnel that remained were no longer expected to play a role in policing. In countering armed threats in Northern Ireland focus has been placed on softer policing techniques and a reliance on intelligence in an attempt to avoid an over-militarised response. The heavy handed deployment of police or soldiers in the past, epitomised by events such as Bloody Sunday, invariably provided one of the 'best recruiting' mechanisms for the PIRA and is blamed for setting off a 'cycle of futile violence' from which Northern Ireland is only just escaping.[59] The emphasis placed on softer policing techniques recognises that intelligence is the most vital element in successfully countering armed groups.[60]

Secondly, in terms of structural change, the composition of the police service has become more representative. Along with decommissioning and prisoner releases, policing proved to be one of the most controversial aspects of the Northern Ireland peace process. Despite making up more than 40 per cent of the population in Northern Ireland, Catholics accounted only for 8 per cent of the RUC in 1998.[61] The police force was not just poorly represented in terms of national identity; only 12.6 per cent of officers were women.[62] The RUC was therefore seen as overwhelmingly Protestant and male. In order to counter this under-representation the Independent Commission on Policing for Northern Ireland (Patten Report) proposed the adoption of 50:50 Catholic and Protestant recruitment to the police over a ten-year period. The Patten

Report acknowledged that a reformed police service in a post-GFA era needed to employ a large number of nationalists, including republicans, if it was to be fully accepted.[63] The result of this recruitment quota was that by 2014 the proportion of Catholics in the police reached 30.4 per cent.[64]

Finally, in terms of political change, Sinn Féin's support for policing in Northern Ireland proved a significant milestone, not just in the Northern Irish peace process but also in the evolution of political change within the Provisional republican movement. In 2007 Sinn Féin took their seats on the Northern Ireland Policing Board for the first time. Not only did Sinn Féin affirm their support for the PSNI, they made a distinct effort to distance themselves from the continued violence of dissident republican groups. McGuinness's 'traitors to the island of Ireland' comment following the dissident attack at the Massereene army barracks in 2009, confirmed the mainstream republican endorsement of new policing structures. Political change was emphasised further in the aftermath of a dissident republican car bomb, which killed Catholic PSNI Officer Ronan Kerr in 2011. Ronan Kerr's funeral proved highly symbolic as unionist and nationalist politicians, GAA players and PSNI officers stood side by side in a demonstration of solidarity. A former member of the PIRA declaring that 'the war is over' and a broad consensus in support for policing have made it difficult for hard line republicans to claim that the reformed police service represents a sectarian force.

It is a credit to the leadership of the Provisional republican movement that throughout the evolution of the group they have maintained relative unity. Despite removing the policy of abstention to Dáil Éireann, and later Stormont, as well as decommissioning and accepting the legitimacy of the PSNI, the voices of dissent have not been able to gather large-scale momentum. The Provisional movement has maintained significant organisational cohesiveness. McEvoy and Shirlow describe how even on the issue of accepting the PSNI, the most emotive issue of recent years, and one of the most powerful gestures of the entire process, '[Provisional] Republican discipline appears to have held firm. The peace process required a continued military presence from the PIRA in order to counter the destabilising threat from dissident organisations. Their management of the potential threat from dissidents has at times been violent.'[65] Whilst Sinn Féin demonstrated a united front politically, the PIRA also remained a cohesive paramilitary presence during the transitional phase of the peace process.

On one level the culture and ethos of policing in Northern Ireland have changed. However, it remains the case for some that in ideological terms the PSNI is still a British police force that represents a colonial and sectarian presence. Dissident publications and propaganda still refer to the police as the RUC. The demilitarisation process involves more than ridding Northern Ireland of visible apparatus of military occupation or policing through disarmament, demobilisation and reintegration. Smyth explains that the process of demilitarisation must not only demilitarise combatants and decommission weapons, this procedure also needs to address aspects of society that have been militarised, including political culture and ideology.[66] The PSNI remain an unwelcome presence in many republican areas and reporting of police victimisation dominates much of the dissident republican narrative. PSNI activity such as stop and search, house raids and routine screening is used by dissidents to express the fact that Northern Ireland has not been 'normalised' and emphasises that resistance to the current political arrangements remains within some republican communities.[67] Despite the structural developments within the security services, tactical change and political support for policing, in ideological terms, the PSNI is still viewed as a colonial and sectarian presence by some in Northern Ireland.

Preventing normalisation

Key to understanding the continued use of violence by armed dissident groups is their desire to prevent the impression of Northern Ireland being a normalised state. Highlighting the continued presence and scrutiny of security forces can potentially create the impression that republican violence is reactionary. According to RSF's Geraldine Taylor, little has changed since the peace process:

> The Brits are still here. They keep telling us there are no troops on the streets, but they are still here. They are in barracks. But anyway we are still under occupation. And when the people react and do something about it, they are called terrorists. How can you be a terrorist in your own country when you are fighting for the freedom of our own country. The terrorists are the British government.[68]

Anti-state organisations engaged in armed resistance often invoke the rights of self-defence in justification of their actions.[69] Therefore, by paramilitary groups claiming the right of self-defence, violence is presented as a reaction to state oppression. Such an argument is typified by the assertion of a republican prisoner:

> All armed struggle is, is a response to the armed presence of the British government and the violent refusal of the British government to allow the Irish nation its freedom. Republicanism does not in any form promote violence nor does it support the initiation of violence. Armed struggle comes to exist only due to the armed actions of those who attack republicanism's advance. When armed actions are taken they are not undertaken as core republicanism. They are a response to armed action against usually peaceful people's offensives aimed at implementing the rights of the nation.[70]

Framing the actions of state security forces as the catalyst of the conflict is an attempt to justify the past, present and future actions of republican violence.

After an attack on two off-duty police officers in the areas of Derry and Dungannon in November 2007,[71] the RIRA issued a threat that it would 'continue to target Crown Forces at a time and place of our choosing'.[72] Between March 2009 and May 2012, forty-three police officers were re-housed because of the threat from dissident republicans,[73] with far more having to increase their home security.[74] The targeting of the police is at one level a physical attack on security services, but is also an attempt to attack the impression of normalisation.

In 2008 Hugh Orde claimed that the chief objective of dissidents was to kill a police officer and thereby fuel political instability.[75] A successful attack on the security forces in Northern Ireland grabs attention. It provides an opportunity for the dissident campaign to be in the international media, spreading the message that there remains the presence of those in Northern Ireland intent on resisting the status quo. Thus according to one dissident:

> If you talk about the six counties we are somewhere below the pecking order when it comes to decision makers in Ireland. They decided to pay attention to us because the IRA were a problem, they had to, it was crucial.[76]

It is suggested that the armed republican campaign is no longer concerned with planting an indiscriminate bomb in a high-profile location, but is more interested in specific targets, especially in reference to the targeting of the police.[77] Therefore, whilst at one level the targeting of police represents opposition to the Sinn Féin agenda it also demonstrates a physical threat which has the potential to gain greater media attention and ultimately presents Northern Ireland as a non-normalised entity.

The evolving international context

Whilst local circumstances are vital to understanding the security situation in Northern Ireland, it is also important to place dissident republicanism within a broader political context. Events such as 9/11 and the attacks in London in July 2005 altered how political violence was viewed in the international arena. In the twenty-first century the British state's policies towards the PIRA and Sinn Féin have been viewed as juxtaposed to the treatment of alternative forms of violence such as the threat posed by Islamic fundamentalism. In July 2005, the PIRA released their final decommissioning statement declaring the organisation had put all arms beyond use. This came just three weeks after the July 7 bombings, which targeted the public transport system in London, killing fifty-two and injuring hundreds more. This was the first ever suicide attack on British soil. Whilst these bombings did not provide a direct impetus for the PIRA decommissioning statement a few weeks later, these attacks altered the context within which acts of political violence were 'tolerated'.[78]

The threat from armed groups to the UK has completely changed in nature. Parallel to the Northern Irish peace process overseen by the Blair government was the growing threat from 'international terrorism', or Islamic fundamentalism. At this time state counter-terrorism policy varied depending on whether the terrorism was international in scope or related to the conflict in Northern Ireland.[79] The British government engaged in a process of accommodation with the PIRA where the Northern Ireland peace process required a process of conciliation to succeed. Simultaneously, Blair described the suppression of Islamic fundamentalism as a 'global struggle' against an 'evil ideology' that he concluded was 'perverted and poisonous'.[80] A distinction was therefore made between different 'types' of terrorism.[81]

The British government avoided comparisons of its policy in Northern Ireland and its support for the global war on terror. Blair insisted on the difference between the terrorism of al Qaeda and the PIRA stating in 2005, 'I don't think you can compare the political demands of republicanism with the political demands of this terrorist ideology we're facing now … My entire thinking changed from 11 September – the belief that you have a different form of terrorism.'[82] The distinction had been made between violent actors that were perceived as 'nihilistic' in nature and others who were treated as rational political actors and could be negotiated with. Such a division resulted in Blair being accused of applying double standards by unionists in Northern Ireland, where the numbers killed should not be used to distinguish between those engaging in terrorism.

Blair's approach to international terrorism in the UK has been described as reminiscent of previous Prime Ministers' approach to armed republicanism in the 1970s, when not only was the idea of negotiating with a terrorist organisation virtually impossible but the demands and objectives of the PIRA were also considered unacceptable.[83] It is also necessary to make the point that much of the language used to describe those responsible for the attacks on London in 2005 is mirrored in the portrayal of dissidents in Northern Ireland today who are similarly referred to as being 'insane' and 'evil' by politicians and the mainstream media.[84]

The root causes argument accounting for the reason behind political violence is unpopular in the zero tolerance climate in the post-9/11 context. The causal relationship between underlying social, economic and political grievances and armed action suggests that there exist legitimate grievances or causes of violence. For dissident republican groups that continue to engage in an armed campaign the international context within which they function has altered dramatically since that of the PIRA campaign. Attacks on New York and London in the early twenty-first century changed perceptions about the nature and scale of terrorism, and subsequently how political violence should be managed. Therefore, armed dissident republican groups today operate in a more hostile environment than that of the PIRA.

Conclusion

The Northern Irish peace process is used as a model for conflict resolution, especially in reference to its inclusivity and engagement with republicans. The inclusion of Sinn Féin in the peace talks served as a carrot to incentivise co-operation, the abandonment of violence and the continuation of peaceful means. Despite the rebranding of Provisional republicanism, Sinn Féin remains relatively unified in that the party has retained most members and indeed expanded. It is now the second largest party in Northern Ireland and is growing on both sides of the border.

Contextual circumstances, such as the desire to prevent normalisation, the claimed need for self-defence (where violence is a response to security service oppression) and the need for more community control are also employed as means to rationalise dissident violence. The use of violence does not lie in the belief it will force the British government to relinquish sovereignty. The strategic rationale, insofar as it exists, is to stop Northern Ireland embedding as an uncontested state, in the hope that a campaign of resistance may grow due to, as yet, unforeseen episodes, such as security force mistakes, which may help encourage support for the 'dissidents' in their claims to the title deeds of the IRA. Dissidents have attempted to utilise measures enforced by the state to highlight the lack of normality. The introduction of counter-terrorism measures such as Section 44 has been framed by dissidents as state repression. Violence is then subsequently portrayed as reactionary, or as a means of self-defence.

Normalisation has made progress in terms of reforms of policing and political structures but there still exist areas that have not made sufficient advances. Ultimately, the police strategy in Northern Ireland cannot eliminate dissident republican violence, but it can manage it. There exists a tendency to deny that any form of political violence could be associated with a legitimate political cause because there is a wish to deny these actors any legitimacy.[85] However, in parallel to the security response it is essential to address existing root causes such as victimisation and social inequality.

Whilst certain armed campaigns may come to an end, as the PIRA's did in the early twenty-first century, examination of Irish history highlights the durability of armed republicanism. There is a long history of armed republican paramilitarism that stretches further back than the foundation of the Provisional movement in 1969. Before the PIRA, there had been many others bearing the same title and carrying on violence in pursuit of a united Ireland. As English explains:

> The Irish revolution of 1916–23, the IRA's bombing campaign in Britain during 1939–40, the same organisation's Border Campaign in Ireland 1956–62 – all of these demonstrate the degree to which Irish republican political violence has been a long term rather than merely recent phenomenon.[86]

Such longevity suggests that the existence of armed republicanism goes beyond specific material circumstances. Historical determinism and tradition play a significant role within Irish republicanism, an aspect that the spoiler discourse does not account for. Whilst the armed campaigns of republican groups throughout history may have come to an end, armed republicanism is not going to evaporate. Dissident republican violence today demonstrates the next phase in this cycle.

Notes

1 See for example, R. Mac Ginty, 'Irish Republicanism and the Peace Process: From Revolution to Reform', in M. Cox, A. Guelke and F. Stephens (eds), *A Farewell to Arms? Beyond the Good Friday Agreement* (Manchester, Manchester University Press, 2006); S. J. Stedman, 'Spoiler Problems in Peace Processes', *International Security* 22, no. 2 (1997), pp. 5–53; J. Darby and R. Mac Ginty, *The Management of Peace Processes* (Basingstoke, Palgrave, 2000); A. Guelke, 'Political Comparisons: From Johannesburg to Jerusalem', in Cox, Guelke and Stephens (eds), *A Farewell to Arms?*
2 J. Darby, 'A Truce Rather Than a Treaty? The Effect of Violence in the Irish Peace Process', in Cox, Guelke and Stephens (eds), *A Farewell to Arms?*, p. 218.
3 See *Guardian*, 'Barack Obama in Ireland praises peacemakers for "ripple of hope"', 23 May 2011; *Belfast Telegraph*, 'Northern Ireland peace can inspire Middle East, says Obama', 26 May 2011.
4 See E. O'Kane, 'Learning from Northern Ireland? The Uses and Abuses of the Irish "Model"', *British Journal of Politics and International Relations* 12, no. 2 (2010), pp. 239–256; *Irish Times*, 'NI politicians coach Iraqis on building peace process', 4 September 2007.
5 *BBC News*, 'International negotiators urge Eta to lay down weapons', 17 October 2011.
6 O'Kane, 'Learning from Northern Ireland?', p. 242.
7 Darby and Mac Ginty, *The Management of Peace Processes*, p. 3.
8 Stedman, 'Spoiler Problems in Peace Processes', p. 8.
9 Darby and Mac Ginty, *The Management of Peace Processes,* p. 8.
10 Stedman, 'Spoiler Problems in Peace Processes', p. 8.
11 *Ibid.*, p. 8.
12 *Ibid.*, p. 6.
13 See Sinn Féin, 'Defending the Good Friday Agreement', Sinn Féin submission to the Mitchell Review, 23 September 1999, www.cain.ulst.ac.uk/events/peace/docs/sf23999.htm.
14 See for example RNU, Critique of the Good Friday Agreement, 14 April 2011,www.republicannetwork.ie/; A. McIntyre in *The Pensive Quill*, 'Republicanism: alive or dying?', 1 January 2008.
15 See Stedman, 'Spoiler Problems in Peace Processes', pp. 5–53.
16 John Murphy, interview with author, Cork, 2 March 2011.
17 D. Muro, 'The Politics of War and Memory in Radical Basque Nationalism', *Ethnic and Racial Studies* 32, no. 4 (2009), p. 675.

18 See M. I. Lichbach, 'Deterrence or Escalation? The Puzzle of Aggregate Studies of Repression and Dissent', *Journal of Conflict Resolution* 31, no. 2 (1987), pp. 266–297.

19 Des Dalton, interview with author, Dublin, 21 October 2011.

20 J. Blackbourn, 'International Terrorism and Counterterrorist Legislation: The Case Study of Post-9/11 Northern Ireland', *Terrorism and Political Violence* 21, no. 1 (2009), pp. 133–154.

21 G. D. Miller, 'Confronting Terrorism and Successful State Policies', *Terrorism and Political Violence* 19, no. 3 (2007), pp. 331–350.

22 E. Newman, 'Exploring the "Root Causes" of Terrorism', *Studies in Conflict and Terrorism* 29, no. 8 (2006), pp. 749–772.

23 See S. B. Blomberg, G. D. Hess and A. Orphanides, 'The Macroeconomic Consequences of Terrorism', *Journal of Monetary Economics* 51 (2004), pp. 1,007–1,032; N. V. Crain and W. M. Crain, 'Terrorized Economies', *Public Choice* 128 (2006), pp. 317–349; K. Gaibulloev and T. Sandler, 'Growth Consequences of Terrorism in Western Europe', *Kyklos* 61, no. 3 (2008), pp. 411–424.

24 M. Olson, 'Rapid Growth as a Destabilizing Force,' *Journal of Economic History* 23 (December 1963), pp. 529–552.

25 T. R. Gurr, 'Sources of Rebellion in Western Societies: Some Quantitative Evidence', *The ANNALS of the American Academy of Political and Social Science* 391 (1970), pp. 128–144.

26 J. Smyth and A. Cebulla, 'The Glacier Moves?', in, M. Coulter and M. Murray (eds), *Northern Ireland After the Troubles: A Society in Transition* (Manchester, Manchester University Press, 2008), p. 177.

27 S. Byrne, O. Skarlato, E. Fissuh and C. Irvin, 'Building Trust and Goodwill in Northern Ireland and the Border Counties: The Impact of Economic Aid on the Peace Process', *Irish Political Studies* 24, no. 3 (2009), p. 339. S. Ryan, *The Transformation of Violent Intercommunal Conflict* (Aldershot, Ashgate, 2007), cited in Byrne, Skarlato, Fissuh and Irvin, 'Building Trust and Goodwill in Northern Ireland and the Border Counties', p. 340.

28 P. Shirlow, 'The Economics of the Peace Process', in C. Gilligan and J. Tonge, *Peace or War? Understanding the Peace Process in Northern Ireland* (Aldershot, Ashgate, 1997), p. 136.

29 *Ibid.*, p. 145.

30 P. Shirlow and B. Murtagh, *Belfast: Segregation, Violence and the City* (London, Pluto, 2006), p. 50.

31 Office of First Minister and Deputy First Minister, *2007 Labour Force Survey: Religious Report* (Belfast, Northern Ireland Statistics and Research Agency, 2009).

32 H M Treasury, *Rebalancing the Northern Irish Economy* (London, H M Treasury, 2011), p. 11.

33 Office of National Statistics, *Public Sector Employment Statistical Bulletin Q4 2010* (London, ONS, 2011).

34 H M Treasury, *Public Expenditure Statistical Analyses* (London, H M Treasury, 2010).

35 Department for Enterprise, Trade and Investment, *Labour Market Report* (Belfast, Northern Ireland Statistics and Research Agency, 2011).

36　See Northern Ireland Executive, *The 100 Most Deprived Small Areas in Northern Ireland: Northern Ireland Multiple Deprivation Measure 2010* (Belfast, Northern Ireland Statistics and Research Agency, 2010).

37　K. Bean, '"New dissidents are but old Provisionals writ large"? The Dynamics of Dissent Republicanism in New Northern Ireland', *Political Quarterly* 83, no. 2 (2012), pp. 83–98.

38　See *Financial Times*, 'A peace to protect', 15 August 2012, p. 7; *Sunday Business Post*, 'Last-ditch bid to snuff out Northern normality', 5 August 2012.

39　Ciaran Boyle, interview with author, Derry, 8 March 2012.

40　Northern Ireland Statistics and Research Agency, *Monthly Labour Market Report*, December 2013, www.detini.gov.uk/labour_market_report_-_december_2013__final_.pdf?rev=0.

41　Northern Ireland Statistics and Research Agency, *Northern Ireland Multiple Deprivation Measure 2005* (Belfast, The Stationery Office, 2005).

42　N. Jarman, 'From War to Peace? Changing Patterns of Violence in Northern Ireland, 1990–2003', *Terrorism and Political Violence* 16, no. 3 (2004), p. 436.

43　J. Evans and J. Tonge, 'Menace without Mandate? Is There Any Sympathy for Dissident Irish Republicanism in Northern Ireland?' *Terrorism and Political Violence* 24, no. 1 (2012), pp. 1–18.

44　Shirlow, 'The Economics of the Peace Process', p. 147.

45　Evans and Tonge, 'Menace without Mandate?', pp. 61–78.

46　Blackbourn, 'International Terrorism and Counterterrorist Legislation', p. 138.

47　See Terrorism Act 2000, 21 July 2000 available at www.legislation.gov.uk/ukpga/2000/11/pdfs/ukpga_20000011_en.pdf, accessed 28 August 2012.

48　In September 2003 journalists and peace protestors were subject to lengthy stop and search and prevented from attending a demonstration in London.

49　*Guardian*, 'Stop and search powers illegal, European Court Rules', 12 January 2010.

50　See *From War to Law: Liberty's Response to the Coalition Government's Review of Counter-Terrorism and Security Powers* (London, Liberty, 2010) available at www.liberty-human-rights.org.uk/pdfs/policy10/from-war-to-law-final-pdf-with-bookmarks.pdf, accessed 29 August 2012.

51　Figures taken from M. McKibbin, *Northern Ireland Terrorism Legislation: Annual Statistics 2009/10* (London, Northern Ireland Office, 2010). Includes all persons charged with offences under the Terrorism Act (2000), regardless of the arrest used.

52　Joe Barr, interview with author, Derry, 8 March 2010.

53　*News Letter*, 'Real IRA boss Munster given prison sentence', 14 June 2005, p. 15; *Belfast Telegraph*, 'Real IRA and four active members jailed', 14 June 2005.

54　John Murphy, interview with author, Cork, 2 March 2011.

55　*Irish Examiner*, 'Real IRA convictions overturned on appeal', 7 May 2008.

56　See for example Jarman, 'From War to Peace?', pp. 420–438; Blackbourn, 'International Terrorism and Counterterrorist Legislation', pp. 134–154; A. Guelke, 'The Northern Ireland Peace Process and the War against Terrorism: Conflicting Conceptions?' *Government and Opposition* 42, no. 3 (2007), pp. 272–291; P. Dixon, 'British Policy Towards Northern Ireland 1969–2000: Continuity Tactical

Adjustment and Consistent "Inconsistencies"', *British Journal of Politics and International Relations* 3, no. 3 (2001), pp. 340–368.

57 M. Smyth, 'The Process of Demilitarisation and the Reversibility of the Peace Process in Northern Ireland', *Terrorism and Political Violence* 16, no. 3 (2004), p. 545.

58 *Guardian*, 'British troops leave after 38 years', 1 August 2007, www.theguardian.com/uk/2007/aug/01/northernireland.military.

59 R. English, *Terrorism: How to Respond* (Oxford, Oxford University Press, 2009), p. 131.

60 *Ibid.*, p. 143.

61 Independent Commission on Policing for Northern Ireland, *A New Beginning: Policing in Northern Ireland* (London, HMSO, 1999), p. 81.

62 *Ibid.*, p. 81.

63 *Ibid.*, p. 81.

64 Police Service of Northern Ireland, 'Workforce Composition Figures' (2014), available at www.psni.police.uk/index/updates/updates_statistics/updates_workforce_composition_figures.htm, accessed 12 February 2014.

65 K. McEvoy and P. Shirlow, 'Re-imagining DDR: Ex-combatants, Leadership and Moral Agency in Conflict Transformation', *Theoretical Criminology* 13, no. 1 (2009), p. 43.

66 Smyth, 'The Process of Demilitarisation', p. 547.

67 See S. A. Whiting, '"The Discourse of Defence": "Dissident" Irish Republicanism and the "Propaganda War"', *Terrorism and Political Violence* 24, no. 3 (2012), pp. 483–503.

68 Geraldine Taylor, interview with author, Belfast, 21 October 2011.

69 See C. J. Finlay, 'Legitimacy and Non-State Political Violence', *Journal of Political Philosophy* 18, no. 3 (2010), pp. 287–312. For more information on the role of self-defence as a justification for armed struggle, see Whiting, '"The Discourse of Defence"', pp. 483–503.

70 Tarlach McConnell, interview with author, Portlaoise Prison, 8 March 2010.

71 M. Frampton, *The Return of the Militants: Violent Dissident Republicanism. A Policy Report for The International Centre for the Study of Radicalisation and Political Violence* (London, ICRS, 2010), p. 16.

72 *Irish Times*, '"Real IRA" issues threat to North police', 28 November 2007.

73 Freedom of Information Request, Request Number: F-2012–02338, available at www.psni.police.uk/police_officers_rehoused.pdf, accessed 24 August 2012.

74 See *BBC Newsnight*, 'Files reveal growing NI terror threat', 28 October 2009, www.news.bbc.co.uk/1/hi/programmes/newsnight/8328309.stm, accessed 29 August 2012.

75 Oral Evidence of Chief Constable Sir Hugh Orde OBE, Assistant Chief Constable Judith Gillespie and Chief Inspector Sam Cordner, House of Commons Northern Ireland Select Committee (HC 1174–i), 5 November 2008, available at www.parliament.the-stationery-office.co.uk/pa/cm200708/cmselect/cmniaf/c1174–i/c117402.htm.

76 Independent Republican Prisoner B, interview with author, Portlaoise Prison, 16 July 2010.

77 See J. Mooney in *The Times*, '"Critical" threat to troops in North', 7 February 2009.

78 Blackbourn, 'International Terrorism and Counterterrorist Legislation', p. 146.
79 See *Ibid.*, p. 134; Guelke, 'The Northern Ireland Peace Process and the War against Terrorism', p. 272.
80 *BBC News*, 'Tony Blair's speech on terror', 16 July 2005, full text available at www.news.bbc.co.uk/1/hi/uk/4689363.stm, accessed 1 February 2014.
81 Guelke, 'The Northern Ireland Peace Process and the War against Terrorism', p. 275.
82 *BBC News*, 'IRA are not al Qaeda says Blair', 26 July 2005, available at www.news.bbc.co.uk/1/hi/uk_politics/4718223.stm, accessed 1 February 2014.
83 Blackbourn, 'International Terrorism and Counterterrorist Legislation', p. 147.
84 S. A. Whiting, '"The Discourse of Defence"', pp. 483–503.
85 Newman, 'Exploring the "Root Causes" of Terrorism', p. 751.
86 English, *Terrorism*, p. 122.

Conclusion

In assessing the ideological basis of dissident republicanism since 1986 there are several conclusions that can be drawn in defining 'dissent', assessing the aims, strategies and tactics of dissidents, and analysing dissident groups. It was not the aim of this book to provide detailed insight into the military operations of dissident republicanism. Whilst there has been a need to provide information on the nature of armed dissident activity, the volume and full range of dissident attacks are difficult to set out due to the limits of space and time, and such information can be found elsewhere.[1] Rather, the research presented in this book is designed to add to the small, yet growing, literature on how to understand the evolution of contemporary republicanism beyond that offered by Sinn Féin. The focus of this research has been firstly, to explore dissent in terms of how and why this occurs within the republican framework and, secondly, to explain 'dissent' as a construction in reference to how public perception of these groups is formed. There is a need to address the volatile tendencies of republicanism and why the nature of the tradition has made it so prone to division. It is within this framework that this research has aimed to provide a detailed examination of dissident organisations and their attempts to legitimise their activity.

Divisions within Irish republicanism: is it still about 'the split'?

Irish republicanism has always been vulnerable to splits and divisions. The fractious and heterogeneous nature of the republican movement has been an enduring characteristic throughout the past century. In exploring why Irish republicanism has been so prone to division some academics have attempted to explain this phenomenon as a cyclical trend where the tension between political struggle and military conflict has provided the regular catalyst in dividing the movement.[2] This category of explanation sees republicanism as comprising an enduring struggle between militarists and politicians, between hawks and doves and between Neanderthal tendencies and progressives. Such explanations, whilst helpful in emphasising endogenous factors, internal tensions and inherent strains in the movement, fail to consider the impact of exogenous factors weighing upon the movement, most notably socio-economic factors and the strategy of the British state.

Other explanations account for the perpetuation of splits by highlighting that Irish republicanism has never been a static entity, but rather is best viewed as a product of contextual realities, reacting to governmental policies and social and economic circumstances.[3] As a result, strategies have regularly altered. On this interpretation, republicanism is less a set of fundamental, rigid principles and more a contextually based articulation of a set of ideas which embrace Irish unification and national sovereignty, but offer considerable tactical flexibility in terms of the means of the attainment of these overarching goals.

Whilst important, there is a need to go beyond social, economic and political circumstances and to consider also the strongly held traditions and the historical narrative attached to Irish republicanism. It is the prominence of tradition within republicanism that helps frame individual interpretation of the movement in its current context. Therefore, individual circumstances come together with historical tradition to create a multifaceted and diverse phenomenon. As a result of such diversity within one tradition, 'the split' is set to remain an enduring characteristic of Irish republicanism.

Throughout this book examination has been given to whether it is possible to define Irish republicanism through set principles and to why Irish republicanism is so prone to division? Can Sinn Féin still be labelled republican and is there such a thing as dissident republicanism? Finally, how, if at all possible, do armed dissident groups defend the continued use of armed struggle? In order to supply the answers to each of these questions it is necessary to draw on the discussions of the previous chapters.

Defining Irish republicanism: are there agreed components?

In considering the emergence of dissident republicanism since 1986 there is a need to explore how such a vast range of interpretations can exist, each claiming lineage to the same tradition. Ultimately, is it possible to present any agreed components to Irish republicanism? It is very difficult to assign the label of republican in the form of 'tick box' criteria. Offering a model of the 'true' republican provides a restrictive and shallow understanding of the tradition, unable to comprehend the space from which alternative interpretations may emerge. It is not the aim of this book to provide a checklist of what constitutes 'true' Irish republicanism. Rather, it is to investigate where and why the fault lines occur within different interpretations. The fault line between 'purist' and 'pragmatist' demonstrates the instability that is inherent in the movement. For both, the goal of unification is the same yet the methods by which to achieve this are diverse; there are those who accept the northern consent principle and need to persuade unionists to change allegiance, and those for whom any acknowledgement of the northern state delegitimises republicanism. It is within the interpretation and application of such ideals that variations occur. The categories of purist and pragmatist are not necessarily representative of any groups and characteristics are not mutually exclusive. But the polar positions of these categories do provide the opposing ends of the republican spectrum to allow us to consider where, if at all, dissident groups as well as Sinn Féin fit on the spectrum. Whichever end of the spectrum groups may occupy, neither can ensure their methods will guarantee success in reaching their ultimate constitutional goal. Consensus exists only in terms of the ultimate objective. Construction of republicanism as a spectrum is more conducive to considering where republican groups today are positioned, as well as how they relate to one another.

The evolution of republicanism: Sinn Féin's modernised brand

Despite the absence of a 'true republican' checklist, Sinn Féin has firm posses-sion of the republican franchise in Northern Ireland. As a result any other groups claiming republican credentials are considered in relation to what Sinn Féin, in their modern form, represent. By utilising constitutional politics within a system that recognises partition, Sinn Féin are accused by republican critics of 'selling out' or compromising their aspirations for political rewards. The former PIRA member Anthony McIntyre has commented that 'in politics as in other areas of life it is often necessary to compromise principles. But there is a gulf between compromise and abandonment that should not be bridged.'[4] It has therefore been necessary to assess the evolution of Sinn Féin and the forces behind such seismic shifts in the party in order to consider whether their claims of being a republican party are still valid.

Sinn Féin has responded to Downsian laws of electoral competition and the need to chase the median nationalist voter, processes which became of greater importance amid military stalemate and public hostility towards armed struggle. As a result, the party expanded their ideas to include a pluralist interpretation of identity and frontloaded the (republican) principle of equality (within the 'Ireland of Equals' rhetoric) at the expense of freedom and territorial sovereignty. By employing constitutional strategy and displacing revolutionary tactics and armed struggle, the party broadened its support base. In terms of the operation of a constitutional republican party, Sinn Féin's moves were logical. By adhering to the rules of party competition and electoral logic Sinn Féin are now in a posi-tion whereby they have far more influence than they ever would have possessed as a mere voice for the actions of the IRA. Because republicanism has been so open to interpretation and therefore harder to define, it is easier for Sinn Féin, despite the compromises made, to claim fidelity to the republican tradition. Understanding this has been essential in understanding how Sinn Féin have utilised republican tenets to explain and justify their seismic shift and how they can continue to frame their actions within the broad and flexible parameters of republican principle.

Rather than employing a rigid framework of republicanism, it is more useful to consider where groups claiming the label relate on a spectrum. This allows us to consider groups in their own right, rather than in relation to Sinn Féin. Therefore to answer whether Sinn Féin can still be labelled republican, there is no more or less reason why they should be labelled republican than dissident groups. The rewards of constitutional politics are greater and have broadened the appeal of the party. It is therefore much easier for Sinn Féin to articulate their position of pragmatic constitutional republicanism as *the* republican mantle.

Is there such a thing as dissident republicanism?

In order to question whether there exists such a thing as dissident republicanism there is a need to go beyond the descriptive analysis of the phenomenon and provide insight into the differing interpretations of the tradition. Exploring the origins, strategies and campaigns of several dissident groups has revealed the complexities in understanding modern day Irish republicanism. In addition to understanding the dissident critique of mainstream republicanism it has been necessary to consider these groups in their own right and not in reflection to what Sinn Féin represent. Using the label of dissident implies defection from republican ideological principles, as well as a challenge to the accepted status quo. In addition, placing a broad range of groups under the same label of 'dissident republican' denies the presence of heterogeneity.

Closest of all the groups to the 'purist' interpretation of the republican tradition is RSF. The ending of the policy of abstention from Leinster House in 1986 was viewed by RSF as a betrayal of the All-Ireland Republic of 1916. The policy of abstention remains the position of RSF today. Whilst many consider this unwillingness to alter their stance as outdated and static, RSF are provided with a sense of exceptionalism in not having compromised their position and retaining fidelity to what they alone see as the only true republican tradition. For groups such as the 32CSM that remained with the Provisionals after the 1986 division, the eventual split was less about the arcane principle of twenty-six county abstention and more about the *modus operandi* of republicanism: the running down of its military capacity and displacement in favour of electoralism. Such alignment to the physical force tradition was expressed by members who claimed that there has to be some sort of 'military solution to the problem'.[5] Positions of principle were also involved; dissidents of various hues unite in opposition to participation in a Northern Ireland assembly, but for most 'dissident' republicans disarmament of republican groups can only be justified after the clear advancement of national goals, not in advance.

Even in terms of militarism there is nonetheless diversity as neither the IRSP nor éirígí believe that 'armed struggle' need be a core component. The IRSP emerged from the socialist wing of republicanism, distinct from the Provisionals, and are labelled dissidents based on their ideological departure. The post-GFA context saw the emergence of the socialist Irish republican political party éirígí. Through dynamic campaigns éirígí have expressed the centrality of socialism and the working-class struggle in answering the national question. The party recognises a need to embrace electoral politics in parallel to active, grass-roots campaigning.

RNU are often mistakenly described as an umbrella organisation for other dissident groups. They refute being the driving force behind the creation of a dissident republican united front, but they do encourage the coming together of republican groups especially over the rights of republican prisoners and opposition to the PSNI. RNU are not a political party yet retain a pragmatic position in respect to the use of electoral politics in the future.

Dissident groups thus emerged at different times, for different reasons and from different branches of Irish republican lineage. They all express differences in their interpretation of republicanism and demonstrate different approaches to electoral politics. Except RSF, all consider the positives of a united 'broad front' to varying degrees and disagree in their views on the utility of 'military' struggle. Groups continue to evolve organisationally, making them harder to define. They have to adapt and evolve as the British state overwhelmingly has the upper hand and therefore dictates the conditions in which dissident groups function. In the Northern Ireland context, the label of dissident has become a construction to collectivise those who oppose the current status quo, and is largely bereft of serious analytical purpose.

Justifying the armed campaign

The scale of change within Sinn Féin, the dismemberment of the PIRA and what was viewed as the 'copper fastening' of partition under the GFA, meant that dissent and opposition to the peace process was inevitable. A number of small groups have emerged resistant to compromise, maintaining the utility of a military campaign. How do militant republican groups that continue to advocate the legitimacy of armed struggle, such as Óglaigh na hÉireann (ONH), the Continuity IRA (CIRA), RAAD (Republican Action Against Drugs) and the Real IRA (RIRA), attempt to justify and rationalise their actions?

Dissidents are often labelled as deluded, evil and obsessed with violence at the expense of peace. Such dominant discourses frame our understanding of dissident groups and the methods they employ. Therefore, to look beyond the label given to dissident groups it is necessary to deconstruct the dominant narrative. All groups that engage in anti-state violence attempt to provide a rationale for their actions. The use of violence does not stem from a belief that it will provide a route to their ultimate constitutional claim. However, it does present an opportunity to provide a physical expression of 'resistance' to the current status quo. These groups, to different degrees, emphasise republican history and claim legitimacy from its supposed lessons. These include the absence of a prior mandate for republican violence at any stage of history, yet its deployment subsequently being fêted, the Easter Rising providing the obvious example. Moreover, the effective threat of force offered by unionists shaped British policy in the twentieth century. These claimed lessons obviate the need to demonstrate a mandate from the living and place republicanism in a sphere of interminable physical force contestation. As a 32CSM member articulated:

> No there is no compromising. If we compromise then the same thing is going to happen – there is going to be splits, there is going to be dissidents, more dissident groups. Do you know what I mean? If we say tomorrow, oh we are going to do it through peaceful means, there are a lot of groups who would have just carried on. People don't realise that, it's not going to stop. There is no solution; there is no peaceful solution to unite the country.[6]

Understanding the prevalence of historical tradition and the attachment to armed struggle is vital in explaining the persistence of the physical force tradition. However, to understand armed dissident republicanism by expressing the phenomenon exclusively in terms of traditionalism and events of the past creates an overwhelming impression of groups being backward looking and stuck in perpetuity in a bygone era. Groups have to evolve to contemporary circumstances and attempt to present actions as a necessary use of force.

In attempting to justify violence, dissident groups identify British forces as legitimate targets and as threats to their community. The range of targets includes the police and British Army, but is extended, in terms of community 'threat', to drug dealers and those engaging in 'anti-social' behaviour. These threats are reinforced at times of tension, with dissidents capitalising on controversies over Orange parades which retain unpopularity within the broader republican community.

The intention is not only to present armed force as either an inevitable response to British involvement in Ireland, or as self-defence, but also to transfer responsibility for the violence to the threat they claim to be opposing. Dissident groups therefore attempt to portray violence as resistance or as a form of self-protection, claiming that despite the GFA, the peace process has brought nothing for certain communities. The mainstream discourse attempting to condemn or undermine groups might damage the broader public perception of dissidents, but fails to permeate the groups themselves. When asked how they felt or how they responded to people labelling them dissidents, a 32CSM member responded with the following:

To me, it doesn't really bother me to be honest … It's a media term from Provisional Sinn Féin. But we didn't change our view. Other people changed their views. Just by going on the TV and calling us micro groups does us no damage at all. It destroys no credibility. You have people saying these people don't have support. These people do have support. They call us criminals, it doesn't wash. They have to say these things to satisfy their own support.[7]

Whilst the term 'dissident' is rejected on the basis that anti-GFA groups believe themselves not to have dissented from republican principles, the meaning associated with the term has been constructed to support arrangements under the GFA. As the opening quote to this book outlined, dissent (armed or otherwise) is defined by those who are in defence of the status quo:

Those who defend status quo relationships of power, or see them as natural and normal, tend to treat any opposition or critique as tantamount to treason or terrorism. That 'another world is possible', to invoke a popular refrain, is nothing less than an ontological challenge to the world that is today.[8]

Sinn Féin, the Northern Ireland executive, the British government, security services and the media have framed the interpretation and understanding of dissent. Therefore, the label 'dissident' can be rejected as a meaningful, analytical term. Rather it is a label to collectivise those republican groups who present opposition or challenge to what is seen as 'normal' and the 'accepted' status quo.

The peace process has not ended the debate on how Irish republicanism is defined. For dissidents, whilst a significant aspect of their campaign is providing a critique of Sinn Féin, there is a void in offering a viable alternative. No group provides an electoral challenge to Sinn Féin. In rejecting constitutional politics as an area in which to gain a mandate or legitimacy, dissidents do not offer convincing explanations of how the continued use of armed struggle, abstention or political campaigning can reach the final constitutional goal, or even why support for each of these is a republican absolute. However, it is necessary to note that there is also no guarantee that Sinn Féin's institutional participation will be any more successful in achieving a united Ireland. A strategy based upon making a hitherto contested political situation work better is far from necessarily the means of its removal. What was once described by a constitutional republican of the Fianna Fáil variety, Charles Haughey, as a 'failed political entity' may be working for the first time in its existence, thanks to Sinn Féin's participation. Making something viable as a means of its disposal might be seen as curious.

The main question for future research into dissent is whether we are now witnessing the last gasp of armed republicanism, or whether this is just another repetition of a cyclical trend inherent in the very nature of the Irish republican tradition. Seeking refuge in historical determinism can only preserve, not advance, the dissident cause. However, as the closing quote suggests, there are those who remain determined to take their legitimacy from the refuge of republican history, however far that takes them:

> We wouldn't regard ourselves as dissidents. What I would say is I have to stand up for what is right and carry on the principles the leaders of 1916 walked after, and I'd be proud to call myself a dissident if that is what it is.[9]

Notes

1 M. Frampton, *The Return of the Militants: Violent Dissident Republicanism. A Policy Report for The International Centre for the Study of Radicalisation and Political Violence* (London, ICRS, 2010).

2 See B. Feeney, *Sinn Féin: A Hundred Turbulent Years* (Dublin, O'Brien Press, 2002); A. Maillot, *New Sinn Féin: Republicanism in the Twenty-first Century* (London, Routledge, 2005); J. Augusteijn, 'Political Violence and Democracy: An Analysis of the Tensions within Irish Republican Strategy, 1914–2002', *Irish Political Studies* 18, no.1 (2003), pp. 1–26; M. L. R. Smith, *Fighting for Ireland?: The Military Strategy of the Irish Republican Movement* (London, Routledge, 1995).

3 See K. Bean, *The New Politics of Sinn Féin* (Liverpool, Liverpool University Press, 2007); R. English, *Irish Freedom: The History of Nationalism in Ireland* (Oxford, Pan Macmillan, 2006); B. O'Brien, *The Long War: IRA and Sinn Féin* (Dublin, O'Brien Books, 1999); R. White, *Provisional Irish Republicans: An Oral and Interpretative History* (Westport, Greenwood Press, 1993).

4 A. McIntyre, in the *Guardian*, 'By shaking the Queen's hand, Martin McGuinness accepts her sovereignty', 26 June 2012.

5 Michael Gallagher, interview with author, Derry, 29 January 2010.

6 Ciaran Boyle, interview with author, Derry, 8 March 2010.

7 Ciaran Boyle, interview with author, Derry, 8 March 2010.

8 R. D. Lipschutz, 'Foreword', in, L. Coleman and K. Tucker (eds), *Situating Global Resistance: Between Discipline and Dissent* (London, Routledge, 2012), p. 1.

9 John Murphy, interview with author, Cork, 2 March 2011.

Bibliography

Primary sources

32CSM, *Background* (n.d.), www.derry32csm.com, accessed 28 November 2011.

32CSM, *Dismantling Partition* (n.d.), www.32csm.info, accessed 2 August 2010.

32CSM, *Entering and Accepting British Political System* (2000), www.32csm.net/p/32 csm-policy-documents.html#!/p/32csm-policy-documents.html, accessed 21 April 2000.

32CSM, *Irish Democracy: A Framework for Unity* (2005), www.32csm.info, accessed 2 August 2010.

32CSM, *Preparing an Irish Democracy* (n.d.), www.32csm.info, accessed 2 August 2010.

32CSM, *Republican Unity: A Discussion Document* (2007), www.32csm.net/p/32csm-policy-documents.html, accessed 2 August 2010.

32CSM, *United Nations Submission* (1998), www.32csm.info, accessed 2 August 2010.

BBC Newsnight, 'Files reveal growing NI terror threat', 28 October 2009, www.news.bbc.co.uk/1/hi/programmes/newsnight/8328309.stm, accessed 29 August 2012.

Department for Enterprise, Trade and Investment, *Labour Market Report* (Belfast, Northern Ireland Statistics and Research Agency, 2011).

Éirígí, 'Elections, Elected Institutions and Ireland's Revolutionary Struggle' (2009), www.eirigi.org/ArdFheis09/elections.pdf, accessed 15 February 2010.

Éirígí, 'For a Socialist Republic' (n.d.), www.eirigi.org.about_us/faq.htm, accessed 15 December 2009.

Éirígí, 'From Socialism Alone Can the Salvation of Ireland Come' (n.d.), www.eirigi.org/pdfs/socialism.pdf, accessed, 26 June 2012.

Éirígí, 'New Year Statement' (2010), www.eirigi.org/latest/latest010110.html, accessed 2 January 2010.

Éirígí, 'Reclaim the Republic', poster (n.d.), www.eirigi.org/pdfs/campaigns/reclaim_republic_campaign.pdf, accessed 17 July 2012.

Éirígí, 'Republican Newry Says No to the PSNI', 14 February 2010, www.eirigi.org/latest/latest140210print.html, accessed 15 February 2010.

Freedom of Information Request, Request Number: F-2012–02338, www.psni.police.uk/police_officers_rehoused.pdf, accessed 24 August 2012.

Great Britain Parliament, *Report of a Committee to Consider, in the Context of Civil Liberties and Human Rights, Measures to Deal with Terrorism in Northern Ireland* [Gardiner Report] (London, HMSO, 1975).

Hall, M. (ed.), *Preventing a Return to Conflict: A Discussion by Ex-combatants* (Belfast, Island Publications, 2009).

Hall, M. (ed.), *Republicanism in Transition: (1) The Need for a Debate* (Belfast, Island Publications, 2011).

Hall, M. (ed.), *Republicanism in Transition: (3) Irish Republicanism Today* (Belfast, Island Publications, 2011).

Hall, M. (ed.), *Republicanism in Transition: (4) The Question of Armed Struggle* (Belfast, Island Publications, 2012).

H M Treasury, *Public Expenditure Statistical Analyses* (London, H M Treasury, 2010).

H M Treasury, *Rebalancing the Northern Irish Economy* (London, H M Treasury, 2011).

Independent Monitoring Commission Report (one to twenty six) (London, The Stationery Office, 2004–11).

Independent Commission on Policing for Northern Ireland, *A New Beginning: Policing in Northern Ireland* (London, HMSO, 1999).

Irish News, 'First Statement issued by the "real" IRA', 18 August 1998, www.cain.ulst.ac.uk/events/peace/docs/rira18898a.htm, accessed 9 August 2012.

Irish News, 'Second Statement issued by the "real" IRA', 18 August 1998, www.cain.ulst.ac.uk/events/peace/docs/rira18898b.htm, accessed 9 August 2012.

IRSP, *Founding Statement of the IRSP* (Dublin, IRSP, 1974).

IRSP, *Republican Socialist Programme for Ireland* (Belfast, IRSP, n.d.)

McKibbin, M., *Northern Ireland Terrorism Legislation: Annual Statistics 2009/10* (London, Northern Ireland Office, 2010).

Northern Ireland Executive, *The 100 Most Deprived Small Areas in Northern Ireland: Northern Ireland Multiple Deprivation Measure 2010* (Belfast, Northern Ireland Statistics and Research Agency, 2010).

Northern Ireland Statistics and Research Agency, *Northern Ireland Multiple Deprivation Measure 2005* (Belfast, The Stationery Office, 2005).

Office of First Minister and Deputy First Minister, *A Shared Future: A Consultation Paper on Improving Relations in Northern Ireland. Policy and Strategic Framework for Good Relations in Northern Ireland* (Belfast, Community Relations Unit, 2005).

Office of First Minister and Deputy First Minister, *2007 Labour Force Survey: Religious Report* (Belfast, Northern Ireland Statistics and Research Agency, 2009).

Office of First Minister and Deputy First Minister, *Programme for Cohesion, Sharing and Integration* (Belfast, Policy Secretariat, 2010).

Office of National Statistics, *Public Sector Employment Statistical Bulletin Q4 2010* (London, ONS, 2011).

Police Service of Northern Ireland, *Police Recorded Security Situation Statistics: Annual Report Covering the Period 1st April 2011 – 31st March 2012* (Belfast, Northern Ireland Statistics and Research Agency, 2012).

Republican Network for Unity, *About Us*, www.republicannetwork.ie, accessed 24 July 2012.

Republican Network for Unity, Bodenstown Address (2007), www.republicannetwork.ie, accessed 26 April 2012.

Republican Sinn Féin Poblachtach, *A Permanent Peace Depends on Ending British Rule Not Updating It* (Dublin, Republican Sinn Féin, 1997).Republican Sinn Féin Poblachtach, *Presidential Address 93rd Ard-Fheis* (Dublin, Republican Sinn Féin, 1997).

Republican Sinn Féin Poblachtach, *Éire Nua: A New Democracy* (Dublin, Republican Sinn Féin, 2000).

Republican Sinn Féin Poblachtach, *Elections and Abstention* (Dublin, Republican Sinn Féin, 2000).

Republican Sinn Féin Poblachtach, *An Address to the People of Ireland* (Dublin, Republican Sinn Féin, 2003).

Republican Sinn Féin Poblachtach, *Saol Nua: A New Way of Life* (Dublin, Republican Sinn Féin, 2004).

Republican Sinn Féin Poblachtach, *Presidential Address 105 Ard-Fheis* (Dublin, Republican Sinn Féin, 2009).

Sinn Féin, *The Politics of Revolution: The Main Speeches and Debates from the 1986 Sinn Féin Ard Fheis* (Dublin, Sinn Féin, 1986).

Sinn Féin, *Towards a Lasting Peace in Ireland* (Dublin, Sinn Féin, 1992).

Sinn Féin, *The Economics of a United Ireland* (Dublin, Sinn Féin, 1994).

Sinn Féin, *Setting the Record Straight* (Dublin, Sinn Féin, 1994).

Sinn Féin, *A Scenario for Peace* (Dublin, Sinn Féin, 1998).

Sinn Féin, 'Defending the Good Friday Agreement', Sinn Féin submission to the Mitchell Review, 23 September 1999.

Sinn Féin, *Agenda for Government: Sinn Féin Assembly Election Manifesto* (Dublin, Sinn Féin, 2003).

Sinn Féin, *Others Promise, We Deliver: 2007 Manifesto* (Dublin, Sinn Féin, 2007).

Sinn Féin Education Department, 'The Split', *Republican Lecture Series* No. 1 (1979).

Internet Resources

32CSM, www.32csm.net/.

ARK (Access Research Knowledge), Northern Ireland Elections, www.ark.ac.uk/elections/.

BBC Hearts and Minds Survey, www.cain.ulst.ac.uk/issues/politics/polls.htm#02.

BBC News Online, www.bbc.co.uk/news/.

Conflict Archive in Northern Ireland (CAIN), www.cain.ulst.ac.uk/.

Conflict Archive in Northern Ireland (CAIN), Results of Elections Held in Northern Ireland since 1968, www.cain.ulst.ac.uk/issues/politics/election/elect.htm.

Economic and Social Research Council (ESRC) 2010 Northern Ireland General Election Survey, results available at www.liv.ac.uk/politics/staff-pages/ESRCSurvey/index.htm.

Éirígí, www.eirigi.org/.

Election Communication Literature, www.irishelectionliterature.wordpress.com.

Guardian, www.Guardian.co.uk/.

Indiana University – Purdue University Indiana Polis Library, www.ulib.iupui.edu/digitalscholarship.

Irish Republican Socialist Party (IRSP), www.irsp.ie/.

National Archives, www.legislation.gov.uk/.

New Republican Forum, http://republican.ie/forum/.

NewsHound, www.irishcentral.com/news/nuzhound/.

Northern Ireland General Election Survey 2001, data available at www.esds.ac.uk.

Northern Ireland Life and Times Survey, 2010, www.ark.ac.uk/nilt/2010/Political_Attitudes/UNINATID.html.
Office of First Minister and Deputy First Minister (OFMDFM), www.ofmdfmni.gov.uk/.
Police Service of Northern Ireland (PSNI) Security Situation Statistics, www.psni.police.uk/security_situation_statistics_user_guide.pdf.
Republican Sinn Féin, www.rsf.ie/.
Republican Network for Unity (RNU), www.republicannetwork.ie/.
RTÉ News, www.rte.ie/news/.
Sinn Féin, www.sinnfein.ie/.
Slugger O'Toole, http://sluggerotoole.com/.
The Blanket, www.indiamond6.ulib.iupui.edu:81/.
The Pensive Quill, www.thepensivequill.am/.
UTV News, www.u.tv/news/.
World Socialist Website, www.wsws.org/.

Interviews

Joe Barr, 32CSM, Derry, 8 March 2010.
Ciaran Boyle, Publicity Officer 32CSM, Derry, 8 March 2010.
Des Dalton, President of Republican Sinn Féin, Dublin, 21 October 2011.
Gary Donnelly, 32CSM, Derry, 16 April 2013.
Michael Gallagher, 32CSM, Derry, 29 January 2010.
Fra Halligan, Irish Republican Socialist Party, Belfast, 1 May 2012.
Independent Republican Prisoner A, Portlaoise Prison, 16 July 2010.
Independent Republican Prisoner B, Portlaoise Prison, 16 July 2010.
IRSP member A, Belfast, 2 June 2012.
IRSP member B, Belfast, 2 June 2012.
Alex Maskey (MLA), Sinn Féin, Belfast, 25 September 2009.
Tarlach McConnell, Independent Republican Prisoner, Portlaoise Prison, 8 March 2010.
Danny Morrison, writer and journalist, former editor of *An Phoblacht*, Liverpool, 8 October 2011.
John Murphy, 32CSM, Cork, 2 March 2011.
Republican Network for Unity member A, Belfast, 1 May 2012.
Sean Oliver, Sinn Féin, Belfast, 25 September 2009.
Republican Sinn Féin member, Belfast, 21 October 2011.
Republican Network for Unity member B, Belfast, 1 May 2012.
RNU member, Belfast, 31 July 2012.
Geraldine Taylor, Vice-President of Republican Sinn Féin, Belfast, 21 October 2011.
Peadar Whelan, Sinn Féin, Belfast, 25 September 2009.

Newspapers

An Phoblacht
An Phoblacht/Republican News
Anderson Town News

Beir Bua
Belfast Telegraph
Business Post

Daily Mail
Daily Telegraph
Derry Journal
Derry News
Financial Times
Fortnight
Fourthwrite
Guardian
Independent
Iris Bheag
Irish Echo
Irish Examiner
Irish Independent
Irish News
Irish Post
Irish Times

Londonderry Sentinel
Magill
Newry Times
News Letter
New York Times
Observer
Republican Bulletin: IRIS NA POBLACHTA
Saoirse
Saoirse Nua
Scotsman
Sovereign Nation
Starry Plough
The Blanket
The Economist
The Times
Weekly Worker

Secondary sources

Achbar, M., *Manufacturing Consent: Noam Chomsky and the Media* (Montreal, Black Rose Books, 1994).
Adams, G., *The Politics of Irish Freedom* (Dingle, Brandon, 1986).
Adams, G., *A Pathway to Peace* (Cork, Mercier, 1988).
Adams, G., *Before the Dawn: An Autobiography* (London, Brandon, 1996).
Adams, J., Morgan, R. and Bambridge, A., *Ambush: The War between the SAS and the IRA* (London, Pan Books, 1998).
Alexander, Y., 'Terrorism, the Media and the Police', *Journal of International Affairs* 32 (1978), pp. 101–113.
Alexander, Y. and O'Day, A. (eds), *Terrorism in Ireland* (London, Croom Helm, 1984).
Alexander, Y. and O'Day, A. (eds), *The Irish Terrorism Experience* (Aldershot, Dartmouth, 1991).
Alonso, R., *The IRA and Armed Struggle* (London, Routledge, 2007).
Anderson, B., *Imagined Communities* (London, Verso, 1983).
Arendt, H., *On Violence* (New York, Harcourt Books, 1970).
Arthur, P., 'Republicanism and the Implementation of the Agreement: An Academic Perspective', *Working Papers in British-Irish Studies* 5 (2001), pp. 5–10.
Atton, C., *Alternative Media* (London, Sage, 2002).
Augusteijn, J., 'Political Violence and Democracy: An Analysis of the Tensions within Irish Republican Strategy, 1914–2002', *Irish Political Studies* 18, no. 1 (2003), pp. 1–26.
Aune, J. A., 'The Argument from Evil in the Rhetoric of Reaction', *Rhetoric and Public Affairs* 6, no. 3 (2003), pp. 518–522.
Barton, B. and Roche, P. J. (eds), *The Northern Irish Question: The Peace Process and the Belfast Agreement* (New York, Palgrave Macmillan, 2009).
Bean, K., *The New Politics of Sinn Féin* (Liverpool, Liverpool University Press, 2007).
Bean, K., 'Book Review: M. Frampton, "The Long March"', *Irish Political Studies* 25, no. 1 (2010), pp. 135–154.

Bean, K., '"New dissidents are but old Provisionals writ large"? The Dynamics of Dissent Republicanism in New Northern Ireland', *Political Quarterly* 83, no. 2 (2012), pp. 83–98.

Bean K. and Hayes, M., 'Sinn Féin and the New Republicanism of Ireland: Electoral Progress, Political Stasis, and Ideological Failure', *Radical History Review* 104 (2009), pp. 126–142.

Beiner, R. (ed.), *Theorising Nationalism* (New York, SUNY Press, 1999).

Bennie, L., Rallings, C., Tonge, J. and Webb, P. (eds), *British Elections and Parties Review, Volume 12: 2001 General Election* (London, Frank Cass, 2002).

Benton, T. and Craib, I., *Philosophy of Social Science: The Philosophical Foundations of Social Thought* (New York, Palgrave Macmillan, 2001).

Berelson, B., *Content Analysis in Communication Research* (New York, Free Press, 1952).

Berlin, I., *Four Essays on Liberty* (Oxford, Oxford University Press, 1969).

Blackbourn, J., 'International Terrorism and Counterterrorist Legislation: The Case Study of Post-9/11 Northern Ireland', *Terrorism and Political Violence* 21, no. 1 (2009), pp. 133–154.

Blomberg, S. B., Hess G. D. and Orphanides, A., 'The Macroeconomic Consequences of Terrorism', *Journal of Monetary Economics* 51 (2004), pp. 1,007–1,032.

Blumer, H., 'Sociological Analysis and the "Variable"', *American Sociological Review* 21 (1956), pp. 683–690.

Bower Bell, J., *The Secret Army: The IRA* (Oxon, Transaction Publishers, 2003).

Bowman-Grieve, L., 'Exploring "Stormfornt": A Virtual Community of the Radical Right', *Studies in Conflict and Terrorism* 32, no. 11 (2009), pp. 989–1,007.

Breen, K. and O'Neill, S. (eds), *After the Nation? Critical Reflections on Nationalism and Postnationalism* (Basingstoke, Palgrave, 2010).

Brewer, M. B., *Intergroup Relations* (Buckingham, Psychology Press, 2005).

Brown, D., *Contemporary Nationalism: Civic, Ethnocultural and Multicultural Politics* (London, Routledge, 2000).

Brubaker, R. (ed.), *Ethnicity without Groups* (Cambridge MA, Harvard Univeristy Press, 2004).

Buhr Giliomee, H. and Gagiano, J., *The Elusive Search for Peace: South Africa, Israel and Northern Ireland* (Oxford, Oxford University Press, 1990).

Byrne, S., Skarlato, O., Fissuh, E. and Irvin, C., 'Building Trust and Goodwill in Northern Ireland and the Border Counties: The Impact of Economic Aid on the Peace Process', *Irish Political Studies* 24, no. 3 (2009), pp. 337–363.

Camus, A., *Caligula and Three Other Plays* (New York, A. A. Knopf, 1958).

Cloud, D. L., 'Beyond Evil: Understanding Power Materially and Rhetorically', *Rhetoric and Public Affairs* 6, no. 3 (2003), pp. 531–538.

Coakly, J. (ed.), *Changing Shades of Orange and Green: Redefining the Union and the Nation in Contemporary Ireland* (Dublin, UCD Press, 2002).

Coakley, J. and O'Dowd, L., 'The Transformation of the Irish Border', *Political Geography* 26, no. 8 (2007), pp. 877–885.

Coleman L. and Tucker, K. (eds), *Situating Global Resistance: Between Discipline and Dissent* (London, Routledge, 2012).

Collins, J. and Glover, R. (eds) *Collateral Language: A User's Guide to America's New War* (New York, New York University Press, 2002).

Connolly, J., 'The Irish Flag' (8 April 1916), in *Collected Works* (Vol. II) (Dublin, News Books, 1988), p. 175.

Cottle, S., *Mediatized Conflicts* (Maidenhead, Open University Press, 2006).

Coulter, M. and Murray, M. (eds), *Northern Ireland after the Troubles: A Society in Transition* (Manchester, Manchester University Press, 2008).

Cox, M., Guelke, A. and Stephens, F. (eds), *A Farewell to Arms? Beyond the Good Friday Agreement* (Manchester, Manchester University Press, 2006).

Crain, N. V. and Crain, W. M., 'Terrorized Economies', *Public Choice* 128 (2006), pp. 317–349.

Cullen, F., 'Beyond Nationalism: Time to Reclaim the Republican Ideal', *The Republic* 1 (2000), pp. 7–14.

Cunningham, M., 'The Political Language of John Hume', *Irish Political Studies* 12, no. 1 (1997), pp. 13–22.

Currie, P. M., and Taylor, M. (eds), *Dissident Irish Republicanism* (London, Continuum, 2011).

Curtis, L., *Ireland and the Propaganda War: The British Media and the Battle for Hearts and Minds* (London, Pluto, 1998).

Darby J. and Mac Ginty, R., *The Management of Peace Processes* (Basingstoke, Palgrave, 2000).

Devereux, E., *Media Studies: Key Issues and Debate* (London, Sage, 2007).

Dixon, P., 'British Policy Towards Northern Ireland 1969–2000: Continuity Tactical Adjustment and Consistent "Inconsistencies"', *British Journal of Politics and International Relations* 3, no. 3 (2001), pp. 340–368.

Downs, A., *An Economic Theory of Democracy* (New York, HarperCollins, 1957).

Edwards, A. and Bloomer, S. (eds), *Transforming the Peace Process in Northern Ireland: From Terrorism to Democratic Politics* (Dublin, Irish Academic Press, 2008).

Eldridge, J. (ed.), *Getting the Message: News, Truth and Power* (London, Routledge, 1993).

Elliott, M. (ed.), *The Long Road to Peace in Northern Ireland* (Liverpool, Liverpool University Press, 2007).

Emerson, R. M. (ed.), *Contemporary Field Research: A Collection of Readings* (Boston, Little, Brown and Co., 1983).

English, R., 'Defining the Nation: Recent Historiography and Irish Nationalism', *European Review of History* 2, no. 2 (1995), pp. 193–200.

English, R., *Armed Struggle: A History of the IRA* (Basingstoke, Macmillan, 2003).

English, R., *Irish Freedom: The History of Nationalism in Ireland* (Oxford, Pan Macmillan, 2006).

English, R., *Terrorism: How to Respond* (Oxford, Oxford University Press, 2009).

Evans, G. and Duffy, M., 'Beyond the Sectarian Divide: The Social Bases and Political Consequences of Nationalist and Unionist Party Competition in Northern Ireland', *British Journal of Political Science* 27, no. 1 (2007), pp. 47–81.

Evans, J. and Tonge, J., 'Social Class and Party Choice in Northern Ireland's Ethnic Blocs', *West European Politics* 32, no. 5 (2009), pp. 1,012–1,030.

Evans, J. and Tonge, J., 'From Abstentionism to Enthusiasm: Sinn Féin, Nationalist Electors and Support for Devolved Power Sharing in Northern Ireland', *Irish Political Studies* 1 (2012), pp. 1–19.

Evans, J. and Tonge, J., 'Menace without Mandate? Is There Any Sympathy for Dissident Irish Republicanism in Northern Ireland?', *Terrorism and Political Violence* 24, no. 1 (2012), pp. 61–78.

Fahey, T., Hayes, B. and Sinnott, R., *Conflict and Consensus: A Study of Values and Attitudes in the Republic of Ireland and Northern Ireland* (Dublin, Institute of Public Education, 2005).

Feeney, B., *Sinn Féin; A Hundred Turbulent Years* (Dublin, O'Brien Press, 2002).

Fernett, R. and Smith, M. L. R., 'IRA 2.0: Continuing the Long War. Analyzing the Factors Behind Anti-GFA Violence', *Terrorism and Political Violence* 24, no. 3 (2012), pp. 375–395.

Finlay, C. J., 'Legitimacy and Non-State Political Violence', *Journal of Political Philosophy* 18, no. 3 (2010), pp. 287–312.

Frampton, M., *The Long March: Political Strategy of Sinn Féin, 1981–2007* (Basingstoke, Palgrave Macmillan, 2009).

Frampton, M., *The Return of the Militants: Violent Dissident Republicanism. A Policy Report for The International Centre for the Study of Radicalisation and Political Violence* (London, ICRS, 2010).

Frampton, M., *Legion of the Rearguard: Dissident Irish Republicanism* (Dublin, Irish Academic Press, 2011).

Gaibulloev, K. and Sandler, T., 'Growth Consequences of Terrorism in Western Europe', *Kyklos* 61, no. 3 (2008), pp. 411–424.

Gidron, B., Katz, S. N. and Hasenfeld, Y. (eds), *Mobilizing for Peace: Conflict Resolution in Northern Ireland, Israel/Palestine and South Africa* (Oxford, Oxford University Press, 2002).

Gil-Alana, L. A. and Barros, C. P., 'A Note on the Effectiveness of National Anti-Terrorist Policies: Evidence from ETA', *Conflict Management and Peace Science* 27, no. 1 (2010), pp. 28–46.

Gilligan, C. and Tonge, J. (eds), *Peace or War? Understanding the Peace Process in Northern Ireland* (Aldershot, Ashgate, 1997).

Graham, B. and Nash, C., 'A Shared Future: Territoriality, Pluralism and Public Policy in Northern Ireland', *Political Geography* 25, no. 3 (2006), pp. 253–278.

Green, J. and Browne, J., *Principles of Social Research* (Maidenhead, Open University Press, 2005).

Guelke, A., *Northern Ireland: The International Perspective* (Dublin, Gill and Macmillan, 1988).

Guelke, A., 'The Northern Ireland Peace Process and the War against Terrorism: Conflicting Conceptions?' *Government and Opposition* 42, no. 3 (2007), pp. 272–291.

Gurr, T. R., 'Sources of Rebellion in Western Societies: Some Quantitative Evidence', *ANNALS of the American Academy of Political and Social Science* 391 (1970), pp. 128–144.

Hanley, B., 'Change and Continuity: Republican Thought since 1922', *The Republic* 2 (2001), pp. 92–103.

Hargie, O. and Dickson, D. (eds), *Researching the Troubles: Social Science Perspectives on the Northern Ireland Conflict* (London, Mainstream Publishing, 2004).

Hariman, R., 'Speaking of Evil', *Rhetoric and Public Affairs* 6, no. 3 (2003), pp. 511–517.

Harris, E., *Nationalism: Theories and Cases* (Edinburgh, Edinburgh University Press, 2009).

Hayes, B. and McAllister, I., 'Who Voted for Peace? Public Support for the 1998 Northern Ireland Agreement', *Irish Political Studies* 16, no. 1 (2001), pp. 73–93.

Hayes, M., 'The Evolution of Republican Strategy and the 'Peace Process' in Ireland', *Race Class* 39, no. 3 (1998), pp. 21–29.

Hearn, J., *Rethinking Nationalism: A Critical Introduction* (New York, Palgrave Macmillan, 2006).

Hogan, G. and Walker, C., *Political Violence and the Law in Ireland* (Manchester, Manchester University Press, 1989).

Holland, J. and McDonald, H., *INLA: Deadly Divisions* (Dublin, Torc Press, 1994).

Hollander, P., 'Contemporary Political Violence and Its Legitimation', *Society* 46, no. 3 (2009), pp. 267–274.

Honohan, I., 'Freedom as Citizenship: The Republican Tradition in Political Theory', *The Republic*, 2 (2001), pp. 7–24.

Honohan, I., *Civic Republicanism* (London, Routledge, 2002).

Honohan, I. (ed.), *Republicanism in Ireland: Confronting Theories and Traditions* (Manchester, Manchester University Press, 2008).

Honohan, I. and Jennings, J. (eds), *Republicanism in Theory and Practice* (London, Routledge, 2006).

Horgan J. and Morrison, J., 'Here to Stay? The Rising Threat of Violent Dissident Republicanism in Northern Ireland', *Terrorism and Political Violence* 23, no. 4 (2011), pp. 642–669.

Hueckel, C., 'Sinn Féin without the IRA: Legitimacy or Loss of Popular Support', *Osprey Journal of Ideas and Inquiry* 31, no. 6 (2007), pp. 1–13.

Irvin, C., *Militant Nationalism:Between Movement and Party in Ireland and the Basque Country* (Minneapolis, University of Minnesota Press, 1999).

Jackson, R., *Writing the War on Terrorism: Language Politics and Counter Terrorism* (Manchester, Manchester University Press, 2005).

Jarman, N., 'From War to Peace? Changing Patterns of Violence in Northern Ireland, 1990–2003', *Terrorism and Political Violence* 16, no. 3 (2004), pp. 420–438.

Kearney, R., *Transitions: Narratives in Modern Irish Culture* (Manchester, Manchester University Press, 1988).

Kearney, R., *Post Nationalist Ireland: Politics, Culture and Philosophy* (London, Routledge, 1997).

Kearny, H. F., *Ireland, Contested Ideas of Nationalism and History* (Cork, Cork University Press, 2007).

Knox, C. and Quirk, P., *Peace Building in Northern Ireland, Israel and South Africa* (Basingstoke, Palgrave Macmillan, 2000).

Kohn, H., *The Idea of Nationalism* (New York, Collier, 1967).

Lee, R. M., *Doing Research on Sensitive Topics* (London, Sage, 1999).

Lichbach, M. I., 'Deterrence or Escalation? The Puzzle of Aggregate Studies of Repression and Dissent', *Journal of Conflict Resolution* 31, no. 2 (1987), pp. 266–297.

Lynn, B., 'Tactic or Principle? The Evolution of Republican Thinking on Abstentionism in Ireland, 1970–1998', *Irish Political Studies* 17, no. 2 (2002), pp. 74–94.

Machiavelli, N., *The Prince* (Chicago, University of Chicago Press, 1985).

Madison, J., 'The Federalist Papers, no. 51', in J. Madison, A. Hamilton and J. Jay (eds), *The Federalist Papers* (New York, New America Library, 1951).

Maillot, A., *New Sinn Féin: Republicanism in the Twenty-first Century* (London, Routledge, 2005).

McAllister, I., '"The armalite and the ballot box": Sinn Féin's Electoral Strategy in Northern Ireland', *Electoral Studies* 23, no. 1 (2004), pp. 123–142.

McBride, I., *History and Memory in Modern Ireland* (Cambridge, Cambridge University Press, 2001).

McEvoy, K., 'Prisoners, the Agreement, and the Political Character of the Northern Ireland Conflict', *Fordham International Law Journal* 22, no. 4 (1998), pp. 1,539–1,576.

McEvoy, K. and Shirlow, P., 'Re-imagining DDR: Ex-combatants, Leadership and Moral Agency in Conflict Transformation', *Theoretical Criminology* 13, no. 1 (2009), pp. 31–59.

McGarry, F. (ed.), *Republicanism in Modern Ireland* (Dublin, UCD Press, 2003).

McGarry, J., 'Consociationalism and Its Critics: Evidence from the Historic Northern Ireland Assembly Election 2007', *Electoral Studies* 28, no. 3 (2009), pp. 458–466.

McGovern, M., 'Irish Republicanism and the Potential Pitfalls of Pluralism', *Capital and Class* 71 (2000), pp. 133–161.

McGovern, M., '"The Old Days are over": Irish Republicanism, the Peace Process and the Discourse of Equality', *Terrorism and Political Violence* 16, no. 3 (2004), pp. 622–645.

McIntyre, A., 'Modern Irish Republicanism: The Product of British State Strategies', *Irish Political Studies* 10, no. 1 (1995), pp. 97–122

McIntyre, A., *The Good Friday Agreement: The Death of Irish Republicanism* (New York, Ausubo Press, 2008).

McKearney, T., *The Provisional IRA: From Insurrection to Parliament* (London, Pluto Press, 2011).

McLaughlin, M., 'A Political Perspective', *Working Papers in British-Irish Studies*, 5 (2001).

Miller, G. D., 'Confronting Terrorism and Successful State Policies', *Terrorism and Political Violence* 19, no. 3 (2007), pp. 331–350.

Minichiello, V., Aroni, R. and Hays, T. N., *In Depth Interviewing* (Melbourne, Pearson Education Australia, 1990).

Mitchell, P., Evans, G. and O'Leary, B., 'Extremist Outbidding in Ethnic Party Systems is Not Inevitable: Tribune Parties in Northern Ireland', *Political Studies* 57, no. 2 (2009), pp. 397–421.

Moloney, E., *A Secret History of the IRA* (London, Penguin, 2002).

Moncrieffe, J., 'Researching with "Violent Actors": Dangers, Responsibilities and Ethics', *Institute for Development Studies Bulletin* 40, no. 3 (2009), pp. 97–99.

Moody, T. W., McDowell, R. B. and Woods, C. J. (eds), *The Writings of Theobald Wolfe Tone, 1763–98* (Vol. I) (Oxford, Clarendon Press, 1998).

Muro, D., 'The Politics of War and Memory in Radical Basque Nationalism', *Ethnic and Racial Studies* 32, no. 4 (2009), pp. 659–678.

Murray, G. and Tonge, J., *Sinn Féin and the SDLP: From Alienation to Participation* (London, Hurst, 2005).

Nairn, T., *Faces of Nationalism* (London, Verso, 1997).

Newman, E., 'Exploring the "Root Causes" of Terrorism', *Studies in Conflict and Terrorism* 29, no. 8 (2006), pp. 749–772.

Norris, P., Kern, M. and Just, M. (eds), *Framing Terrorism: The News Media, the Government and the Public* (New York, Routledge, 2003).

O'Boyle, G., 'Theories of Justification and Political Violence: Examples from Four Groups', *Terrorism and Political Violence* 14, no. 2 (2002), pp. 23–46.

O'Brien, B., *The Long War: IRA and Sinn Féin* (Dublin, O'Brien Press, 1999).

O'Day, A. (ed.), *Terrorism Laboratory: The Case of Northern Ireland* (Aldershot, Dartmouth Publishing, 1995).

O'Doherty, M., *The Trouble with Guns* (Belfast, Blackstaff Press, 1998).

O'Kane, E., 'Learning from Northern Ireland? The Uses and Abuses of the Irish "Model"', *British Journal of Politics and International Relations* 12, no. 2 (2010), pp. 239–256.

O'Leary, B., 'Analysing Partition: Definition, Classification and Explanation', *Political Geography* 26, no. 8 (2007), pp. 886–908.

O'Leary, B. and McGarry, J., *The Politics of Antagonism: Understanding Northern Ireland,* (London, Athlone Press, 1996).

Olson, M., 'Rapid Growth as a Destabilizing Force,' *Journal of Economic History* 23 (December 1963), pp. 529–552.

Pain, R. and Smith, S. J. (eds), *Fear: Critical Geopolitics and Everyday Life* (Aldershot, Ashgate, 2008).

Paletz, D., Fozzard, P.A. and Ayanian, J. Z., 'The IRA, the Red Brigades, and the F.A.L.N. in the New York Times', *Journal of Communication* 32, 2 (1982), pp. 162–171.

Pape, R. A., 'The Strategic Logic of Suicide Terrorism', *American Journal of Political Science Review* 97 (2003), pp. 343–361.

Patterson, H., *The Politics of Illusion: A Political History of the IRA* (London, Serif, 1997).

Pettit, P., *Republicanism: A Theory of Freedom and Government* (Oxford, Oxford University Press, 1997).

Philps, M., 'English Republicanism in the 1970s', *Journal of Political Philosophy* 6, no. 3 (1998), pp. 235–262.

Picard, R. G., 'How Violence is Justified: Sinn Féin's *An Phoblacht*', *Journal of Communication* 41, no. 4 (1991), pp. 90–103.

Pocock, P. G. A., *The Machiavellian Moment: Florentine Political Thought and the Atlantic Republican Tradition* (Princeton, Princeton University Press, 1975).

Porter, N. (ed.), *The Republican Ideal: Current Perspectives* (Belfast, Blackstaff Press, 1998).

Rafter, K., *Sinn Féin 1905–2005: In the Shadow of Gunmen* (Dublin, Gill and Macmillan, 2005).

Richards, A., 'Terrorist Groups and Political Fronts: The IRA, Sinn Féin, the Peace Process and Democracy', *Terrorism and Political Violence* 13, no.4 (2001), pp. 72–89.

Ruane, J. and Todd, J. (eds), *After the Good Friday Agreement: Analysing Political Change in Northern Ireland* (Dublin, University College Dublin Press, 1999).

Rousseau, J. J., *Discourse on Political Economy and the Social Contract* (Oxford, Oxford University Press, 1994).

Sanders, A., *Inside the IRA: Dissident Republicans and the War for Legitimacy* (Edinburgh, Edinburgh University Press, 2011).

Sarma, K., 'Defensive Propaganda and the IRA: Political Control in Republican Communities', *Studies in Conflict and Terrorism* 30, no. 12 (2007), pp. 1,073–1,094.

Shafir, G. (ed.), *The Citizenship Debates* (Minneapolis, University of Minnesota Press, 1998).

Shanahan, T., *The Provisional Irish Republican Army and the Morality of Terrorism* (Edinburgh, Edinburgh University Press, 2009).

Sharrock, D. and Davenport, M., *Man of War, Man of Peace* (Basingstoke, Macmillan, 1997).

Shirlow P. and McEvoy, K., *Beyond the Wire: Former Prisoners and Conflict Transformation in Northern Ireland* (London, Pluto Press, 2008).

Shirlow P. and Murtagh, B., *Belfast: Segregation, Violence and the City* (London, Pluto, 2006).

Shirlow, P., Tonge, J., McAuley, J. and McGlynn, C., *Abandoning Historical Conflict? Former Political Prisoners and Reconciliation in Northern Ireland* (Manchester Manchester University Press, 2010).

Silke, A., 'Rebel's Dilemma: The Changing Relationship between the IRA, Sinn Féin and Paramilitary Vigilantism in Northern Ireland', *Terrorism and Political Violence* 11, no. 1 (1999), pp. 55–93.

Smith, A. D., *National Identity* (Harmondsworth, Penguin, 1991).

Smith, M. L. R., *Fighting for Ireland? The Military Strategy of the Irish Republican Movement* (London, Routledge, 1995).

Smyth, M., 'The Process of Demilitarisation and the Reversibility of the Peace Process in Northern Ireland', *Terrorism and Political Violence* 16, no. 3 (2004), pp. 544–566.

Smyth, M. and Robinson, G. (eds), *Researching Violently Divided Societies* (Tokyo, United Nations University Press, 2001).

Stedman, S. J., 'Spoiler Problems in Peace Processes', *International Security* 22, no. 2 (1997), pp. 5–53.

Strom, K., 'A Behavioural Theory of Competitive Party Politics', *American Journal of Political Science* 34, no. 2 (1990), pp. 565–598.

Stuart Ross, F., *Smashing H Block* (Liverpool, Liverpool University Press, 2011).

Sunstein, C. R., 'The Republican Civic Tradition', *Yale Law Journal*, 97 (1988), pp. 1,539–1,590.

Sweeney, G., 'Self-Immolation in Ireland: Hunger Strikes and Political Confrontation', *Anthropology Today* 9, no. 5 (1993), pp. 10–14.

Taylor, M., 'Introduction', in Currie P. M. and Taylor, M. (eds), *Dissident Irish Republicanism* (London, Continuum, 2011), pp. 1–16.

Taylor, P., *Provos: The IRA and Sinn Féin* (London, Bloomsbury, 1997).

Taylor, P., *Behind the Mask: The IRA and Sinn Féin* (New York, TV Books, 1998).

Taylor, R. (ed.), *Consociational Theory: McGarry and O'Leary. The Northern Ireland Conflict* (London, Routledge, 2009).

Tonge, J., "'They haven't gone away you know": Irish Republican "Dissidents" and "Armed Struggle"', *Terrorism and Political Violence* 16, no. 3 (2004), pp. 671–693.

Tonge, J., *Northern Ireland* (Cambridge, Polity Press, 2006).

Tonge, J., "'No-one likes us; we don't care": "Dissident" Irish Republicans and Mandates', *Political Quarterly* 83, no. 2 (2012), pp. 219–226.

Tonge, J., Braniff, M., Hennessey, T., McAuley, J. W. and Whiting, S. A., *The Democratic Unionist Party: From Protest to Power* (Oxford, Oxford University Press, 2014).

Tonge, J., Evans, J., Mitchell, P. and Hayes, B., 'The 2010 Election in Northern Ireland: Evidence from aggregate and ESRC Survey Data', Data presented at The 2010 Electoral Change in Northern Ireland Conference, Queen's University, Belfast, October 2010.

Torres Soriano, M. R., 'The Road to Media Jihad: The Propaganda Actions of Al Qaeda in the Islamic Maghreb', *Terrorism and Political Violence* 23, no. 1 (2010), pp. 72–88.

Tugwell, M., 'Terrorism and Propaganda: Problems and Response', *Conflict Quarterly* 5, nos. 1–2 (Spring, 1986).

Von Clausewitz, K., *On War* (Princeton, Princeton University Press, 1989).

Von Tagen Page, M. and Smith, M. L. R., 'War By Other Means: The Problem of Political Control in Irish Republican Strategy', *Armed Forces and Society* 27, no. 1 (2000), pp. 79–104.

Walsh, P., *Irish Republicanism and Socialism: The Politics of the Republican Movement 1905 to 1994* (Belfast, Athol Books, 1994).

Weinstock, D. M., *Republicanism: History, Theory and Practice* (Portland, Frank Cass, 2004).

White, R., *Provisional Irish Republicans: An Oral and Interpretive History* (Westport, Greenwood Press, 1993).

White, R., 'Issues in the Study of Political Violence: Understanding the Motives of Participants in Small Group Political Violence', *Terrorism and Political Violence* 12, no. 1 (2000), pp. 95–108.

White, R., *Ruairí Ó Brádaigh: The Life and Politics of an Irish Revolutionary* (Bloomington, Indiana University Press, 2006).

White, R., 'Structural Identity Theory and the Post Recruitment Activism of Irish Republicans: Persistence, Splits, and Dissidents in Social Movement Organizations', *Social Problems* 57, no. 3 (2010), pp. 341–370.

Whiting, S. A., "'The Discourse of Defence": "Dissident" Irish Republicanism and the "Propaganda War"', *Terrorism and Political Violence* 24, no. 3 (2012), pp. 483–503.

Wilford, R. (ed.), *Aspects of the Belfast Agreement* (Oxford, Oxford University Press, 2001).

Wilkinson, P., 'The Media and Terrorism: A Reassessment', *Terrorism and Political Violence* 9, no. 2 (1997), pp. 51–64.

Wilkinson, P., 'Politics, Diplomacy and Peace Processes: Pathways Out of Terrorism?', *Terrorism and Political Violence* 11, no. 4 (1999), pp. 66–82.

Williams, R, *Marxism and Literature* (Oxford, Oxford University Press, 1977).

Zagorin, P., 'Republicanisms', *British Journal for the History of Philosophy* 11, no. 4 (2003), pp. 701–712.

Zarakol, A., 'What Makes Terrorism Modern? Terrorism, Legitimacy, and the International System', *Review of International Studies* 37, no. 5 (2011), pp. 2,311–2,336.

Zartman, I. and Rasmussen, J. L. (eds), *Peacemaking in International Conflict: Methods and Techniques* (Washington, United States Institute of Peace Press, 1997).

Zenker, O., 'Autochthony and Activism among Contemporary Irish Nationalists in Northern Ireland, or: If 'Civic' Nationalists are 'Ethno'-cultural Revivalists, What Remains of the Civic/ethnic Divide?', *Nations and Nationalism* 15, no. 4 (2009), pp. 696–715.

Zetzel, J. E. G., *Cicero: De Republica. Selections* (Cambridge, Cambridge University Press, 1995).

Index